TOWNSCAPE WITH FIGURES

By the same author

Auden: An Introductory Essay
The Uses of Literacy
W. H. Auden
Teaching Literature
Speaking to Each Other:
Volume 1: About Society
Volume 2: About Literature
Only Connect – On Culture and Communication:
The BBC Reith Lectures 1971
An Idea and Its Servants: UNESCO from Within
An English Temper
The British Council and the Arts (joint)
An Idea of Europe
(with Douglas Johnson)
A Local Habitation:
Life and Times, Volume I: 1918–40
A Sort of Clowning:
Life and Times, Volume II: 1940–59
An Imagined Life:
Life and Times: 1959–91

As Editor

Your Sunday Paper
The Future of Broadcasting
(with Janet Morgan)
Main Principles of Public Service Broadcasting
Quality in Television
Liberty and Legislation

TOWNSCAPE
WITH FIGURES

Farnham: Portrait of an English Town

———

RICHARD HOGGART

Chatto & Windus

LONDON

First published in Great Britain in 1994

1   3   5   7   9   10   8   6   4   2

© Richard Hoggart 1994

Richard Hoggart has asserted his right under the Copyright,
Designs and Patents Act, 1988 to be identified as the author
of this work

Published in 1994 by
Chatto & Windus Limited
Random House, 20 Vauxhall Bridge Road,
London SW1V 2SA

Random House Australia (Pty) Limited
20 Alfred Street, Milsons Point, Sydney,
New South Wales 2061, Australia

Random House New Zealand Limited
18 Poland Road, Glenfield
Auckland 10, New Zealand

Random House South Africa (Pty) Limited
PO Box 337, Bergvlei, South Africa

Random House UK Limited Reg. No. 954009

A CIP catalogue record for this book
is available from the British Library

ISBN 0 7011 6138 8

Printed and bound in Great Britain by
Mackays of Chatham PLC, Chatham, Kent

To Mary with love

CONTENTS

CONTENTS

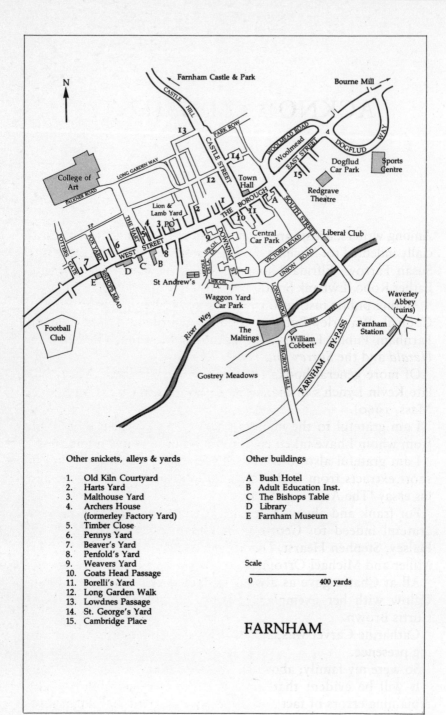

N

Farnham Castle & Park

Bourne Mill

College of Art

Town Hall

Lion & Lamb Yard

St Andrew's

Waggon Yard Car Park

Central Car Park

Redgrave Theatre

Dogflud Car Park

Sports Centre

Liberal Club

Football Club

The Maltings

'William Cobbett'

Gostrey Meadows

Waverley Abbey (ruins)

Farnham Station

CASTLE HILL
PARK ROW
CASTLE STREET
WOOL MEAD ROAD
Woolmead
EAST STREET
DOGFLUD WAY
LONG GARDEN WAY
FALKNER ROAD
THE HART
WEST STREET
DOWNING ST
THE BOROUGH
SOUTH STREET
VICTORIA ROAD
UNION ROAD
LONGBRIDGE
ABBEY STREET
FARNHAM BY-PASS
FIRGROVE HILL
POTTERS GATE
FOX YARD
BISHOP'S MEAD
MIDDLE CH. LA.
UPR. CH. LA.
LWR CH. LA.
River Way

Other snickets, alleys & yards

1. Old Kiln Courtyard
2. Harts Yard
3. Malthouse Yard
4. Archers House (formerley Factory Yard)
5. Timber Close
6. Pennys Yard
7. Beaver's Yard
8. Penfold's Yard
9. Weavers Yard
10. Goats Head Passage
11. Borelli's Yard
12. Long Garden Walk
13. Lowdnes Passage
14. St. George's Yard
15. Cambridge Place

Other buildings

A Bush Hotel
B Adult Education Inst.
C The Bishops Table
D Library
E Farnham Museum

Scale

0   400 yards

FARNHAM

ACKNOWLEDGMENTS

Among writers, artists and commentators on Farnham, I am especially indebted to: Michael Blower, Ashton Booth, John Dodgson, Susan Farrow, Elfrida Manning, W. E. Newman, Jean Parratt, Father Robo, Ewbank Smith, Nigel Temple and Sir John Verney.

Among public institutions, I am glad to thank: Surrey County Council, Waverley Borough Council, Farnham Town Council, Farnham Public Library, the Farnham Museum, the *Farnham Herald* and the *Surrey and Hants News*.

Of more general books I owe a particularly large debt to the late Kevin Lynch's brilliant *The Image of the City* (Cambridge, Mass, 1960).

I am grateful to the many authors, most of them long dead, from whom I have taken epigraphs and other short quotations.

I am grateful also to Messrs. Faber and Faber for the use of short extracts from Auden's poem 'In Praise of Limestone' and his essay 'The American Scene'.

For frank and always helpful readings of this essay I am very grateful indeed to: Geoffrey Goodman, Alex Graham, A. H. Halsey, Stephen Hearst, David Lea, Muriel McNaughton, John Miller and Michael Orrom.

All at Chatto gave as always sustained help, especially Jenny Uglow with her exemplary editing. So did Michael Shaw of Curtis Brown.

Catharine Carver was, again as always, a wonderfully sustaining presence.

So were my family; above all, my wife Mary.

It will be evident that none of them is responsible for any remaining errors of fact and the inevitable errors of judgment.

PREFACE

'Not at all your kind of place, I'd reckon', said a friend on her first visit to us at Farnham. Fair enough; she knew under what circumstances we had arrived in far West Surrey but wondered, I suppose, why we had stayed. That was almost twenty years ago.

An accident brought us here. In mid-1974 we were living in Paris and expecting to do so for about six to nine months more. Then our landlord asked for his flat back, for October; he had been recalled by the Quai d'Orsay.

No point in moving all our furniture within the city for a few months only. We decided to find a place in England, move our furniture there and spend the last few months in a furnished flat.

I had no job in England and our children had all moved south. We decided to look for somewhere within an hour of London by train. We found Farnham.

Farnham; late 1993.

The axis of the earth sticks out visibly through the centre of
each and every town or city.

OLIVER WENDELL HOLMES,
The Autocrat of the Breakfast Table

ON A CERTAIN KIND OF WRITING

I do not hear enough, in economy books, of pies and puddings. A man lives in and for the delicacies, adornments, and accidental attributes of life . . . this is not the philosophical, but the human side of economics; it interests like a story.
Robert Louis Stevenson, *The Amateur Emigrant*

Stevenson's chirpy passage can remind us that Virginia Woolf was mistaken in accusing Arnold Bennett of being so obsessed with the 'thisness' of things that he was unable to see the transcendence of what may seem the 'ordinary' details of life. Bennett found transcendence precisely by feeling his way through that thisness; as in the immensely moving description of Sophia's feelings on seeing, so many years after he had deserted her, the dead body of her husband, Gerald Scales.

Almost forty years ago, in preparing what was meant to be a teaching-aid, (*The Uses of Literacy*), I was led instead to write about Northern working-class life in the twenties and thirties, and about modern mass-culture and its likely effects on that life. So strong did these new interests become that later attempts to write a novel and a play foundered, no doubt from natural inability but also because the impulse to see social and cultural meanings everywhere possible constrained the imagination, made it difficult to see material, events and above all people as unique, not necessarily representative. To see all those as, instead, in some ways indicative of a society and its trends was difficult but, to people like me, heady; truffle-hunting with a, possibly plastic, pig's nose. After a while you begin to think you know when you have got it right, when it rings true; and when it is dead, inert; you may of course be wrong, kidding yourself; either way.

There are quirky but supporting comments on all this from many major writers. Auden:

> In grasping the character of a society, as in judging the character of an individual, no documents, statistics, 'objective' measurements can ever compete with the single intuitive glance. Intuition may err . . . but documentation . . . must err in a field where completeness is impossible.

Not having that degree of assurance, I resort quite often to 'it seems' and the like.

And then Henry James, reporting the answer of an English woman novelist 'of genius' who was asked where she gained her knowledge of the way of life of French Protestant youth:

> These opportunities consisted in her having once, in Paris, as she ascended a staircase, passed an open door where, in the household of a *pasteur*, some of the young Protestants were seated at a table round a finished meal. The glimpse made a picture; it lasted only a moment, but that moment was experience . . . She knew what youth was, and what Protestantism; she also had the advantage of having seen what it was to be French, so that she converted these ideas into a concrete image and produced a reality.

That must be enough here but the passage, in James's *The Art of Fiction*, goes on wonderfully to trace the relations between experience and 'the condition of feeling life in general so completely that you are well on your way to knowing any particular corner of it'. Flaubert was more compact: 'Induction is as good as deduction. . . . No doubt my poor Bovary is suffering and weeping in twenty different French villages at this very moment.'

So, though there can be no proof, this is not to say that your efforts are fruitless or inalienably ill-judged. There can be no proof of the 'truth' of a novel any more than of discursive impressionistic writing. Yet the varying emotional pressures behind discursive writing can be as revealing as those of fiction. It was not fortuitous that the chapter in *The Uses of Literacy* that drew most interest was the most personal, that called 'Scholarship Boy'.

There are also, in discursive social writing as much as in autobiographical, intense problems of selection. To repeat: how do I know that this incident in my life, or in the common life of Farnham or of anywhere else, reverberates, resonates, with meanings indicative in some way of other people's experiences also, is not simply a moment I am hung up on, niggled by, and would like to make general rather than revealing about me alone, my tastes, my limits? For myself, I have to recognise the 'Primitive Methodist syndrome', the tendency to see all such moments and images, as the lay preachers in the Hunslet (industrial South Leeds) chapels congenitally saw them, as moral parables.

There are constant problems of angle, the position from which you approach any incident at all – from how you saw it, or from how it must have appeared to others, or from a would-be dispassionate perspective.

Most difficult of all is the matter of tone, for that determines the very texture of the language you use. The incidence of 'I' in the text is a good first guide to how far the writer has thought about tone. In autobiography (though in discursive social observation based on personal experience such as this, a little leeway can be allowed) tone will be decided partly by the writer's thoughts about the nature of the medium chosen and partly by the writer's own character. A writer who uses a winning, partly pert, partly prat-fall, twee or pally, manner has simply picked up the easiest verbal kit. For one such as myself, anxious not to seem to be enveloping the reader in his own hot breath (and in this probably exhibiting and sharing with most readers an English, don't come too near, reticence), the beginning of the search for the right tone is the definition of right distance. How far should you be from the reader, how far from the material? It can be a deflective procedure and not all readers like it and some will then charge you with face-saving cageyness. Keeping your distance can be overdone. But some form of it, some use of it, is essential to discursive writing using personal material if it wishes to make itself more than personal.

Last, and this is something to be glad of, you can learn something everywhere. As much as in the novel this kind of writing can run away with you; your incidents and people can refuse, as Lawrence said, to be nailed down but will get up and run off with the nail, become bigger than you knew; your flat characters can against your expectations become round. If you are sensible you will let all that happen. My Aunt Ethel did that in the first volume of my *Life and Times*; I did not know how strongly I was still emotionally involved with her memory, until a woman novelist pointed it out; I knew at once she was right. So, distancing or not, we do reveal ourselves and should not resent that. Whatever devices we use, we are all the time, and however submerged the realisation may be, creating a portrait of a personality – ourselves – and may then begin to act more and more like the picture of ourselves we have created.

Similarly, I now know better how deep is my dislike of the sense of class or, perhaps more and more now, of status-distinction in England. But as to places like Farnham, we are talking chiefly about the old sense of class and of its surprising tenacity. It is said that in Farnham pubs and clubs where middle-class professionals meet the most taboo of all topics is, precisely, class. That sounds like a response to something known to exist but not happily acknowledged and so accommodated by tacit silence.

In view of all the above I have finally decided to use, as still the most relevant, the old nomenclature: working-class – lower middle-class – middle-class – a slight admixture of upper middle-class chiefly from the surrounding villages – and a growing group of professional-semi-classless newcomers.

Much the same elements of self-knowledge can come from what reveal themselves as favourite uses of language, and especially of images. As in the recurrence of the figure of climbing, and of ladders, in this and others of my books. The source of that is not difficult to locate.

A reviewer fairly asked on what grounds I could habitually address my imagined audience as 'we' since that word seemed to invoke a group of readers with shared interests, and who knows if such a group still exists; almost certainly they don't, was his implication. I believe him wrong, but that argument is for another place. Similarly, words for judgments of value are needed but not easily available, not safe. The old ones begin to look like nineteenth-century Ruritanian State Railway Bonds, uncashable. In the absence of a common currency, I fall back on words such as 'decent' and 'shabby'. And what do those mean, another reviewer rightly asked.

So for various reasons I have been led to write one more book which aims, by looking at a particular place and its people, to offer some 'representative significance'; whilst also recognising unique characteristics. The trickiest element in writing of this kind is to find the proper balance between the two aims. If the book so focussed on the special nature of Farnham that it appealed to hardly anyone who did not live there or have a prior interest in the town then it would have failed. It would have failed not because the book was focussed on one small place – so are many books, whether discursive or fictional, and some have had all the more success precisely because of that. It would have failed because I had not made the place seem interesting, in its own right, to people who had not heard of it until they began to read.

'Representativeness' is more difficult than 'uniqueness'. So many characteristics of towns 'like this' are bound to be shared that it may seem otiose to mention them; yes, of course, they do this in Farnham as they do all over the place; and yes the same winds of cultural change blow through all our streets; why bother to say so?

Partly because it can be useful and interesting to trace common habits and styles; and because it is surprising how many people have not thought of them as widely shared patterns, or thought about what they might mean: the vast commitment to voluntary good works, to neighbourliness, to what we used to call 'hobbies' (and especially the central importance of a good hobby to people in deeply boring, if also continuously demanding, jobs), and to bargain-hunting; to name only four areas.

More important, is putting a finger on those habits which are at points of change and trying to indicate what those changes are, even in matters which seem so everyday as to be little worth thinking about. One of the themes of this book, again more prominent than I expected, is the importance of shopping, its revelatory importance. And a recurrent sub-theme is the way in which the supermarkets have taken over from most other kinds of local shop, displacing some styles and meanings and creating others. There are other such changes and continuities and we all sort-of-know about them in our heads and know that they must be affecting the whole of Britain.

That is the sort of moment, the kind of hinge, at which particular local observation can emerge into the 'representative'. It is different from the physical description of the particular town, and from its other 'uniquenesses'. Both can be right, true, and both should have their place; there is no reason at all why they should quarrel.

When an observation about Farnham points outward to an important general issue which affects many if not most towns and cities I have moved out and talked about the national issue: the condition of architecture and town-planning, the state of the National Health Service, of the Public Library Service and of local government; or the growth of violence on the streets, and so on.

Much of all this comes down to continuities and changes, to noting how both are expressed in this time and this place and how they are also going on elsewhere: the continuing chauvinism, the taking-the-world-for-granted, the absence of a sense of history; and the secular changes, notably those in sexual habits and attitudes. Funny, though; I find myself at ease about the particularities of description and would be sorry if they were often felt not interesting enough to be worth their space. I am less secure in presenting things which seem also to be representative. That is why there appear, perhaps too often, locutions which jog the reader, which say: 'Look, this isn't just Farnham; it's typical.' Such elements should almost always speak for themselves.

Another frequent theme which has emerged in the writing of this book is a quarrel with some people who are politically on the Left, as I am. Obviously, I am not politically Conservative; there are continuing criticisms of Conservatism here and of the class-snobberies of the Conservative-voting middle-class. There are attacks on the greed of naked capitalism and on its unavoidable urge to break out and reassert its predatory nature even against whatever restraints are placed on it. There are, throughout, attacks direct and implicit on capitalism's handmaiden, con-

sumerism and its engines of promotion, notably PR activities and
advertising. All that has been brutally and insensitively promoted by the Tory governments of the last decade and a half,
governments whose record on many things which affect our
intellectual and imaginative – and humane – life is shameful.

So: not a Conservative and not a Liberal Democrat; a Socialist
but a centre and central Socialist and unwilling to be reassigned
towards the Right by those who are further left or who, if they
have moved more and more to the left, have comfortably taken
the definition with them so that they remain or think they remain
at the central marker beacon. I am a non-Christian, ethical
Socialist or socialist Humanist; that is a long tradition and calls
up phrases little used today, such as 'Commonweal' (the sense of
brotherhood) combined with 'personal freedom' (before group
loyalty). I therefore dislike all absolutisms, ideologies, single
solutions, blueprints and dogmatisms. We have seen that future
and it didn't work; not that we should have needed the evidence
of late 1989 to learn that absolutism in thought and centralism
in government destroy human rights. Just as absolutisms lead to
tyranny so, left alone, open capitalist societies are inhumane,
catch-as-catch-can; but they can be, if we fight to keep them
that way, to some degree open; open to judgment, regulation and
correction.

This is a non-utopian position and recognises the fallible, the
inevitably compromised and qualified nature of experience itself;
two steps forward, one-and-a-half back; it does not expect people
to be or to become saints and equally hesitates to write them off,
except under extreme provocation, as villains; it recognises, as I
say more than once in the pages which follow, that we belong to
one another. Here the mundane details of life, the humane sense
and the best art meet; muddy ground and one where we practise
a language which, unless it too is constantly kept under watch,
itself becomes muddier and muddier; but not shifting ground,
not endlessly relative because compass-less and hence ready to
go with whatever new wind blows. So one plugs away, goes on
going-on.

Above all, since it is essential continually to oppose the tendency of open capitalist societies to keep their members below the
level of critical literacy, so that they shall further those societies'

purposes without becoming awkward, above all one goes on demanding as essential to a democracy better education for people of all ages, better journalism, a broadcasting system which recognises the public interest as against that of the market, support for the arts and intellectual life as the air-holes which, as well as being good in themselves, can help discourage a 'democratic' society from becoming a populist society – which would predictably continue to call itself democratic. At present many in this society, far too many for its health, are sub-literate.

My own socialism distrusts some of the activities and much in the language of the Left when it assembles in small or large groups. I do not mean only or most importantly the discovery of corruption in Labour local councils, though that should shock us more than would corruption on the Right. I mean, for example, that I switch off when the Labour Party, led by the platform, sings 'The Red Flag' at the close of the party's annual conference; that is coterie-self-deception of a high order. So is the blokeishness of trade unionists who talk less about the members or the men than they do about 'the lads' or 'my lads'. There are other and larger bad habits, especially the habit of intolerant, abusing distortion of opposing positions. (Coleridge comes to mind: 'I have seen gross intolerance shown in support of tolerance'). That too should shock us more than such a practice on the Right; socialism is nothing unless guided by both respect for the truth and charity in pursuing it.

Of such failings, the two most important are the identification of many on the Left with an often insensitive anti-racism and with a cloth-eared political correctness in language; together, they damage well-considered anti-racism and deflect attention from genuinely prejudicial uses of language. Both emerge as illiberalism and anti-intellectualism: the first, here, in the description of an engagement with a specialist at the Royal Surrey County Hospital; the second towards the final pages, apropos the current uses and misuses of the word 'community'. Erving Goffman has a warning which is relevant here – on the bad habit of 'confronting everyone else with too much morality'. Too bullheaded, selective, partial or misapplied morality, one could add.

I have been told that to refer to the assistants in, for instance, Boots and Woolworth's as 'girls' is now an insult, that that title should be used only up to the age of sixteen. Middle-aged, respectable working-class women in Leeds used to refer to themselves and their friends, rather archly, as 'girls': 'all girls together', 'Come on girls, let's be devils and have another little one'. It is all very curious and fascinating. One can say that the 'youths' from the sixth-form college come to 'spot the talent' in Boots (their phrase not mine). There is no female equivalent of 'youth'. You can just about describe those 'boys' as 'lads' on the lookout; you can't really say they are looking over the 'lasses' (that tips over into the folksy). You can't say those boys – lads – youths – young men – are looking over the 'assistants', without half-implying that some of them are at the least bi-sexual. Seeking advice in Boots, I am likely to say delicately: 'The young lady on that counter [not 'the young woman'] told me that I would find . . .' Yet I still think of them up to, I suppose, the mid-twenties as 'girls' and am not at all aware of insulting, belittling, patronising them. It is all very much more complicated and interesting than those who tell me I must drop 'girls' after sixteen seem to recognise. A wonderful language.

Other arguments with people on the Left, not so much quarrels as differences of emphasis, are more interesting because they are about the reliability of observation and of interpretation; but at bottom they also draw on political assumptions.

It has rightly been said that my earlier descriptions of working-class life almost entirely omit the world of work, are women-centred. That is certainly a limitation. The explanation is that I was brought up in a predominantly women's world, a house with four women in it, all eager for me to 'get on' (which meant to 'get out'), and one man rapidly breaking-down through drink. I would in those days have been pushed into the world of work, of men's work, at fourteen had I not – the only and the first boy for streets and streets all around – gone to grammar school and so become almost entirely detached from the life of those streets and of the heavy industry within them.

An irony is that in the present book I am back on home ground; that is, saying a lot about women, hardly anything about men's heavy industrial work. For two reasons: Farnham is not an industrial town; you do not see the men going to work at the factories in droves each morning. Farnham is above all a servicing town, servicing its own inhabitants and those from several miles around who either work nearby or live there and commute elsewhere to work. So it is a shopping town and a provider of mixed professional and near-professional services. And in these activities the main change in the last three decades or so has been the increase in working-women, especially married women. So again men figure less, but this time with clear justification.

The present book now reveals a contradiction. I have sometimes been said to have drawn a picture of working-class life which, partly because it is largely non-political but chiefly because it lays great stress on the practice of 'neighbourliness', verges on the sentimental. I say later on why that judgment seems mistaken, whilst also apologising for not recognising that 'neighbourliness' is a widespread not a class-based habit.

The contradiction is that the same people, whilst rejecting any description of working-class life which, they fear, might make working-class people seem 'soft', just as strongly resent hard judgments on the habits of some working-class people. Working-class people must be strong in extrovert political rectitude, but none must be described as brutal or cunning, even in their own ways. To describe the particular forms of cunning and harshness in bosses is all right. There is a passage later, apropos young men in what used to be called a milk-bar, about the way such judgments by social determination reduce people as responsible individuals.

In subsequent years the Left's refusal to face this contradiction, this politically inspired distortion in thinking, has grown stronger. It may be argued that this greater intensity has been caused, forced upon them, by the more heartless distortions of Thatcherism. Even so, a reactive argument such as that will not do. A sound socialism should not trade-off in that way.

It was with such a bundle of literary, intellectual and social impulses that I set out to describe the typical, the unique, the humdrum and the strange life of this small English town towards the end of the century.

PART ONE

PEOPLE AND PLACES

CHAPTER 1

THE OLD MEN AND
THE FIRST-CLASS
COMMUTERS

They are the lords and owners of their faces.
Shakespeare, *Sonnet 94*

Most mornings they stand in front of Argos for an hour or two, on the tiled part which sets the long plate-glass window back from the pavement; often a sort of Laurel and Hardy, Shallow and Silence, Don Quixote and Sancho Panza pair. Two old working-men, a big one and a little one. That is a composite, not a particular, picture. There are several old men who use that space but usually only two at a time; men with some common characteristics.

Just standing there, backs to the window of goodies; not really looking out with an apparent interest or any other reaction at the people passing, not really focussing but yet not looking down, more like seeing and not seeing something about eight feet ahead and five feet up; blinking away the rheum at regular intervals, according to the weather. They seem not, certainly not, to be watching the world go by; that is the phrase which comes to mind from habit, and has to be at once thrown away; along with the other evasions in attitudes and language which beset portraits of English places, and especially of villages and small towns.

They are not talking either, the old men, except for occasional short comments from the corners of their mouths, whilst the heads stay facing straight ahead. What might they be saying – picking up some running items of domestic news? Mentioning something that caught their eyes in the day's *Sun* or the week's *Farnham Herald*? Commenting on the passers-by? If it is the last, they've perfected the art of seeing and noting but not being seen to be seeing and noting; they are as adept, as expert, as unobtrusive as bidders in an auction room.

At first they seemed slightly shabby. Their clothes are old-fashioned and in dead colours, the uninspired browns and greys of cheap men's materials, drab rather than shabby. (The women's counterparts nowadays tend to the gaudy. The two styles are just the opposite of the way birds are feathered.) These ill-fitting trousers and jackets could do with a bit of pressing but not mending; they are clean. The very shiny black boots suggest war service. We were taught to put polish on, spit on them and 'bone' them with the back of an old toothbrush. Unexpectant clothing, a world away from the bright, casually disposable clothes worn by their brothers and sisters who come back now and again from Canada, the States, Australia, New Zealand; like birds of paradise. Still, shell-suits are now all over Britain; not for the old men, though; they'd look like uneasy, chain-store Santa Clauses.

An archetypical conjunction. Long-retired chaps with nothing to do and hardly any money to spare, even if they have hobbies. Washed up on the shore for the final phases of their lives, on the shallow ledge which is Argos's forecourt. Presumably the firm set the window back so that more people could be accommodated, unencumbered and unencumbering, to survey the tiered cornucopia of desirable things, consumer durables and nondurables and unendurables; for the garden, the kitchen, the beach, sports, travel, health-and-beauty care, leisure, DIY; costume jewellery and pet accessories, the cavalcade of toys.

Argos – with what was Bejam and is now Iceland (the leader in frozen foods) – is one of the chief icons of the consumer society, very precise, very well-directed at today's not classless but cross-class audiences; at the increasingly thick middle band of those who now have something to spare at the end of each month; not the poor, old and out-of-work and not the well-to-do who go for 'designer' this, that and the other. Even within its thick band of customers there are distinctions; some who buy Argos's electrical goods with reliable brand-names joke at that plethora of costume jewellery.

The body of the catalogue offers respectable objects at reduced prices. Apart from the large windows, and a few eye-catching bins of goods, no display but that huge coloured book representing all the stuff stacked on shelves at the back, called up by computer once you have made your choice. Late-twentieth-century marketing which has creamed off much High Street trade and will itself, they say, be succeeded in ten or twenty years by home-computer-shopping.

And there, right in the front-middle of the display, are the old men, the other side of the same society, those who are unlikely ever to turn round and go into the shop, the hardly-ever-buyers of anything and the never-buyers of the glossier goods most of us are now used to having. The old men belong with those for whom to spend £25 in one go would still seem like a mad lashing-out of money, those who can't say to themselves: 'Well, it's only like ten bob in my early days.' Ten bob! That could have been a lot.

At least the manager at Argos doesn't move them on, though no doubt he has the right. Surprising that, since they might well seem a bit of an affront to him or to his customers, likely to put off some of them. British tolerance? A shrewd sense that it might make him and his shop seem harsh even to his own clientele? Perhaps he had to refer to Head Office for advice. At any rate, he seems to leave them alone, ignore them—or did; I haven't seen them for a month or two.

So do virtually all those who go past: buggy-pushing mothers, working-class people as old as they are but still occupied in one way or another, retired army officers and their wives, retired clerks and shopmen and shopwomen, retired boffins from the Royal Aerospace Establishment, down the road at Farnborough (it is now a Defence Research Agency, a suitably executive name), commercial travellers weaving in and out of shops, their cars in a park a few hundred yards away, and the odd executive and local professional.

Where do they live, the old men? At a guess, most of them on one of the bigger council estates – with wives who don't come out much any more and would rather not have them under their feet all day. Or widowed and living, reasonably content or made to feel a nuisance, with a daughter and her family, or daughter-in-law.

Clearly, they have nothing to do which regularly takes time and attention. Perhaps they now and again do a bit of shopping for the household. It would seem they do nothing in the garden, perhaps out of disinclination or lack of skill or because they have decided that the dogs and cats would foul or the kids nick whatever they managed to grow. So they do not have allotments. Obviously, they lack exercise; they are pale. They are not long-term townees; their build, their clothes, their stance says that; but neither are they country people; Farnham, being on the very edge of Hampshire, which is the first substantially agricultural county in the South-West, still has a fair number of displaced or visiting rural people. They have a touch of George Sturt's 'Bettesworth'; they may not still belong to the land but they retain some of its ways. These old men look rather as if they have always worked in or around this sizeable, part-country, part-urbanized, part-market town, part-commuter centre. Not in the shops or on the surrounding land but as general workmen, loaders, warehousemen, packers, perhaps truck drivers. So once work has been finally given up there is no physical centre to, no focal point in, their daily lives. Street corners in town are bustling, offer no place to be still; Argos's front has become the equivalent of a corner of the village green though they have never themselves known a village, in all probability. But they seem to feel the need for a sort of central resting-point.

I called them working-class because that is what by habit and demeanour they still are, have always been in their work and in where they live. If, as those polished boots suggest, they saw service in the last war, it was probably as soldiers. Like most of the gunners in my own regiment, assigned to a service, not choosers; most would come back to their old jobs and stay with them for forty years; no ladders of promotion, no changes or transfers, the only wage increases those the union negotiated; and then retirement, to the same council house. Nowadays they'll have their State Old Age Pensions. The sorts of job they had would not have been likely to offer a separate occupational pension, contributory or not. They may qualify for extra social security benefits, having no savings. If they live with the generation behind them, and if those relatives aren't grasping, they are not likely to be charged much for bed and board. It's still a thin going-on, though.

They look not all that well-off, at the bottom of the heap, just because so many, those in work at almost any level and age, are today so much better off. Those in their old jobs now have wages larger than anything their predecessors who retired only a dozen years ago could have imagined. These old men and their wives have in some ways fallen out of society, are not worth the wooing by politicians or admen or PR people. What do they feel when they see the commercials on the box for the latest zippy Peugeot or new fancy drink or increasingly exotic holidays? 'Discretionary spending' is a phrase which does not apply to them and which they would hardly understand.

But it would be wrong to call them 'the underclass'. That sounds too much like a boxing-in, too relegating, too side-lining – though economically and socially it is substantially accurate. I would even prefer 'lower' or 'lowest' class; that's suitably straight. They are the final survivors, part-urban but still part-rural in a town which has itself undergone, is still undergoing, those sorts of change – from the genuine market town Sturt knew under the south-western edge of the Hog's Back, serving for centuries West Surrey and East Hampshire, to today's mixture, with commuting executives at various levels more and more evident.

At the opposite extreme from the old men are the first-class commuters. It is commonly said that, being one of the most prosperous towns in Britain, Farnham has more of those than most towns of its size; the local paper recently reported that one third of the men are in banking or other of the financial professions. Their habits are no less well-grooved than those of the old men. There are many more second-class commuters, of course. I am avoiding the bromide 'standard-class' as one should also reject the idiotically mercantile substitution of 'customer' for 'passenger'. British Rail's PR men live in a synthetic semantic world of their own, even more than most of their kind. Some years ago they sought to persuade passengers – *English* passengers – that powdered tea was better than leaf. It was probably more profitable. Forced to back down quite soon, they sought spurious credit by announcing that now you could get a cup of real, good old English-style leaf-tea on their trains. They'll be telling us next that we are lucky to breathe good English air on their trains.

The service from and to Farnham is surprisingly good (even though the rolling-stock is very old, and the seats scuffed by casual boots and shoes), whatever the routine and predictable grumblers say. You can travel the forty-two miles to London every half-hour in under an hour from very early morning to very late at night, and more often at peak periods. There is usually parking-space at the station. So the town particularly attracts people who do not have to be at their desks sharp on nine or who have irregular hours. People working in the mass-media like it, and tend to push out into the little contiguous villages which help make up the town's almost forty thousand.

The most evident of the upper-crust, the first-class season-ticket holders, are – again like the old men – inveterate clus-terers. Dropped from the large Volvo, the Range-Rover, the Mercedes by their wives – the pair of obligatory retrievers or other breed of big dog behind the obligatory back-grid – or after they have put the BMW or Jag. in the car-park, they walk straight through the small booking-hall to their precise congregating-point on the platform. Naturally, they know their train's configuration and so the exact point at which the first of the first-class carriages will stop. And they know who will be there each morning and who is away on a business trip.

Naturally also, their clothes are chosen according to a narrow range of customs: dark suits usually with broad stripes, black or what used to be known (in a phrase unacceptable today) as 'nigger-brown' City bowlers or trilbies, shirts with bold thick stripes – often on a pale pink base, gold cufflinks which look like presentation or Christmas presents (the cuffs are occasionally 'shot' forward so as to keep the cufflinks just showing), regi-mental or regimental-style ties, on a dark base with a small, tastefully neat logo, shiny black shoes, rolled umbrellas. Plainly, the hair is cut in the City, not in Farnham. If an overcoat is needed it is likely to be dark but tightly cut like a British Warm or 'bum-hugger'; and velvet collars are favoured. There must be, there are, changes in these fashions for clothes, though they are slight and slow. But who sets them off? Who started the acceptance of those boldly striped shirts, or the velvet collars? Trend-setters in the City? Lloyd's Names with sufficient boldness? Certain magazines? Once a change has started the rest is a matter of peer-group-copying. There are one or two American financial experts, living for the time being in the Surrey uplands, their children at the American school not far down the line; sartorially these men soon look much like the natives.

With the umbrella they also hold the *Daily Telegraph* and/or the *Financial Times* or *The Times*. Hardly ever the *Guardian*. Now and again, you may these days see an *Independent*. Some of the younger ones, well enough advanced to be allowed to travel first-class but not yet as high as they seek to be, draw papers from their executive cases and go to work. One only very rarely sees a book and, on the occasions when I am being paid to travel first-class, I have not yet seen a mobile telephone. It would be frowned on not only as an interruption of such talk as there is (not very much) but because it would be thought to be showy on so short a journey. Those phones, along with the Walkmen, are more common in the second-class, sometimes flourished and shouted into as a sign of status, like the two-door, souped-up Toyota in the car-park.

The prototypical group here are all men; how are their fixed habits composed, the styles for talking, for greeting, for reacting, for smiling and for the differing lengths of smiles, for the twisting on the heel and back again in the way which signifies a semi-colon in the conversation, for drawing in or leaving out others, for recognising the pecking order, for all those subtle and unconscious forms of communicating which go on in almost all groups?

These styles are based, first and foremost, on public-school or fee-paying independent day-school styles, and especially on those of the sixth forms; on the group manners forged in the first eleven, the first fifteen and the Prefects' Common Room. These are the styles of people who feel themselves by nature and nurture slightly superior to the herd. Not greatly or securely superior since their schools have not usually been among the top half-dozen or so of the 'great' public schools. I have seen enough of men from Winchester, Eton, Harrow to be fairly confident of recognising their differing conversational manners – chiefly an assured unassertiveness – and their shared, unchallenged and hence understated confidence. Most of these men are a few bob short of that level.

The group-style is mid-range public-school sixth-form, residential or not. Their manners of speech are posh without being particularly fluent; they do not have the confident elisions, the slur, of the upper public schools; this is more often money-cute idiomatic and slightly doggish. No comprehensive has breathed over these men and hardly a maintained sixth-form college. They each slot into place in the morning conversation as smoothly as an expensive London bar's inner doors.

There is the Head Boy who probably has the most important job among them, in the City; there is a still slightly hesitant younger man on his way up; there is a fortyish one who mildly flatters the Head Boy, and one who looks as if he drinks too much at lunchtime in Town. And quite aside, usually alone though now and again someone will approach him deferentially, is one of Farnham's fairly numerous captains of industry who lives a few miles out. He will probably be met by the limousine at Waterloo, does not engage in conversation and, matching in this way some of the younger men on the way up the ladder, works on his papers or studies the *Financial Times* during the journey. Not now, or perhaps ever, groupy. Always good at figures but never School Captain of this or that; but with a tight, decisive mouth from before he was thirty.

Around this group move a mixture of other regulars and of those who go intermittently up to town to shop, see an exhibition or a play or film; these last usually after nine, when the cheap-day tickets in second-class become available, allowing OAPs to go to London even more cheaply, for two-thirds of the normal fare. Surprisingly, young secretaries don't much congregate but stand, a bit back, stroking or turning their engagement rings like one-bead rosaries, or preoccupiedly biting their nails to uniformity. A neighbour, a retired scientist, holds his viola; he is going to have it valued and then he and his wife will slip over to the Royal Academy, starting with a cafeteria lunch there. Two or three ill-paid directors of national charities, travelling second-class, nod at each other as they wander down the platform where, though you have further to walk when you reach Waterloo, the compartments are less crowded. Three or four small groups of middle-class, middle-aged women are off on a fairly regular – once a month or so – shopping trip plus lunch. The booking clerk says Thursday is their favourite day; perhaps because the shops stay open later and Friday is a busy day at home, getting ready for the weekend. Six or seven girls and boys, in full private-school fig, are off down the line to Woking or Brookfield. A fair number of minor executives make up the crush in the second-class.

The first-class group are not crushed and do not squeeze. The rules of manners hold right through to getting on the train and taking a seat. And there we may leave them, at least for the time being. But not quite. For I have been circling around one thing which ought to be said about them as a group.

These faces are almost all unattractive, and not just because one or two show signs of over-eating and drinking. It would be an error to call them ugly since ugliness is a matter of birth. And those born ugly can have beautiful faces, lovely expressions, the mark of inward stillness. There is little sign here of an inner life of calm or contemplation. Or of that other kind of interesting and attractive face, one marked by earnest self-doubt, by a thoughtful concern about what one is making of one's life.

I am not criticising these men as individuals. Rather, the point is how very much our public faces are determined by the personae our occupations offer us, and by those they exclude; how much our faces become set, in signalling day after day the attitudes we have had to become used to using professionally. Time and experience and thought etch their particular and telling stories on all our faces; and are reflected in our eyes, from the shining and expectant to the watchful and hooded. It may be that the faces of most of these men, if freed from the expressions which seem to be required when they are operating within the competitive professional world, become softened, relaxedly gay, warm, kindly; they may be good husbands and fathers; the older ones may have had a 'good', a brave, war; they may be well-practised in neighbourliness. But here the faces are watchful, calculating, knowing. They would not use such a vulgar expression as 'no flies on Charlie' but they hint at a more sophisticated

variant of it. Such laughter as there is is brief and often suggests
schadenfreude; there is little irony, and wryness would be a
wrong note, as would self-deprecation; unless it involved a safe
area such as an incident at golf. The range of permitted,
accepted, learned expressions is remarkably limited. Most have
lived-into but few have well-lived-into faces. You know at once
that none of them is an academic, a cleric, working for a charitable cause, a shop assistant, a skilled technician. When another
neighbour, an FRS – the town has a few of those, happy to be
almost entirely unrecognised – passes them on the platform, his
expression, engrossed, lined with deep real thought, makes the
group look like stereotypes; in very good suits.

You can't help regretting, naïve though some will call it, that
all this is so often the price of capitalist democracy; just as the
dour, heavy, not-to-be-pushed-around, watchful faces of Mos-
cow apparatchiks told you something about the Communist
system and how to climb within it. You know, of course, that
almost all these men will vote Tory habitually and that to discuss
it with them would produce a litany of received opinions. That
is likely to be one firm common quality, their confidence in the
interpretation of the world as it has been handed on to them, at
home, at school and during their professional training, their
subaltern days – an interpretation they have entirely accepted.
Not at all an intellectual world, though certainly intelligent and
sharp; not at all an imaginative world or given to musing on the
best that has been thought and said. But certainly a complete, an
all-embracing world within whose perspectives and panoramas
they, their wives (who tend to look harder; perhaps it is one of
the costs of trying to look younger, that hard facial lining) and –
they simply assume until perhaps shaken – their children also can
live in assurance and comfort; as most seem to do. Perhaps one
of the younger men, or one of the much older who is now looking forward to soon leaving the rat-race, may have a conversion
sufficient to make them at least half-think of voting Liberal
Democrat. The others, the majority, stay in the boat.

And at weekends? Gardening for some, certainly – the most
common weekend activity of those in all social classes who own
their own homes. It doesn't help to bridge class-distinctions even
though we all bump into each other on Sundays at the Garden

Centres. But at least it is, though class-divided, a civil and civilised and civilising occupation which most of us practise, from the allotment and its rickety hut to the sit-on, power-driven mower.

Golf, naturally. In spite of some exceptions, still a class-identified, professional middle-class, Rotary and Masons' pursuit; at its peak the club-house and its ritual drinks before lunch on Sunday. Then there is walking the dogs. Some people beagle. Given that Farnham is at least semi-commuter-land, that seems to be stretching to the innermost limits the boundaries of country pursuits. More part of the ex-urbanite pattern are those who drive to Blackbushe and drone their single-engined planes along the Wey valley and over the town on Sundays.

Have I come near to at least implying that the first-class commuters deserve less human sympathy than the old men on Argos's forecourt? If so, that was not intended. Some of the wells of memories and impressions you tap at the back of your head when writing seem fuller and more engaging than others. Or some memories draw much more powerfully than others on your deep-seated sympathies – and lackings of sympathy.

So it is easy to feel a more immediate sympathy with the old Argos men, those who don't go up to London from one year-end to another, than with the first-class commuters. Partly because the first are so much to one side, have such a discarded air, demand pity. Also because their work has not given them catch-as-catch-can, calculating expressions. As we saw, mid- to upper-middle-class executive professions, especially in financial institutions, do not encourage attractive expressions in faces or language. Looking at people such as these you may try hard to be as charitable as possible; but it would be a fudging lie not charity to say that the faces and the language in themselves suggest comely lives, the devotion of good schoolteachers or the disinterested patience of craftsmen, or the selfless absorption of a good scholar or scientist. The faces and the language may, of course, in this instance as in some others, be misleading masks.

But neither do their lives appear to have given the old men faces engraved with the wisdom which may sometimes come from decades on the land, or from practising a fine craft. Or if they have experienced some of these things it does not now show. They do not look beaten, downtrodden; but neither do they look fulfilled, grave and learned in some important human art. They look a bit lost, set down here, now, as change flashes past them. They are at the side-wall of a dance-hall in which they now find no place, and little if any spirit, even to take the mickey out of some of the things that are going on and past them. With the first-class commuters they form the opposing outer brackets of the ranges of characters in this town. Comparing the two kinds directly, one has to agree yet again that private faces in public places really are nicer, if not wiser, than the opposite.

There are many others, many other kinds of inhabitants here, from the hard-working, usually admirably hard-working, local councillors to those who live quiet, neighbourly, suburban and sub-suburban lives in the private estates, the council estates and the scattered houses of the villages; from all such as those to the slipshod, the feckless, the crooked and the brutish. Naturally.

CHAPTER 2

FARNHAM, ROMORANTIN-LANTHENAY AND TOWNS IN OUR HEADS

In the city, time becomes visible.
Lewis Mumford

Art is upon the town.
J. A. McNeill Whistler, *Ten o'Clock Lecture*

Cobbett was born in Farnham and did not lose his early love for its rural and town life, its interest as a particular model of the English market town. George Sturt recorded it with sympathetic precision during a long moment of change. Even today, behind all the middle-class mercantilism and the commuters' smart styles and the council estates' ups-and-downs we can see many of Cobbett's and Sturt's continuities. These two are the historic tap-roots for understanding this place, such a place.

Like similar English towns with a sizeable middle-class, Farnham has many snobberies and jobberies; and their convolutions are endlessly interesting, if often irritating. It is also full of people doing good for others, without payment or expectation of external reward, and of a solid close neighbourliness in all its parts. It is fresher and more graspable than a big city and escapes the claustrophobic range of activities which villages, whether long-settled or largely commuter villages, can entertain. My wife and I have grown to like Farnham but not mainly for the reasons to be found in the usual portraits of small English towns.

I cannot recall the exact moment when I decided to write about Farnham. As you finish writing about one subject how does another, like an imaginative heart-murmur, more and more draw itself to your attention? Partly because, as I said in the Introduction, it becomes the latest magnet for a bundle of your continuing interests and partly for reasons as chancy as finding some unusual coloured stones on a beach. My coloured stones were Cobbett (1763–1835) and, even more, George Sturt, or 'George Bourne' (1863–1927), best known for *The Wheelwright's Shop*. Until we came here I had not realised that both were Farnham men; and with precisely a century between their births. Cobbett was very much more than that, became a national and international figure; but some of his strengths, his peasant strengths as Ebenezer Elliott called them in his obituary poem, were those which the town and district still like with some justice to claim for themselves.

Cobbett was a towering figure, hugely robust – a John Bull, a prolific writer and a man of prolific other activities, political and social. I admire him but have little in common with him except for a touch of driven puritanism and a special hatred of the humbugging of hierarchies, the pretensions of placemen and the incivilities of presumed status; what he called, in his *Advice to Young Men*, 'the supple crouch of servility . . . and the hectoring voice of authority'.

Cobbett was undoubtedly the more greatly gifted individual and the greater writer but I feel personally nearer to Sturt. Sturt was a quieter, more solitary and ingrown man (he had ill-health), and his works much more intimately than Cobbett's portray Farnham, its occupations and its people; this was round about the turn into our century, when the town and its hinterland began unmistakably to change from a rural crafts-based and market area to a modern-servicing, very small-scale-industrial and commuter town and district.

I knew those books from university, prompted by reading F. R. Leavis's praise of them, and later from teaching adults. I had always been a little uneasy with the didactic way Leavis and some of those most influenced by him seemed to use Sturt; and that reflected for a long time on my recollected view of Sturt. I had not looked at the books for thirty years. When I did I was deeply impressed, far more impressed than I expected; and more understanding of Leavis's promotion of them.

For one thing, Sturt writes very well indeed, with the elaborate qualifications and conditionals which the attempt to describe people in time and in relation to their social and physical landscapes needs and rarely has. He is unshakeably humane but not sentimental; his portraits are entirely unglamorous; he can be sharp – as in his descriptions of class-snobberies which I quote later – but is not vengeful or rhetorical. Like the best writers in this field he lets his generalisations emerge from the 'thisness' of his accumulated detail; like one who is blind for the time being he runs his hands carefully and respectfully over the great mass of material until it yields its shape to him; then he quietly offers it to you.

By these means he refreshes your sense of plain but important truths: about how the labourers he knew, faced with a nasty but dangerous emergency, simply expected to do something about it themselves, to become muddy, filthy and soaked through, to put themselves at risk, not to hang back and wait for 'Them' to take over, not to expect someone to send for the police or the doctor. Sturt recovers also the weight of some apparently banal working-class sayings, and of many inescapable facts of that life: such as that it is much harder simply to manage the household budget if it is cut to the bone week after week than it is to manage a budget which contains something to spare, a bit of 'play' within it.

Few small towns and their surrounding areas have had so sensitive and sympathetic a delineator and tracer of change as Farnham had in Sturt. Few such places have had two native sons such as Cobbett and Sturt, each of whom, though in different forms and manners, celebrated their small town in an intimate, loving but wholly unparochial way. Each of them was absorbed by and tried to capture in words the texture, the grain, of English rural and rural-urban life; its sturdiness (for they were English in the bone) and its limitations – especially through the divisions, and so the injustices, caused by the sense of class and status. It would be for me an over-reaching and an alien exercise to try to write like a twentieth-century Cobbett. But I am not being falsely modest when I say that time and again I have wished I could write as well as Sturt about modern Farnham. I cannot, but hope I have learned something from him.

There will be later references to both men, but nothing substantial. It was tempting to include much more but this is a book
about modern Farnham and its representativeness, not a history.
These few pages have been included chiefly because my redis-
covery of Cobbett and Sturt was an impulse towards this enterprise. Perhaps the warmth I have shown will encourage others to
read these two – especially the more neglected Sturt.

We had never before lived in a place like Farnham: southern, still
part-rural, generally prosperous, part ex-urbanite. I found
myself teased every time I walked in town by the differences from
the North, from working-class districts there, by the different
light and air and manners; and teased by the similarities. Then I
began to read two kinds of book other than those of Cobbett and
Sturt: those which described the lives of particular towns other
than Farnham; and those by Farnham's own local historians.
The latter are a large and on the whole admirable company; they
love the town but do not glamorise it. Some portraits of other
towns have the same good qualities, and those by professional
social historians follow their own specialist disciplines.
    As for the rest, they are all too often folksy and flattering,
Thornton Wilder's *Our Town* done into corny English, *Dear
Octopus* as a discursive celebration of a district not just of a
family. That would not do at all; that was one aspect of what I
had been resisting for many years, of what seemed misreadings of
English culture or, more accurately, cultures. If parts of this book
seem tart that may be because this reaction to the droll writers
has still not been sufficiently measured and controlled.

One other long-standing but hitherto not much examined interest
led towards this book: townscapes, the shapes of towns and the
relations of those shapes to the towns' daily life. That interest
had been given a push, just before we came to Farnham, by
Kevin Lynch's *The Image of the City*. I have indulged myself so
far as to write a dozen pages here about townscapes generally.
They can of course be skipped, though I would think that a pity
on the whole.
    That long interest and the impact of Lynch found a focus on a
journey through France in the early eighties. We came upon

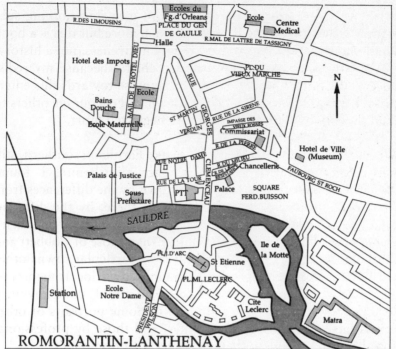

Romorantin-Lanthenay on an early summer evening and thought
it seemed amiably nondescript: as might befit a provincial town
of about forty thousand – a bit bigger than Grantham or Farnham – where nothing very much happens now. Many decades
ago, in the early heady days of the automobile, it was one of the
main French centres of precision development in engines. The
run-down buildings of the Matra works are or were (it is some
years since we were in the town) right in the centre, entered by
an importance-asserting large archway. Matra seems to have
been bought out by Renault. They now make their Espace station-
wagons just outside town, in one of those sets of functional
blocks which you see across the fields on the outskirts of such
towns, as the Route Nationale by-pass pulls you round them; the
crystal, the cutlery, the plastics factories.

You could call Romorantin the south-east gateway to the
haunting landscape of Alain-Fournier, the Sologne; it lies rather
flatly between the Loire and, nearer, the Cher; outside is deeply
and rather dully agricultural land. Its heart has changed very
little over a couple of centuries. The river Sauldre isn't very large,

but at the place where the town began it makes a southward bend and in doing so leaves one modest, one small and one very small island; all so built-up or wooded that you hardly notice them. The middle one is the bottom end of a park which then spreads north-east over a bridge on to the mainland; an exceptionally imaginative visual idea. The biggest island holds at its centre the main town church, St Etienne.

You can see much the same, often prettier and in more striking landscapes, in many parts of France; and England. Presumably that is why few tourists have heard of this place. It does have one extremely expensive hotel whose restaurant has two Michelin stars, so no doubt gourmets seek it out. It has only thirteen rooms plus three apartments, at upper London prices; many of the diners will have to get back into their cars and go. The only other hotels (two) which Michelin recognised in 1993 added only twenty more rooms. Not at all a tourist honey-pot.

We knew nothing about it that first time. We stopped the night there because we were heading south-east on D765 from the Sologne; it was nearly seven o'clock, time to find a bed; Romorantin was the only sizeable place not too far down the road.

We took a walk after supper and were caught. The early evening, not the busyness of the working and shopping day, is best for your first look at a town new to you; it yields its underlying physical character then, and suggests the relation of that character to the daily and continuing rhythm of the place, the circulation through its arteries, its heart, its liver, its kidneys, its lungs. If it is a particularly attractive town it is likely to be, after seven in the evening, like an intelligent beauty who has given up being on show to visitors and become preoccupied with herself.

So that first night in Romorantin we were caught not by the old works, though they have an industrial-archaeological charm by now; nor by the old centre, though that is pleasant enough. I had met Kevin Lynch only a couple of years before. In the generation after Lewis Mumford he was the most imaginative writer I have known on towns, and as much an eye-opener as was Erving Goffman on Gesture (both died relatively young). Lynch had mapped out and named some key characteristics of towns to which I had been responding for years without getting round to defining them. Such as 'edges', 'landmarks' and, most important of all, 'nodes', those focal points which hold a town together, meeting-places, where the rabbit-tracks (which he calls 'paths', simply) cross. If a town has no such network it is hard to make sense of, to feel easily or soon at home in.

Romorantin flows from square to square (those are the most important nodes), up streets and alleys of different widths and lengths, down over the river and back again, some of it old, some of it new. But it all coheres; you could hold it in your hand; you feel immediately at home there, inspired to walk, accepted if only for the time being. More straggly and incoherent places seem colder, less accommodating, if not actually unwilling to accept you and off-putting.

Bigger places can have that feel; the ring of Barcelona before political changes let it burst its bounds must have had it; but that is rare. A medium-sized city such as Norwich, sensitively handled or simply because it is out on a limb, can keep the sense of wholeness. The pattern of nodes and rabbit-tracks has to be reasonably near the centre, manageable on foot; but not necessarily of one period. They are not all contemporary with what European towns' Tourist Boards like to signpost as the 'Historic Centre' – the Cathedral, the old market square and Town Hall, the cluster of carefully preserved medieval houses. The ideal size is probably between fifteen and sixty thousand; in this century, that is. Above that, the needs of industry and commerce are likely to have worked against it; and well-defined class divisions, especially in housing, set in. Below that, the unity is there or it is not; it may be obvious but too small to occupy the imagination for long, or non-existent, as in a featureless straggling village.

Most of Umbria's hill-towns have this unity and that is why, probably, so many of us are first and only half-consciously at ease in them. Aix-en-Provence is a classic, a superb example of the genre; but now overrun. Another outstanding beauty, much less well-known, is Ascoli Piceno, on the Marches running to the sea, east of Southern Umbria. The physical harmony is so great that you are in danger of romantically assuming that the life it sustained in its heyday had that kind of harmony too.

Most towns in Europe, especially after modern developments, have lost the feeling of wholeness, if they ever had it. Look at the disaster inflicted on so many Pennine stone townships in the insensitive sixties; their irregular, holding-together reef-knots – the cobbled market squares – were destroyed and replaced, from mass-produced designs, by trivially uniform shopping centres. Blind local government and persuasive developers came together. The feeling of agoraphobia in many American small towns arises just here – they are spread out straight to four horizons, with little opportunity for social and psychological relationships to weave tortuously between space and buildings so as to hold them together. Nevertheless, so strong is our need for such connections, even such towns can come to be 'raw towns that we believe and die in'.

Some elderly English market towns have, or had, evolved into comprehensible shapes too – evolved rather than being built like that (a most difficult operation, as most of our new towns show). In the middle of writing these pages I read again Lawrence on the Nottinghamshire mining villages and small towns. That passage used to seem more a tirade than a sustainable argument, using overdone comparisons with Italian hill-towns. It is easy to respond to their harmony, variety, sense of people's occupations and recreations being recognised and valued, in spite of the harshness and rigidity of much else in their cultures. But though a quick comparison of their physical setting with that of Eastwood makes a sharp dramatic point it isn't greatly relevant; cultures are not, partially or across centuries, thus transferable.

Nor do we need such sleights-of-hand to be shocked by those mining villages. We can, of course, refuse to be shocked, since we know about the drives of nineteenth-century capitalism. The land-owners wanted to get at the coal under their fields as quickly and as cheaply as possible. The miners were drawn in from existing towns and villages some miles, often many miles, away. Public transport hardly existed; the early unions, where they existed, were ineffectual. So the owners put up, in the middle of the fields, those rows on rows of basic housing. You could say – I could certainly say – that the houses in Lawrence's 'Bottoms' were superior to many back-to-back terraces in the towns, to such as the Hunslet terraces I grew up in; and the air was better.

Yet if you go back to Eastwood today, on its pleasant slope down to the tiny River Erewash, and look at those houses, many still occupied, thrown up in straight lines without any regard to the lie of the land or to the communal needs of people – except for the boozer – you are startled, shocked again, at the power of that economic drive and that disregard for how the workers lived which was so solid that it allowed the owners to leave out of the plans anything which would have deflected them from getting most rabbit hutches for most 'hands' out of the available acres. No irregular square on the top of the hill, no irregularity in the rows of houses, no sinuosity to meet that of the landscape, no thought about the most relevant materials. Except for its technological fecundity and its commercial thrust, a barren and loveless culture, a culture which regarded most workers as little more than beasts of burden and, by treating them as near-beasts, led them further down that road. We *should* still be shocked by evidence such as this.

That was a by-pass within a by-pass, set off by remembering the Italian hill-towns and then Lawrence's comparison of them with his own home town. It also underlines the attractiveness of what may seem at first sight ordinary-looking places, such as Romorantin. They body out the common need in a town for a range of places to meet, for well-used and well-remembered tracks, for odd surprises as you come round corners, for not feeling overborne, or assigned to a lowly position, for having a place to move around in just as much as the next man, whoever he might be.

All that has so far made the characters of such towns seem too unitary, as though there is only one, the same, map in each person's head. But we create our own towns in our own heads, to our own image, according to our own needs. We each have our own psycho-social map and resist others which might quarrel with or question ours. One couldn't claim to a stranger that Leeds is an easily accommodated or accommodating city. But as an adolescent I had, like most of my peers, carved out a manageable core, my Leeds; bounded by the public library and Lewis's on the Headrow, the Majestic cinema and City Square, 'Woollies' and Briggate, the Market and Vicar Lane. It worked, in practical terms; but didn't have the complex, receptive feeling of the kind of place I have been chiefly talking about.

So: many sets of nodes and rabbit-tracks for each town, many mental maps; and all overlapping in space and time and very much else. At the least there are as many maps as there are social

and other groupings; at the extreme, almost as many as there are
individuals who respond to such vibrations. You might easily
have an aerial map of the town, duly showing the streets, squares,
buildings. To indicate its inner coherences you would need a
different map for as many kinds of preoccupation as its citizens
practised or you could manage to note. If those separate maps
were on tracing paper, each in a different colour, and you then
piled them neatly on the basic black-and-white town map, you
would have an enlightening impression of their deviations and,
again, their overlappings.

So much for space. But if you could you would also need to
show another dimension, to show also deviations and overlaps
in time. You could invent a game called 'Rabbit-tracks and
Nodes' in which you provided the players each with a differently
coloured map, its focal points and paths named, and asked them
to identify exactly who, what groups or what individuals, used
each; and if possible when.

All this is, as so often in human activity, a sort of weaving. In
our use of the places we live in, we are psycho-sociological
weaver-birds, creators of nets to hold us up and together – linked
at least with those we wish to be together with, spinners of webs
of habit as tough as those of spiders, congenital knitters without
needles and usually without knowing what we are doing or
making inside our heads, and then marking out with our feet.

There is, though, for each town, a thick central tree – a trunk
and branches – which is most used, though its uses and its users
change constantly. And for each individual there is likely to be a
basic, a most often repeated, track-pattern: from home to railway station or bus-stop, office or shop; then to pub or club or
merely home again each weekday; and a similar core pattern at
weekends. To which, for virtually everyone, multiple variations
have to be added.

The maps change by age; and by class, to which is linked
prosperity. Among British town shops Woolworth's used to be,
was for decades, the chief working-class point of reference;
nowadays it has lost its magic. The supermarkets dominate and
are, between each other and within themselves, class-graded,
though rarely single-class. Then there are the occupational, the
commercial and the social routes.

More interesting are the changes by time of day, by who uses what when. From the mundane to the slightly bizarre – an underground supermarket car-park may be, after nine in the evening, the place where teenagers drink and deal in drugs. During the day and through the week the supermarkets themselves will accommodate a complicated pattern of class-changes. For an hour or so after the eight-thirty opening middle-class housewives in the second car will dominate; working-class wives will arrive later if at all during the week. The corner-shop on the council estate is dearer but nearer and buses are few. Thursday mid- to late afternoon is again a favourite middle-class time for quite big shopping (unless they have gone up to London); perhaps that's another way of moving one sizeable chore from too near the weekend. Saturday is the most clearly defined day – again, middle-class people move in briskly soon after opening time; working-class people, for whom weekend shopping is more leisurely, more of a bit of a break for both husband and wife, are much more numerous on Saturday afternoon and often end the trip at a café for tea.

There are intermittent but intensive temporary routes, often unexpected-hazard routes: for a sequence of visits to the health centre or local hospital, or to a solicitor, an estate agent, the local authority 'Locality Office'.

It is plain from the above examples alone that tracks and nodes change as society changes. There are at least two surprises here; that some new facilities, such as supermarkets and multiple sports centres, are absorbed effortlessly; and that the absorption is often by modification, by making the new provision fit the old set of assumptions about the way life is best lived; unsurprising proof of the tenacious hold of class habits and distinctions.

It follows that some of the same nodes and rabbit-tracks have been used since the towns were founded. They were natural stopping-points and ways-to-get-around from the towns' beginnings and still are. Leicester is quite a large city, going on three hundred thousand, but its market has been for centuries the principal focal point for all groups within its boundaries and around; and the late twentieth-century planners preserved that character when they decided the market needed a face-lift. Some other such transplants have also worked well; others have torn the hearts out of towns, not – it should be obvious – simply the physical heart. They have cut the historic arteries, the living interconnections, broken the weave, destroyed the web, revealed a lack of understanding of the cultures of towns, of the fact that each town has a specific and complex life, partly shared with others like it, partly unique to itself; and that the best first way towards understanding that society is by watching where people walk, where they stop and meet and talk; and then by taking the walk yourself.

And now, as with those other impulses and influences, Cobbett and Sturt, and just as regretfully, I must leave Romorantin-Lanthenay and its like, except for a few further references. It is time to turn directly to this time, this place, Farnham.

Farnham does not reveal its congruities easily or soon. This is probably because it hasn't a very dramatic setting or vestiges of a particularly vivid past, or present; it had troubles during the Civil War; Edward Thompson notes that the first private Bill of Enclosure, passed in 1710, concerned Farnham Park and was strongly resisted locally; there was very slight bombing in the last war. It has pre-historic elements – the earliest recorded village in Britain – and Roman, but substantially the town began as and took its name from a Saxon settlement, round about the sixth century; on water-meadows ('fearn-hamm') by the shallow banks of a small river only ten miles old, the Wey.

This part of Surrey became the South Kingdom of the Middle Saxons. They had penetrated west to the great forests of what is now Hampshire, making a bulge with Hampshire on three sides of Surrey. The Wey rises in a field to the west, well into Hampshire since Farnham is only a mile from the county boundary; the river's north branch then wanders through fields till it reaches the town, slightly sideways on, semi-detached, not central. Soon afterwards it reaches a meadow and becomes rural again. Its site there can be called a valley, but the main impression is of low meadow. Startling to think that even in the last century the townsfolk used still to bathe there naked, sewage notwithstanding – the first main sewer arrived in 1887. A few still bathe there but not naked. There would be a march of embattled established citizens if they tried that today, even in a more or less cleaned-up river.

The flatness soon gives way, but not dramatically, and the change doesn't much take away from that first impression of almost East-Anglian-like meadow. The abrupt western edge of the curiously flat-topped, seven miles or so long, final North Down – the Hog's Back – is near on the east. On the north side, three or four hundred yards from the river and running directly away from it, and starting at what is still the town's dead centre – though the sixties developers did their dim best to displace that centre – there is a bit of a slope, about a quarter of a mile long and gentle until the last hundred yards: Castle Street, still one of the finest streets in Southern England, very wide so as to take a market though it doesn't nowadays except for three or four stalls; lined with houses from several centuries, some fine, some workers' cottages; and on the middle right-hand side a row of almshouses given to the town by Andrew Windsor, Esq., of Bentley, in 1619: 'For the Habitation and Relief of Eight Poor Honest Old Impotent Persons'. Castle Street is, of course, part of the Conservation Area of 1970 and has nineteen listed lamp-posts. Park Row ('Loo Lane'), just off its middle, had a listed loo, but unfortunately that is now offices.

The river goes away, meanders on, east and a little north, round the southern edge of the Hog's Back, through Godalming (from there it is still navigable; it used to carry some commercial traffic). Then Guildford, and on to join the Thames at Wey-bridge.

Castle Street is crowned by a Norman keep and a castle which is a hotchpotch from several centuries but still striking and grand, especially seen from the bottom of the street. It was for centuries the seat of the Bishops of Winchester. The Harrow Way and the Pilgrims' Way to and from Winchester pass the Castle. The Bishops had a very large park for hunting deer and, though much of that has been eaten away, three hundred acres remain. They are matched on the other side of Castle Street, to the west, by a sizeable accidental open area – shallowly sloping fields once central to Farnham's prosperity as a premier hop-growing centre. From the facing slope, Cromwell's troops bombarded the Castle.

Every so often developers' eyes light up at the thought of how many profitable executive dwellings they could cram into all that space – 'having a favoured location near to town centre but with privileged views over this highly sought-after Surrey residential area'. So far all efforts have failed, not only, it is said, because of the campaigns of the land's defenders, but because of inheritance battles. It is rented by a local farmer with a fine herd of Friesians and a well-nourished ecological conscience; so Farnham also has a working farm within the town boundaries. The large open fields – the hop-fields – are criss-crossed with public rights of way. Has any other town, in so populous a part of England, so large a walking area so near its modern working centre?

So open land comes right into the town's back-yard from three sides. The Pilgrims' Way from Winchester snakes across those hop-meadows, round the Castle and east for Chaucer's City of London and Canterbury. And, down by the river, the water-meadows have been too soggy to tempt developers and are also preserved. Thus, there are two superb air-holes – places to breathe – next to the centre of the town.

Now the shape of the living town, its heart for centuries and still today, begins to show itself. The fulcrum – it is not a node since it has no resting-space and is a busy junction – is the point where the bottom of Castle Street meets at right angles the middle of the hundred and fifty yards or so of The Borough. That has been for long the commercial core. Sturt's family had a shop at number 18 there, roughly where Halford's is now and, when they moved, they did not go outside that stretch.

Farnham has a pre-war by-pass, running east and west beyond the river on the south. But there is still enough semi-local traffic to keep the Castle Street/The Borough junction far too busy for the town's peace of mind. Even so, a bench or two facing the junction would be appreciated and adopted by the old men at Argos; and new plans should eventually reduce the weight of traffic.

At its western end The Borough meets Downing Street which has curved up from the old road to Waverley Abbey, only a couple of miles away but now separated by the by-pass. Sampson's Maltings is down there, still on the town side, by the river, not far from where Downing Street starts and heads uptown.

At its eastern end The Borough meets an early bit of fairly brutal town-planning – South Street, which was in 1868, as New

Road, cut in a straight line from the town over the river to the railway station. A branch line from Guildford had appeared in 1849; the Farnham–Aldershot–London line, still our artery, opened in 1870. South Street downgraded the curvy route to the station via Downing Street. At its start, at the junction with The Borough and East Street, are the only traffic lights in the inner town, and they are just on its edge.

The length of West Street is still a testimony to Farnham's prosperous days, when the corn-growers, the hop-growers and the ancillary merchants put up large, brick, terraced residences. A splendid group of town-houses, especially on the south side, proclaims that prosperity and consequence. Not all the Georgian frontages are genuine but the overall effect is excellent, the main stem of a straggly, curvy, irregular, architecturally varied progress. The most interesting building is Willmer House, now the Town Museum. It has, said Pevsner, 'one of the finest cut brick façades in the country' – but is otherwise very odd. West Street ends after half-a-mile, just after the next line of almshouses. Trimmer's, the brewer gave those; Sampson, also a brewer, endowed some at roughly the same place, but they have been moved. Brewing and charity went strongly hand in hand in Farnham. From this point you can feel the country, Hampshire, beginning; Petersfield to the south, Winchester to the west.

The story is different on the east side. Predictably, The Borough yields to East Street; we have only photographs to tell us how that used to look at its inner part, how it related to the town centre. It pointed to London; on the pavement edge of a faceless little modern piazza there has been left an old milestone: 'London 42 miles'. In the sixties, just clear of the designated historic area, they made a two or three hundred yard swathe for commercial development; hence the 'piazza', a small bow in the direction of a sense of community, of circulating space; there is one unwelcoming bench, like a bale deserted in a scruffy field; and all is dead since it is inorganic to the town's pattern of activities.

'The Woolmead', they call that pile; a nod by naming to a bit of mistaken history. Typical of that kind of sixties architecture which makes you think its design was knocked out on an architects' drawing-board in London, by an apprentice using a basic model which one of the senior partners had himself knocked out and pinned up. 'Functional', if that word is dismissive; with one or two 'embellishments' tagged on; these also are inept, would-be historical nods. Some of the old townscape begins again, eastward, after the 'development' has finished. But by then the street is, apart from some good elements, a disorderly straggle; the Woolmead, that dangling participle, that architectural 'and . . . er', that blasted space, has sterilised the ground between The Borough and the rest of East Street, has cut one of the town's main arteries. So the planners added a disembodied, anonymous, one-way system out there, plus the obligatory and equally faceless trading estate.

You stand and look and wonder. Why did the council permit this? Not, in this town, because of local corruption, the lining of pockets. Rather because that style of 'development' was in the air all across Britain and was still felt to be more important than preserving the best of the old and trying to make sure that the new and the old lived together harmoniously or contrasted inter-estingly – which is not to make a case for pastiche. Nor at that time did many local authorities have adequate environmental and planning staff; or the habit of consulting outside experts who might offer unpalatable, braking, advice. Local government in Britain has many virtues and we like to hymn them. It also has some gaping inadequacies, notably of imagination, whether his-torical or of the present.

Why did the architects commit this kind of atrocity? Because they too were caught in a misguided set of doctrines (they don't merit being called even 'ideologies')? Or was this sort of thing, for the graduates once they were on the town, merely cheap work which gave quick and reasonably profitable returns, espe-cially if you used virtually the same matrix wherever you worked? One does tend to have too idealised a view of people in the major social professions – of doctors, dentists, solicitors, architects. But some are slipshod, some sail close to the legal wind and some are just bent. Those architects who thrived on routine, repetitive, culture-blind work in the sixties – such as the Woolmead, and most high-rise flats around the country – should be more ashamed than those (though they were probably no more than local jobbing builders, not graduates) who obeyed the mine-owners in

Lawrence's area almost two centuries ago. That the local councillors agreed to their proposals, from the best of short-sighted motives, does not absolve the architects.

Half-hidden just off Downing Street to the west is a beautiful complex; the fourteenth-century parish church of St Andrew's, with Cobbett's large stone-cabineted grave just outside its main door. Then the double-fronted Rectory and three little lanes of cottages, the lot making a square completed by the edge of Downing Street. But this area is left aside, to one side, contributes nothing to the town's circulation nowadays. That fact has preserved it, but as a dead though beautiful space. Even old people do not sit there, on the three unobtrusive benches.

Just below this group, and also across on the other side of Downing Street, two large central areas have been levelled to make car-parks. At least they are just spaces, not out-of-place high buildings; and some of them have, fortuitously, opened fine vistas of the local vernacular, domestic and small-scale commercial, architecture; small, red-rustic brickwork and hanging pantiles. The most important car-park, the Central, does that but is itself marred by a particularly ugly small supermarket and one which doesn't know what to do with its own gubbins. Multi-storey car-parks would be the worst step of all. Seen from the old hop-fields the town still offers a long, low-level, eighteenth-century panorama, one of the last left in England. It must have looked even more haunting at night, when the streets were lit by gas; that lasted until as recently as 1960.

After all this effort to make sense of Farnham's centre physically, I realise that it doesn't on the face of things make much sense. Time for another attempt. The river flowing past just on the southern edge, the Castle sitting up there, not entirely connectedly, on the northern slope; in the middle the east–west straight line, with The Borough's central few hundred yards – still crowded with shops – fastening East and West Streets together; and out of The Borough, at right angles, Castle Street itself. A sort of upside down 'T', it all makes.

But there was a good complication to Farnham's pattern, and much of it is still there. When you get your eye in, you see that Farnham is a town of snickets, ginnels, passageways, alleys, yards – Harts Yard, Factory Yard, Timber Close, Penfolds Yard,

Steep Mead Lane, Fox Yard, Church Passage, Potter's Gate, Beavers Yard. Two of the biggest, the Lion and Lamb Courtyard and what is now called Borelli Yard, have been re-created by inserting some copy-architecture side by side with renovated buildings. St George's, off Castle Street, has kept up that line. Sympathetic twentieth-century buildings which lived easily with what remains of the old – which is a fair amount – might have been a better solution. But what we now have is far preferable to sixties unimaginative dereliction. Or to the post-modernist stuff now going up in other parts of the town, the latest blindly followed craze, all twirls and fussinesses – tarty frills encasing a tough, hi-tech shell (J. Edgar Hoover in drag) – or like Edwardian Nonconformist chapels trying to be important and striking. Perhaps in forty years another Betjeman – or a cheaper version of him from a school of architecture – will discover great merits in them.

The more sympathetic re-creations are a bit like film-sets but on the whole these yards work, though the shop rents are horribly high and deter almost all local initiatives. Too small to attract the big national chains, they tend to be rented by a variety of 'exclusive', expensive and often short-lived businesses; some of which go bust at almost predictable intervals. Other alleys, as yet unreconstructed, still house small craftsmen or, now more and more, small modern enterprises – often to do with communications technology, and employing only a few people.

So: a main 'T'-shape formed by the chief few streets, scarcely any natural congregating-space such as a square, but lots of little squiggles where the alleys take off from the three arms of the 'T'. In short, Farnham has few nodes. But it is not agoraphobic. It is full of rabbit-tracks, many of them dead-ends but interesting and useful, still part of the town's daily life. It just holds together.

But not all of it holds together physically or psychologically. In any town, you can usually tell instantly when an enterprise has put itself out of the organic area. At the far end of the appalling Woolmead, where East Street proper now begins, is a crooked, swirly corner, with one-way systems peeling off in four directions, a small island in the middle where pedestrians may take breath for a moment after and before risking their lives. Probably the rent for the shop on that corner is not high; it faces away from the town, over the traffic island towards a motor-firm's large repair yard; a near-final fringe area. A second-hand bookseller has taken it over. An interesting shop with good local interests. But you have to remind yourself to go along there and to remember the nearest car-park; you would hardly ever be likely just to come upon it, to pop in on the way to somewhere else. In a small town two hundred yards can make so wide a difference. Perhaps the bookseller will survive on postal trade.

In many ways, a typical English story; some sensitivity and care for the sense of place and community; not less, perhaps more, visual and cultural-social illiteracy; maybe a little corruption, more blind parochialism. It could have been worse; it might have been much better.

Farnham was never a squierarchical town; it had one or two good country houses, just outside, such as Moor Park; but none of their owners was the town's squire or lord of the manor; there was no nearby aristocracy, let alone royalty. We had more of that in Leeds, of all places, with the Harewoods – married into royalty – a few miles up the road. Farnham was from very early on a burghers' town, a merchants' town, a brewers' town, a corn-factors' town, a wheelwrights' town, a masons' town, a solid shopkeepers' town, a middle-class-dominated town; all of which produced right in the place's heart that splendid range of town-houses, especially from the eighteenth century, and the various almshouses.

Cobbett's shade broods over all, from that free-standing, rail-encircled tomb at St Andrew's, and his bust in the Museum garden to his birthplace two hundred yards away hard by the main Maltings; that was a farmstead but is today part of a particularly noisy pub, for long the Jolly Farmer and now – wouldn't you guess? – the William Cobbett.

So only a little digging takes you back to the Farnham of one, two, three and four centuries ago: in the street names – and now the car-park names – Waggon Yard, Dogflud, Maltings – the surnames still on some of the businesses, those odd snickets, the curious gables, the pantiles, the hung tiles, the steeply raked roofs, the small, warm, ruddy brickwork – and in some of the faces and some of the accents of the more obviously working-class people.

Before the First World War the poor were very poor indeed
and many drank far too much. As always, that was the most
common cheap release. It was not at all a genteel town, as many
like to think of it; even today, they are wrong in that, at bottom.
It was rough, especially when the hop-pickers were in town.
Today the Wey, as it passes the exact centre of the town, winding
through the two or three hundred yards of Gostrey Meadow,
past the swings and the shaggy sand-pit, is as tamed as a muni-
cipal geranium bed. The shades of those common people who
used to bathe there naked have fled.

The hopping and brewing accounted for the great number of
pubs in Farnham – at one time, pro rata by population the
highest number of any British town. By the late nineteenth
century the behaviour of some customers became a national
scandal. Finally, in 1902, because of the 'shocking scenes of
debauchery and drunkenness enacted in the town', the magistrates closed a few; over 80 per cent remained. By 1914 only
twenty had gone. There are still a great many. The tougher local
youths, many of whom live in the council housing estates and are
often recorded in the Magistrates Court as 'slater and tiler', have
regular weekend punch-ups with the squaddies from Aldershot.

The poverty of the Farnham working-people until after the
Second World War and their addiction to drink are both best
exemplified in the sizeable number of brick loos. There are still
four in a one-mile stretch in the town centre. 'Built like a brick
shithouse,' they used to say in Leeds of, especially, a strapping
young woman. Farnham's loos would have to be built of
armour-plating to withstand the Saturday night depredations by
the soldiers and the rougher locals, working- or middle-class. The
most comely and haunting loo is a neat, free-standing, small-
brick, single-storey structure, except for one dormer window set
in the roof-slope: like an unskilled worker's bungalow, fronting
directly on to West Street. To left and right are arched doorways,
entries for men and women respectively. In the centre is a tiny
dwelling with sash windows and lace curtains; still very neatly
kept. Today the occupier does not have to clean the loos as a
condition of tenancy – beer and poverty don't go quite so hand
in hand. Presumably the smells will not pass through the walls;
but they will come out of the two lavatory doorways and that

pungent mixture of beer, fags and stale urine will waft in whenever the little house's door is opened. Saturday night after eleven
o'clock or so must have been – must be, since there is still a
handful of pubs within very easy staggering distance – a night-
mare of shouts and smells. What a strong sense of the place
allotted to working-class people is indicated in that architectural
invention; I trust it is listed, as the one in Castle Street was, for
there must be very few left, few such congealed class-monuments.

Apart from the Castle, the numerous fine houses in West
Street, Castle Street and a few other places, the centre of Farnham does not have many spectacular buildings. Generally, its
important old buildings are workmanlike, solidly bourgeois
rather than full of public circumstance – as compared with what
may be found in a town of that size which can boast, say, a
cathedral and its appendages.

Cobbett is, once again, a good name to invoke; like Cobbett,
some aspects of Farnham are deeply English, incorrigibly provincial – proud of having invented the two-minute silence on
Armistice Day, and of its connections with Tubby Clayton, one
of the founders of the inter-denominational Christian fellowship, Toc H, started at Poperinghe during the First World War.
Farnham is ordinary in the grain, not given to great flights of the
imagination or intellect, solid, reliable, likely to do a good crafts-
manlike job on the things it knows and has known for centuries.
It seems fitting that in the second half of the eighteenth century
Augustus Montagu Toplady wrote 'Rock of Ages' there – in
West Street; he was born in the building which now houses
'Elphick's – founded 1881'. The three T's – Toc. H., Two
Minutes Silence, Toplady: no trio could better capture the essen-
tially English pieties of Farnham.

It also seems fitting that in our own century that very English
music-hall and film star (and, later, Mrs Dale of Mrs Dale's
Diary), Jessie Matthews, should have lived in Farnham. Sprung
from the London working-classes, she too ended up in West
Street, on the Downing Street corner above a pub of which she
was licensee (now an estate agent). But she was kept upstairs
there, Farnham believes, because her husband was jealous of the
customers' glances. I'd have stared at her. Her 'Tiptoe through
the Tulips' and 'Evergreen' ('When you've got a little springtime

in your heart, you can laugh at all the wintry winds that blow'),
in that light, removed, thin, virginal yet knowing, cockney voice
which had been transformed into gentility, almost itself transformed the Parkfield Picture Palace in Hunslet into a transcendent garden centre.

In this century Farnham's building history is predictably mixed,
but has exceptionally interesting elements. There is a lifelessly
Palladian Memorial Hall at the far end of West Street, built to
commemorate those who died in the First World War. It sits in
a field, like an abandoned nag put out to grass, forgotten.
Presumably it still belongs to the town but in eighteen years I
have seen hardly any activity there. 'The Morgue', locals call it.
Sometimes a town meeting is held there, usually ill-attended.
Shabby and forlorn-looking, it has acquired a kind of spectral
sub-dignity; the Miss Haversham of Farnham's buildings.

The by-pass, now exceptionally polluted, saved the town from
the worst jams and the worst pressures to knock buildings down
so that the juggernauts could more easily edge round the corners.
Latterly, the centre has been designated as a historic preservation area; and there is 'green land' and the less secure 'white
land' round much of the built area. Edwin Lutyens was brought
up in a nearby village and one of his early commissions was for
the Liberal Club in South Street, of 1894; still there and entirely
characteristic. There's an odd Lutyens house outside too. One
afternoon, up a lost little lane a few miles out of town, we came
upon a Lutyens/Jekyll place, as haunting as anything in *Le
Grand Meaulnes*. An early-middle-aged, professional couple had
inherited it and were straining to recover and maintain it. It was
lovely, dream-like, but only to be prevented from becoming an
incubus if you had so much money that you didn't need to bother
about the expense of other people's labour; or were retired early
on a good pension, and enjoyed both good health and a gardening passion.

Lutyens's work is far less important to the town than that of
the truly local architect, Harold Falkner. Falkner was at bottom
a pasticheur but it was pastiche born of love. He saw that a small
town such as Farnham, with a particularly compact core, could
not easily tolerate large and assertive buildings, though he accepted many of the two or three centuries-worth of styles which

had learned to live together there. He raided old houses about to
be demolished and took bits that suited his magpie genius; and
he designed houses made up of those bits, but houses which
somehow settled together – in his eclectic, solitary, driven qualities he was like a minuscule, very English Gaudí, though not
given to bright colouring; his buildings should not have worked
but somehow they usually did.

In the early thirties Falkner and his great supporter C. E. Borelli,
a councillor and successful jeweller, gained agreement to clear
away some fussy nineteenth-century public buildings at the bottom of Castle Street; the free-standing Corn Market had gone
decades earlier. Falkner's replacement Town Hall buildings are
just right. What Falkner thought of the bizarre Nat. West building which faces the several centuries of Castle Street domestic
architecture and blocks it off, I do not know. It shouldn't be
there; it has a high false frontage as in films of American West
townships. You expect to see the wood-supports behind its
façade, or the sheriff loping across to an assignation with des-
tiny; or to spot a crew filming. It is all white, cream and pale
fawn against the surrounding brick and some half-timbering. But
it has settled in nicely, the Barbara Cartland of Farnham's public
monumental face. I imagine Falkner did not quarrel with it. And,
finally of the mercies, British Rail have so far had the wit not to
damage the little late-Victorian station up its quiet bit of a
side-road. Today, the descendants of the sixties' developers, now
with their flat, country caps, their double-vented jackets, highly
polished brown shoes and boldly striped shirts, prowl the town
like scavenger birds, or urbanised foxes in search of promising
waste-bins. They are on the look-out for whatever bit of possible
infill may still exist – a longish garden here whose owner may
not be able to resist a hundred thousand pounds or so for that
bottom strip of land, a spare bit on a corner where a building
doesn't quite meet the road-line; any spot on which the local
chancers can stick a few cheap or not so cheap des. res.

Nowadays the Council's environmental officers, well abetted
by the Farnham Society, do all they can within their limited
powers. Earlier members of the local authority staff committed
one of the worst road-development atrocities in Britain. To allow
the traffic to flow better along the by-pass about a quarter-mile

from the town centre they made what is said to be the largest roundabout in Europe. It entirely encloses a hamlet so that the inhabitants have to get to and fro between home and the mainland either by one road entry off the right-hand lane, or through a tunnel or, and this is not an exaggeration, by risking their lives crossing the busy three- and four-lane complete circle now made by the main Guildford road where it crosses the Aldershot/Farnborough road.

Today Farnham's council housing, and that of many another borough, is better designed than much private work. It is fashionable to laugh at what some people add on to their formerly council-owned houses once they have bought them, but that too is a trivial snobbery. The new owners are obviously and understandably influenced by some middle-class tastes; they are fulfilling an aspiration, a dream of a place to call your own, such as better-off people have. Changes may come later, so long as home-owners are not seductively but relentlessly led by the nose through the enticements of the home-embellishment salesmen. And better that than stuff and taste foisted on them as suitable for their place and status by a would-be benign local council or government.

CHAPTER 3

NATIVES AND NEWCOMERS; YOUNG AND OLD

The crowd, and buzz, and murmurings.
Abraham Cowley, *The Mistress*

We be all good English men.
Alfred Lord Tennyson, 'The Revenge'

Even though towns like Farnham – as compared with, say, the closely massed industrial areas of big cities – are socially mixed, are there a few main groups which taken together make up most of their present inhabitants? The question seems at first easy but looked at more closely becomes difficult. You could say, and it is just worth saying, that in Farnham the biggest more or less cohesive grouping runs from the respectable and usually comfortable working-class to the comfortable middle-class; that at one end are some depressed or very poor, lower-or-non-respectable, or struggling working-class people; and that at the other end are the successful professional and executive people, many of whom live in the surrounding villages, in new developments or scattered on the outskirts. But that is only the beginning of a beginning of a way to mark the distinctions. There are others, and they can all be true and tell something.

There are those who live and work in the town, of whom some are native, some not. Some still live in small rural cottages tucked into the odd corners near the centre. The council estates house mainly local people; the older among them still have a West Surrey/East Hampshire rural burr; they often go back a long way. When Mr Cobbett came to mend one of our taps and saw all the books he told us with assured pride that he was a

direct descendant of William Cobbett. Many younger people
have lost the local burr; it has been ironed out by school or, more
persistently, by broadcasting. They have a South-East working-
class but otherwise non-regional, flattened, nondescript way of
speaking – one of the national or large-regional accents which
have emerged in the second half of the twentieth century and
owe their origins chiefly to mass-communications.

Many among this group may go abroad on annual package
holidays to places they would not have heard of thirty years ago;
but most go up to London only very rarely. Three hundred
pounds or less may get you to the Costa Brava, accommodation
and some meals included, for a fortnight once a year. Set against
that, even a train day-return to London at about £13 a go, plus all
the costs once there, looks much less of a bargain. But all-in coach
trips to Guildford or even London, which include a popular
musical, are affordable from time to time.

Others, slightly-to-well up the social and financial scale, may
see London more often. They may head occasionally for the
Royal National Theatre, the Royal Festival Hall (both very near
Waterloo Station), even the Barbican; and to well-spoken-of
plays and classical concerts. These make up the middle-range of
inhabitants and daily workers in the town – those employed at
several levels but not manually in the small to medium industrial
and commercial concerns on the trading estates, those who
manage the local shops or the branches of national chains and
are themselves local, and those who serve in them; and, near the
top of this range, the living-in professionals (some brought in,
like Nonconformist ministers, by their national enterprises and
moved on in due time – as also in the banks – but urged by Head
Office to become strenuously part of 'their local community'
whilst they are here). Do they ever get together socially, as a
displaced group? You see them wandering round their branches,
especially during their first few months, hands clasped behind
the back, eyes darting. And there are, right at the top, the solicitors, the estate agents, the GPs, the dentists, the travel agents,
the more comfortably retired.

More complex, more scattered and still encroaching are those
who live in or near the town but work away from it. As a
dormitory town Farnham started early; the distance from London

was short enough to ensure that it had an early railway line, but far enough to ensure that its commuters were well-to-do. Not quite a large snoring dormitory and not quite the country. At the end of the nineteenth century South Farnham on its slope, looking north over town and castle or south towards Hindhead and Haslemere, was designated for expensive housing. The typical houses there are on wide avenues, detached, each in a fair bit of ground. They breathe substance above the young executive level, but not the substance of the corporation Chief Executive. He goes further out to those bigger houses and larger gardens, set back from the road and in amongst the trees; so hidden that as you drive down these narrow and well-tree'd local roads you could think you were in the depths of the country, rather than in a well-disguised but well-populated Surrey ex-urbia. You are then into the land of the Range-Rovers (or, for the slightly flashy, the Isuzu Troopers or Jeep Cherokees) the dog-grills and the horsy or doggy rear-screen stickers: 'I love bulldogs', 'Happiness is a bulldog', 'A dog is for ever, not just for Christmas', the green Wellington boots and Barbour jackets (both beginning to go out, as they are taken over from below), the secluded prep schools and retirement homes, the piney, sandy, good air.

Farnham has roughly the same population as Grantham (where my brother lived) but doesn't feel anything like as big. Grantham is the market town for a large Lincolnshire hinterland; it attracts the headquarters of some county and district services and commercial enterprises; it is just off the A1(M), at that point about a hundred and ten miles on its way up to Edinburgh; it is on the Inter-City line taking the same four hundred mile journey. It has a large, irregular, market square which still operates as an important entrepôt for rural produce. It is a local sub-capital.

Farnham is in many ways overshadowed by Guildford, four times bigger, nearer London so more bustlingly a commuter town and an exceedingly prosperous one, though in the first half of the nineties feeling the effects of the recession. It has an uninspired modern cathedral, a newish university, a pre-London-run theatre, a large county hospital, one or two fair-sized industrial works, the national offices of some enterprises which, because of modern communications technology, can leave Lon-

don for cheaper, more spacious and healthier sites – concerns
such as large insurance companies. It has very large supermarkets,
vast DIY stores and the other customary, town-edge consumer
temples. It is on a main railway line and has a motorway-standard
road running as near into London as Putney. The well-lined
commuters of West Surrey have been generously treated by the
Department of Transport. Guildford's stores define its solid
chunk of better-off clientele. It is beautifully sited on one of the
last shoulders of the North Downs with the River Wey winding
along at the bottom of its High Street. But, for one who lives in
Farnham and is glad to visit Guildford for certain kinds of
shopping, it is not as attractive as Farnham, too glossy, too
shinily executive; you can't really believe that rural England is
near, as near as it actually is.

Farnham is an exploded and fragmented town, a necklace
town, a small semi-rural town surrounded by a beaded cord of
villages and hamlets which are all officially part of it. Most of
the villages have to some extent yielded to the demands of – and
the financial advantages from – executive developments. Most
put them on the village edges, in winsomely named 'Closes',
'Meadows', 'Fields', Queen Anne style 'Homes' coiling round
each other on bulbous semi-closed avenues which turn their
backs on the road and the old parts of the villages.

Quintessential among such village extensions are those at
Bourne, a couple of miles south of Farnham, down the other side
of Firgrove Hill. That was George Sturt's village; he lived in Vine
Cottage, Vicarage Lane, and took his pen-name from the place
as it had taken its name from the stream which wanders through
it towards the Wey. In Sturt's day Bourne still showed that it had
been, was still being, wrested from rough common land by poor
cottagers, most of whom made a mean living from their bits of
ground and odd jobs round about and in Farnham – a half-
hour's walk away, up and down. Sturt focussed on the old
childless couple, the Bettesworths, the grinding hard work they
had known all their lives, their tiny filthy cottage, their devotion
to each other, and above all their decency and how it was
enshrined in forms of speech and in local accents which had not
much changed for centuries. At one point Sturt noted that in
Bourne itself there was not much sense of class-distinctions (at

another point he reported angrily that they did exist); even in his day those distinctions were plain in Farnham as in any town or city.

Towards the end of his writing Sturt noted that a new kind of person was coming in, taking over the cottages and, as we would say, gentrifying them. The minor-executive developments which now greet you as you drop down the hill past Sturt's lane-end are the inevitable extension of what he saw beginning.

Sturt also, in a book less well-known than his Bourne books, describes the style and pace of life at his uncle's farm over Frimley way, a few miles north of Farnham. Now the M3 cuts through Frimley and there, and at Fleet nearby, the old bits have been swallowed more even than at Bourne. These are now executive townlets umbilically held by and generated by the motorway; not cheap but (their builders and buyers hope) rising-executive in dominant style. The gardens are well-kept and their homes more Heal's than IKEA, more Poggenpohl than Magnet; in the evening the executives jog round the avenues or get in a round of golf or take the dogs for a walk or the daughter for her riding lesson. The favoured supermarket is Waitrose and they have a big, new one. Volvos and Peugeots – often station-wagons – are common, BMWs and Mercedes less so at present.

A few years ago there was an accusation from the pulpit that wife-swapping (typical that it's not called husband-swapping) abounds in these areas. Apparently house-keys are, at a party, all thrown in a bowl on a coffee-table and picked out at random. Odd, that – a pig in a poke seems an apt image. Or can they identify the keys which belong to the person they wish to bed? In that case they'll have to be quick or they'll not get the keys they want. It all sounds hardly credible; probably it's a Modern Myth, a deceptive lure to titillate and deceive cultural trend-spotters, especially those who like sexy anecdotes.

The estate agents' windows delineate the nature and style of house movements, especially among middle-range executives who are seeking the more-or-less country air, reasonable nearness to London, lots of private schools at all levels and congenial enclaves. The glass case on the up-platform of Farnham station is even more vicariously interesting than the estate agents' windows in town, as a revelation of what the upper executives, those who have 'arrived', seek – six or seven acres a few miles out,

loose-boxes (the most evocative phrase in all such advertisements), a pool, servant's quarters (lower down we have 'granny
flats'). Plenty of establishments like these are changing hands at
any one time.

The favoured idioms of the estate agents have a common,
culturally unreal, linguistic base at all levels; but at the upper
level they stretch towards a more rarefied, creepingly subservient
air. 'Delightful', 'period style', 'adjoining' and 'splendidly maintained' can appear at any level. For the bigger establishments we
move into: 'superbly appointed', 'commanding – extensive –
spacious', 'exceptional specifications', 'beautifully proportioned',
'immaculately presented' (sounds like a dish at the Tour d'Argent,
or an entry in a TV-ballroom-dancing competition), 'enjoying
views over the open countryside', 'comprising of a wealth of
unique features', 'a magnificent gentleman's residence' (Gentleman's Relish in the larder, no doubt). A stage world of language,
a world similar in its marmorial unchangingness to that of the
'In Memoriam' columns of the newspapers, a world which has
fallen in love with certain ingratiating verbs, adverbs and adject-
ives – *'enjoying* views', *'immaculately presented'* (that's Jeeves-
land or sub-Howards End). It is hard to imagine estate-agent
trainees of any intelligence seriously adopting this jargon, but
they do. Perhaps they have it in a box in the office, like chunks
of ready-made-up type-face, so that drafting a house description
is easy, only a matter of putting together the bits which seem
reasonably relevant. Perhaps they make a few private notes after
a visit: 'A Maples sitting room' = 'superbly appointed and
presented drawing room'; 'open outlook at back' = 'enjoying
favoured views over unspoilt Hampshire'. A world of its own, a
linguistic backwater into which few currents from the modern
world penetrate, though no doubt the 1993 Act on misrepres-
entation will disturb it. No wonder Roy Brooks caused such a
stir not long after the war when he described houses, disadvantages and all, in demotic and cheerfully rude English. What a
country! It accepts for decades a crass linguistic gentility and
then succumbs instantly to the language of a music-hall comic.

To what sort of communities do these commuting executives
belong? Sometimes to their villages, to parts of their villages, if
the villages still have communal lives of their own. Sometimes to

more narrowly executive clubs and societies – golf, of course; perhaps Rotary or the Lions; perhaps to amateur theatricals; perhaps to none of these things, since they may well be too tired on most nights.

Not many will have a strong sense of this place and this time, and times before. In a Bourne estate few would respond to the name George Bourne, or to Sturt; or, as they walked to the village paper-shop or the pub, would have a sense of the shadow of old Bettesworth and his kind tramping those paths year on year after many a long day's work and sometimes calling in for a pint; few would know that their neat garden was probably once a plot worked for decades to provide basic vegetables for a family living on what would be today the equivalent of only a few pounds a week. A sense of history is compounded of a sense of roots and a sense of change; it can bring respect for those whose sweat fell on the soil year after year as they swung their hand-tools, soil now cared for with power-mowers and sophisticated fertilisers. All this no more than half-a-century ago, a short time, less than one life-span; before television, fridges, freezers, cam-corders, micro-wave cookers, lap-top computers, cordless phones, answering machines, widespread car ownership, foreign holidays.

To regret this two-dimensional, this without-time, sense of the world, is not to be nostalgic; nor does it aim to make easy fun of executives' aspirations and styles of life. Like most of us, they are trapped in their time; and the main engines of communication in their society do not suggest that respect for the past is a good thing to nourish; they imply the opposite, not so much by active rejection as by either a denaturing and weightless nostalgia or by a sheer ignoring. For most of these executives their professional life could have landed them in any one of a thousand similar developments of similar housing. And tomorrow they may be required to move on, two hundred miles, to another similar estate. In such circumstances you do not carry much idea of a collective memory; your history starts a short time back, is captured not in books but in the framed wedding-and-onwards photos on the mantelpiece and coffee-tables, is the history of your nuclear family, its future one of 'short distances and defin-ite places'.

*

That is one way of trying to identify some of Farnham's main groups – on the one hand through those born into the town and working there, together with those who, though not born there, now earn their living in its shops and offices; and on the other hand through those for whom the town is a dormitory, a pleasant enough dormitory but little more than that, a liveable-in backcloth.

There is a more colourful pattern, which includes those who live there from choice, have retired to it, and those who work an easy car-ride away; and some who commute to London but are minority kinds of commuter.

The retired services group, mainly military, are likely to have spent some of their time as serving officers at Aldershot or perhaps Bordon, a few miles on opposite sides of town, to have liked the area and especially Farnham and its more immediate surroundings and so to have settled there on leaving the service. They range from a Field Marshal (not Montgomery; he was seven or eight miles west, in Hampshire, but came in to the local Post Office weekly, in his chauffeur-driven car, to collect his Old Age Pension; the most expensively collected of any British State Old Age Pension) down to captains, and no doubt to some NCOs and ORs, though those are not so evident.

A good number of the retired senior officers serve on the local Council and work hard and, in their own prescribed terms, well. Some start small or not so small businesses, and sometimes succeed; or tend their gardens assiduously. One used to stand at the bottom of Castle Street, a picture of rural health, selling fine bushes he had grown himself – looking like a character from Hardy who had strayed in from the wrong cast and caste. We knew him only as The Major. Others play golf and some regularly help their wives with the shopping. Yet others do good works in the traditional English manner, especially for the Maltings which has the right cachet.

The ideal-types among ex-service officers are as recognisable as a detective-constable in plain clothes. They wear good-quality hacking jackets and heavy drill or whipcord trousers, always clean and well-creased; their brown shoes have a mirror-like gloss as though they – not their former batmen since few can now afford to employ them – have 'boned' them night after night; some still wear desert boots and revert to the short-arsed British Warm overcoat in winter; a Panama hat may appear in summer. The impeccably clean jacket and trousers and the shiny shoes are a mark of retired middle-class men in general. A puzzling phenomenon to those of us whose jackets, trousers and shoes look soiled after three days' wear. Perhaps they or their wives – 'We can't have you going out looking a mess' – get up each morning and freshen all their clothes, for the wives are almost as well-pressed as the men.

Because some of them cannot altogether give up walking (or talking when out-of-doors) as if on a parade-ground, they tend to appear – in civvies – flat-footed, with slightly turned-in toes. They are fond of flat country caps with sewn brims, like the army's 'cheese-cutters', and in this they join hands with the horse-loving folk outside town; and now, with the younger 'developers'.

Living next door to us in our early years here was 'an old India hand'. He was not, we were told, a former serviceman but had passed many years running a successful business in India under the Raj, made money and settled in Farnham for his last couple of decades. The widow of a true 'old India hand' of the military kind was just up the road, now devoted to saving dogs and cats from unhappy fates. She and the commercial old India hand did not get on, ostensibly because of quarrels over animals but deep-down because of social antipathy. Our immediate neighbour occupied himself with golf and stiff drinks. He was not likeable and eventually his second wife left him. He had a heart attack but managed to persuade a middle-aged golfing lady to move in and look after him. I used to go in to ask how he was. One evening he invited me to join him in a gin. The living-in lady was in the kitchen of the largeish house. He lifted his hands, clapped loudly and called: 'Chota peg for the sahib.' She brought one, looking poisonous.

As we saw on the station platform virtually all people in this middle-class professional group will habitually and almost automatically vote Conservative, of course. As it happens, the local MP has been for years the better kind of Conservative so those Socialists who also greatly value the constituency attentiveness of MP's have had their lances blunted here. We may still vote Labour, as a matter of endlessly hopeful principle.

There are other small enclaves: the Royal Aerospace Establishment is in a dull, featureless and centreless part of Farnborough and so many RAE boffins live in Farnham. They tend to be highly civilised, especially since some came over as refugees from Hitler's Europe; and they are very musical. The Establishment has its own chamber orchestra. It is a truism, well exemplified here, that great theoreticians, especially mathematicians, have a special feeling for music, particularly of a non-operatic kind.

There is also that smaller group of commuters, erratic not true commuters since they do not have to be in their offices at set times daily: broadcasters who no longer feel the need to be daily at the centre of things, a few actresses and actors who can learn their roles best in quiet surroundings, a journalist or two, a couple of writers; all partially released by their word-processors, answering machines and faxes. Farnham swallows them without a hiccup and seems almost entirely unaware of them; which is part of its attraction. They are in the town but not of it. They can go shopping without much risk of being pointed out.

And there are some usually unhappy fly-by-nights (though that is the last thing they wish to be), typical products of the eighties and nineties. They are redundant executives from various levels and occupations – salesmen, above all, pushed out when sales fall away. They have lost quite good salaries, BUPA insurance, the company car, an expense account. They receive a silver if not a golden handshake and wonder what to do. They listen to the Tory government's urgings about individual initiatives and realise that they had always wanted to run their own show. Farnham's golden, commercial T-piece (Downing Street as the bent vertical, The Borough and the first couple of hundred yards of West Street as the horizontal) always has a few shops up for sale or to let; and it has its solid group of prosperous middle-class people as possible customers. But they are economising: the last dealer in fine furniture closed a year or so ago.

Shall it be wine for the discerning, or greetings cards that are winsome but not twee, or picture-framing for those who won't buy Boots clip-on plastic offerings (there are four framing shops), or Far Eastern pseudo-antique junk, or excitingly modish clothes for women or for men from eighteen to thirty-five, or – most hazardous of all – a swanky restaurant where *cuisine nouvelle* still meets *cuisine minceur* in dishes which look more like minimalist Japanese art than food and whose raw materials don't put much strain on the budget? And the name? One word, preferably; and even more preferably a plural or possessive – SCRIBES, VOLCANOS, TOPERS, BOURGEOISIE, TRENDS, TENDENCIES, THE PAPERWORKS, CELEBRATIONS, TEMPTATIONS, CHILDHOOD MEMORIES and, the most poignantly self-conscious, touchingly reaching out: BUT IS IT ART?

For a few years in the eighties Farnham enjoyed a hi-tech prosperity, but in the early nineties the slump developed in almost all areas, from working-class teenagers to the previously 'secure' professional. We had then the usual stories of men still going, properly dressed, to the railway station or even into London each day, to a job which no longer existed. Those may be inevitable myths. But it is now easier to find a nearby place in the station car-park than it was in the eighties.

So the redundancy-payment entrepreneurs suffer early. Often their offerings are in their nature things people buy when they are flush, luxury top-dressings. You go past such shops after three or four months and see that yet another has gone bust. Most of their occupiers creep away in a day, or two at the most. If they have been formally declared bankrupt you may see the large bailiff's locks on the doors, put there by men whose manners tend not to be those of the genteel middle-class; they are half-cousins to wheel-clampers. The estate agents look around for another client, perhaps another gambler or romantic, and meanwhile let the premises for a small rent or free to yet another charity selling second-hand clothes and books, British bric-à-brac and Far Eastern crafts.

The previous tenants disappear quickly, as though they had never been, had never set foot in Farnham. The tenants of a fancily-styled bakery left cartons of 'farm-fresh' eggs on the counter. Such a business becomes another statistic in the awful monthly totals of failed enterprises. It is doubtful if many of them are driven into bed-and-breakfast accommodation provided by the local Council; but life with parents or in-laws after all this time and all those hopes must be full of stresses – until something turns up, or some job is taken out of desperation. The unattractive face of minor capitalism, eighties and nineties style; glossier than the lives of salesmen driven in the thirties to sell newspaper subscriptions from door to door; but still these men are their descendants, their descendants who went to grammar schools or potty private day-schools, or took a polytechnic course in Business Management or a correspondence course in Dynamic Salesmanship – and found too late that the only people likely to be left with jobs, or able to flit comfortably and as need be from one new course to another, are the course inventors and the PR men who promote their trash.

There is a small stage army in the streets, so well-known that they seem villagey not urban: the former ex-service officers, followed by the man who tickets you for parking too long in the Borough car-parks, the ruddy-faced and hugely white-haired window-cleaner who seems to have the contracts for most of the centre shops. He seems as much a part of the streets' moving-furniture as the women parking wardens who patrol those few places that still have a yard or two available for free, two-hour parking.

Now and then a policeman or policewoman appears, walking with a slightly self-conscious air as though to say: 'Look, policing on the beat again.' Few know them or respond to them. They are different people from the village or small-town bobby we have met in so many whimsical books. They are Surrey County policemen assigned to the Farnham station, past Downing Street just by the river. No doubt they do their best if you are in trouble; and they are overborne, especially at weekends, by drunken vandalism and dangerous brawls. But one doesn't easily or soon think of them as a part of Farnham's being. As with so many elements of town life the local paper, by paying attention to the public appearances and pronouncements of the resident Superintendant, tries to incorporate him and his office into the town's sense of itself.

Occasionally, a few punk-rockers (and I mean punk-rockers, even in the nineties) appear from the council estates and wander through town. Yet 'wander' is not the right word for their special and characteristic way of walking. They move quite quickly, bouncing off the balls of their feet so that the shoulder-chains rattle and swing slightly forward, and the cock's-comb-like quiffs of the Mohican hair-dos bob slightly up and down, front and back, as though looking for grain. The Farnham worthies who opened the first few council houses at the beginning of the century would have been outraged; they hand-picked the occupants, for respectability.

At the bottom of Castle Street is one of the finest and largest fruit-and-veg stalls in the South of England. It is manned entirely by cheerful balletic young men whose mental arithmetic seems astounding and is entirely trusted by almost all the customers – but not by the occasional one who enters each purchase on a small calculator as he goes through his list.

Quite soon, the women of Farnham – especially the middle-aged, middle-class women – seem more interesting than the men; though that may indicate more about me than about Farnham or its women.

I come back again and again to women of that age and class, their clothes, their ways of walking, of holding their heads, their crimplened or, better, crystallised hair, their predilection for trilby hats, usually from Burberry's or in the Burberry style (they give an explicitly mannish air – 'the mann'ish trilby and the brogue-stiff shoe'). Combined with short waxed jackets or padded gilets and tailored cord trousers they are formidable and forbidding; Coventry Patmore would have run away as quickly as he could. They employ extraordinary similarities of expression and of voice and accent ('Thenk you *so* much'; or, higher up the scale, 'Thenk you *vair* much'); it is all unattractive, especially when addressed to someone felt to be lower in the scale. Such a woman, rightly rebuked in a car-park for a very dangerous manoeuvre, offered no apology but moved off with an over-the-shoulder: 'I don't feel like arguing today, thenk you.' A real pro.

Another tiny but illustrative incident. I was in a supermarket one Friday morning, waiting behind such a middle-aged woman who was next to be served. The man who was checking out his groceries emptied the trolley and moved perhaps a yard away from it so as to have more space to sort out his shopping bags. He did not at that moment pull the trolley with him. The hard-hatted lady next in line called to him without hesitation, in

a voice which would have carried twenty yards, not the one yard
needed to reach the man: 'Do you intend to leave that trolley
thare?' It was premature, rude, stupid. What made her think she
could call out in that tone of voice to anyone? Would she have
done so to someone more obviously of her social status? Why
couldn't she have waited until she saw whether as soon as the
man had paid he reached back to pull the trolley with him? Did
she live in a world of sharp-eyed assessing, low-level suspicion
of others, especially others who might not seem quite of her
kind? It would be easy to argue that such a petty, truly petty, incident tells us something about one woman only, a neurotic, bad-
tempered, perhaps not very well woman, or one a bit off-colour
that day. Maybe it does, to some extent; but it also speaks for,
reveals something of the common style of, a whole class of
women, especially those of a certain age.

It is hard to be charitable to such women, at least to their public
presences. One can explain much in their manner by the powerful influences of their sub-culture, as we saw with the first-class
commuters. We can say that they may very well be excellent
wives, mothers, neighbours, sturdy and unflagging in voluntary
good works; and that may often be so. But we then have to avoid
patronage, what can soon become a reducing of them by an
explaining-away of their public manner, making them into mere
clones of their social group. For their public presences are often
displeasing because soon displeased, defensive/aggressive. Whatever their private virtues, their public faces are the female counterparts of those of the first-class commuters twisting on the points
of their umbrellas as they wait for the up-train. At that point I
remember again the typical Sturt woman; the aged, dirty but
innocent face of Lucy Bettesworth and the patient virtue of Ann
Smith whom Sturt celebrates in the final chapter of *A Farmer's
Life*.

And are the men really, as they seem, rather less unattractive?
Are the women usually as dominant as they seem to be when
they are shopping accompanied by their husbands? The women
often have the air of, if not wearing the trousers, at least of
carrying the verbal stick to fend off intruders, outside those
areas in which the husband is the boss and knows the rules of his
place. It is, after all, the wife who day after day treats with the

woman who comes in to do some cleaning, with the plumber who might prove to be fly, with the carpenter who exceeds his estimate and tries to talk his way out of it, with the door-to-door salesman who might be on the lookout for some portable property to lift from the garage when she isn't looking. Perhaps it is all such continuing and recurrent experiences which make her develop that suspicious, pursed-up manner, that voice which has all the off-putting character of a large and large-beaked bird's call to warn you off her eggs.

On the whole, husbands do not have the temptations to develop this range of protective practices, this lack in many public encounters of gentleness and at least initial courtesy. It is a great pity, all in all, but one does have to say that the dominant out-of-door manners of many middle-aged, middle-class English women would have to be placed low on a scale of true gentilesse. You may bet that almost all such women did not go to one of the current great social levellers, a university (or what used to be called a polytechnic or other place of higher education) and certainly not to a comprehensive school. Instead, they were probably sent to a private school, perhaps boarding, perhaps not, but certainly to one whose socially segregating purpose was at least as high and probably higher than its educational.

A small by-way. As with the discovery of my interest in women of that sort, there comes another surprise. A reader of a book about my early life said he had been amused to discover a sexual reference every few pages. That was a great exaggeration; there were several sexual anecdotes, instances, as there no doubt will be in this book. It was as surprising, though not momentous, to have their recurrences pointed out as it is to recognise now the many appearances of supermarkets here.

There are also lots of anecdotes which have no sexual content; perhaps they do not strike some readers' inner eye as sharply as those that do. Still, there is more than that to these repetitions. Stories with a sexual edge are often more sharply informative than most others, especially in England; and funnier, or sadder. Like comedians suddenly showing their underwear in a middle-class drawing-room comedy, they pull away the social pretences, show the old Adam at work, the continuance of country roughness behind the suburban gentility, the visual comedy and

oddity of the sexual act – particularly if you think of it being
performed by the pompous and publicly self-assured, the big
bow-wows.

So it all emerges in old or new forms, in the habits of some girls
when they go boozing in pairs on Saturday nights through apparently neat and tidy Farnham, or early-middle-aged executives
moving down their neat drives to those rumoured wife-swapping
parties. The English interest in and practice of sex may be no
stronger than that of the French, Germans or Italians; the peculiar proportions in the mix of overt puritanism, primness and
rough practice in our attitudes to sex are all our own – and
certainly do not include a disgusted recognition, as in Swift's
'Celia shits . . .'

As to the middle-aged, middle-class ladies, enough has been
said for the time being. They are a strikingly discernible but
relatively small group of women – much smaller in number than
the working wives; and of them there is a greater variety. Today,
'working women' cover a very large range in ages. There are
many of the old style, much as I knew them as a boy, those who
simply have to go out to work – often as cleaning women in
homes or offices – because if they did not the ends of the family
budget would not meet; as, now, do many women who are single
parents. Others, again from a wide range of ages, work because
they and their husbands are happily but sometimes rather
nervously (what if one of us were given the sack?) caught up in
the revolution of rising expectations. Their parents might well
think that their sons and daughters had enough to live on with
the husband's salary alone; but that is to miss the point. Their
children's generation reach out now, have reached out for at
least a couple of decades, to central heating, a washing-machine,
perhaps a dishwasher and the other electronic objects I listed
earlier; and all these increase outgoings on gas and electricity.
Then there is the phone and perhaps a smallish car on HP; but
not, in many instances, school fees, for we are talking about
careful working-class people or the bottom fringe of the lower-
middle-class (which is why the accents and the ages at the
check-outs can vary fairly widely; another instance of the supermarkets' blurring of edges). By now, four out of five Farnham
women are in service occupations.

Soon the wife's salary is absorbed as a necessary part of the regular family income, even if the husband is in work. Common to the idea of the wife working is the decision to use her wages to pay for a foreign holiday each year. Another main impulse is to escape from boredom, to be part of a group with shared interests. In January the conversation in lulls at the check-outs is about what holiday is being considered, in autumn about what it was like. And though many foreign holidays – to Florida, say – may seem not to cost unreachably more all in all than the same amount of time in Blackpool, to take a family of four and be generous when you are there and bring back presents will not be found out of most husbands' wages. A wife putting in twenty-five to thirty hours a week will pay little tax and what is left will easily cover such a holiday. This is an important force behind some wives' decision to work though some may feel able to wait until they have got the children on their feet, when the youngest is about five years old. These women are the backbone of the supermarkets' employment pattern, not the young unmarried women, nor the few young men from the sixth-form college who come in on Saturday mornings, nor the occasional sixty-odd-year-old man whom a change in 'recruitment policy' has brought out.

Among the young women, from sixteen to about twenty-five, by which time many of them have married, there is a delicate pattern, grading, pecking-order of posts. One should allow, though, for the way in which the Saturday morning temporaries of both sexes ignore, cut across, this pattern; they are most of them floaters, as willing to work in Woollies as in a health-food shop; all depends on the wage offered.

Yet the pattern, even on Saturdays, isn't quite as fluid as I have just implied. You are more likely to find a manifestly middle-class girl in the health-food store, probably serving with a ring-fence insouciance, than you would find her in Woolworth's. The regular Woolworth's assistants are mostly working-class and regard what they are doing as a proper job; and tend to stay with it. The young men in the branches of the national chains of cobblers are, like those on the fruit-stall, cheerfully, or rudely, their own masters; perhaps the area managers only come round occasionally. The women in the travel agents are very respectable working-class or lower-middle-class, and intelligent. They have to be or they wouldn't last long, even though in some the geographical competence is not strong. Theirs may be fairly low down in the vast list of new occupations spawned by modern communications technology – from jumbo-jet pilots to unsolicited telephone saleswomen – but the work is taxing and sometimes exerts considerable pressure. These clerks – all women – have to have 'more about them' than most in their district – just as, at slightly more highly regarded levels, have the secretaries to estate agents and, even more, solicitors, and those entirely hidden away from the public in the accounts departments of the bigger stores and the supermarkets. By the time you reach the much more expensive shops – well-established jewellers, typically – the sex line has become blurred; you find men as much as women, so long as they have all reached the required level of appearance, speech and competence.

Female gentility is all-embracing at the 'better' women's clothing shops, but that is only to be expected since many of the adventurous owners have served their time in expensive shops in larger places or in the more expensive parts of big stores. Marshall and Snelgrove's tortured accents live on. The most tortured of all, in accents and manner, are to be found in our local branch of one of the newly privatised industries. That is staffed by three ladies in early middle-age, in twin-sets; not middle-class but secure lower-middle-class; they would be likely to say that they only work for pin-money or for a foreign holiday somewhere away from the crowds. The showroom is stuffed with expensive new equipment. They glide from the back with a fluted: 'Can I help you, sir?'

You explain that you are not there to buy a new glossy piece of large machinery but to ask if they stock replacement grommet-brushes for your electronic what-not, since yours has packed in. Their faces, which had fallen the moment you said you didn't want to buy any of the large gear on display, now express momentary consternation so that you realise they do not know what a grommet-brush is. Nor do they know if they can be obtained from area office. They say this nevertheless in voices which suggest they haven't much time for people who try to replace a grommet-brush instead of throwing the old machine away and getting a shiny new one from them. You almost expect them to say: 'Nowadays all the best people replace their major domestic equipment each year.'

By this time you surmise that if they have had any training at all it has not given them a modest knowledge of spare parts and of where they can be obtained. It has been entirely concerned, in this new commercially aggressive Britain, to introduce them not to the idea of a public service but to ways of 'shifting' large pieces of new equipment (about which they know no more than the sales patter), with a percentage commission every time they manage it. You, wanting your grommet-brush, don't interest them; and can't; so you slightly disconcert them as well. Their lack-of-interest shutter comes down as though they were running late on a Saturday evening and due out in an hour for whist or, more likely, bridge. Still, they are unlikely to use that most killing of all Pontius Pilate phrases towards dissatisfied customers: 'Don't blame me. I only work here.'

Most interesting of all are the assistants – again, all women and mostly young – in Boots. They are fresh-looking even without their fresh-looking regulation clothing; they look what my Aunt Ethel would have called 'nicely brought up girls' and no doubt are; and they are, again as Aunt Ethel would have said, 'Very obliging. Very obliging indeed.' Their well-learned: 'Ken l help yeow, sir?' is contemporary-commercial speech carried on mixed East Hants/West Surrey vowels. Youths, from the sixth-form college for example, just happen to slip in there after afternoon school to buy another tube of hair-gel and inspect the talent. If you are over twenty-five some of the talent can, in turn, look through you as they serve you, as to someone from another planet. There is predictably a group of older women, usually on the pharmacy counter, stalwarts of many years, now long married and still fresh-looking and helpful if occasionally inclined to be a bit imperious; they've been around and know a lot about their counter, and a fair amount about the dispenser's business too.

But the characteristic Boots assistant is in her late teens to early twenties, obviously not an academic type but usually shrewd; and, though more and more begin with a partnership, most still look forward to marriage and a family. Such aspirations at their

level and in their kind of life change extremely slowly and can be
as much a sign of the amiable working of their parents' married
life, of the snug and secure atmosphere in which they have been
brought up, as they are indications of a merely routine and
conventional mind. It is unlikely if many of them are Saturday
night pub-crawlers. But they are not easily fazed. As I was waiting
my turn one day a man of about thirty-five asked for two dozen
condoms. His small and neat wife looked away as though detached; the two children weren't paying much attention; the
assistant served him as unaffectedly as though he had asked for
cough drops. So she should, of course, and perhaps she would
think my invisibly raised eyebrow an extraordinary reaction; but
perhaps only to be expected from someone of that generation.
Boots is a good example of one kind of chain-store which fits
into and helps strengthen a strong, continuing element in the
pattern of English provincial life at one of its levels; the reluctance to change, the assumption that marriage, children, a 'proper'
going-on, a house-proud wife and a home-living, reliable and
affectionate husband make a natural and desirable goal.

Walking round and looking at all this you are left with some
interesting questions: presumably Boots train their local managers unusually precisely on just the sort of staff they should
appoint? How many years do the girls serve on average? Do
most leave to be married? What proportion come back at some
point after marriage? What proportion give unbroken service
from their appointment onwards for, say, twenty years or more?

* * *

I feel chilly and grown old.
                Robert Browning, 'A Toccata of Galuppi's'

'O, Sir! you are old' – but not truly a 'Senior Citizen'. At a time
when, as we all have been reminded again and again, the proportion of Old Age Pensioners is steadily increasing, Farnham has
its fair share and perhaps more, since it has had so warm a place
in the hearts of many who have worked round about. One result
is that its old people cover a wider than usual social spread,
probably wider than those in some of the favoured South Coast
retirement towns – from the retired top military brass, distin-

guished scientific boffins, ex-London stockbrokers, to teachers of various kinds; most of these will have professional occupational pensions. And then there is the majority, the locals – from the not-well-off old men who stand on Argos's forecourt to others with a better going-on, those who are still comfortable working-class and lower-middle-class.

The retired middle-class – like most of us – are a fairly well-defined group who follow well-defined, habitual, unchanging, mental and physical tracks. If you hold a door open for an elderly upper-middle-class professional in Farnham he is likely to use that: 'Thank you *vair* much' form; most people will say: 'Thanks'; young people say: 'Cheers' or 'Ta, mate' . . . or 'mite'. (A woman lecturer at a London college rebuked my door-holding male chauvinism with: 'Fuck you.') Not long ago, an elderly man said 'Cheery-bye' to me as he moved off; but that form is as dated as *Brief Encounter*.

Elderly Farnham people of the middle-class, though not necessarily implying 'Not in my back-yard', rightly look warily at most new building developments and are members of the Farnham Society and their local Residents' Association. They go regularly to the Maltings and many lend a hand there. When the Farnham branch of the University of the Third Age (U3A) was proposed we should have been able to guess it would attract a crowd to its inaugural meeting. There must have been about two hundred, virtually all of them middle-class; we were only allowed to squeeze in, at the back, instead of having to come to an overflow meeting a week later, by telling them we would be away at that time.

U3As began in France and took root in Britain through the enthusiasm of the Cambridge don Peter Laslett. I do not know what he thinks of them now or what the French think of the British variant. But if the Farnham proposals on that launching-day, and their fulfilment now, are typical, the work does not deserve its grand name. It encourages butterfly interests in a promiscuous range of subjects. Odd to think that a century and a half ago the Extension movement for university education was set up by the old universities. Later, the Workers' Educational Association was founded, partly to insist on the need for sustained study in depth, if the interest of the universities was to be gained and out of respect for the presumed potentialities of working-class students. Two hundred yards from the Farnham meeting there are dozens of classes available from the county adult education service and from the University of Surrey, but that particular group of U3A proponents making their enthusiastic pitch seemed to have no knowledge of them or of the achievements of Mansbridge and Temple and Tawney in that precise field. Not all U3A branches may be like that but what has arrived in Farnham is the educational equivalent of an inset in a Sunday colour supplement: 'Quick and Painless Guide to the Best in Modern Art/Music/Literature'. One could, of course, make out a case to justify its existence; but, given the history of university extra-mural education, it should not be called university work. To its credit, though, Farnham's U3A is involved with the town's Oral History Project; that is exactly right.

Some of the retired middle-class are well-heeled enough to patronise from time to time one of the expensive restaurants in West Street. Not long ago I saw a Queen Mary toque there, the first sighting since the war. Many others among the middle-class retired seem to spend a good deal of time worrying over their stocks and shares. Perhaps in part that is a sort of hobby, in its own way enjoyable. Shall I switch to that? Take out a few shares in this? Have a mild flutter on that? They take the *Financial Times*, are regular readers of the Personal Finance columns of the broadsheets and regular listeners to – and writers to – Radio 4's 'Moneybox' programme; and presumably regular writers to their brokers. They are regular listeners, too, to much other than 'Moneybox' on Radio 4; it is their channel pre-eminently – but also much broader and better than its general reputation might suggest. The letters to 'Moneybox' confirm the worrisomeness of stocks-and-shares-holding to a lot of people. So do the grumbles, as of those who feel they have been robbed, at the great drops in Building Society interest rates from 1992 onwards; that is enough to make some threaten to defect from the Conservative Party. At the far end of that set of nervous attitudes are the people who fall for the promise of extraordinarily large profits and are ruined by such as Barlow Clowes. The non-worriers are much more prudent and rather more interested in finding out what is the minimum number of shares which will allow them to qualify for shareholders' perks – discounts in a corporation's shops, privileges on Channel crossings and air journeys.

That is a world of its own, alien to yet another cluster of old people. These are the ones who pick over the marked-down goods in the supermarkets. Those are usually to be found in a large container at the end of a known aisle; tins with dents in them, damaged packets, items which simply have not taken on, have not 'moved'. The surprise here, in Sainsbury's at least, is how little is knocked off – 2p off a battered tin of soup; 10p off a small tin of prepared meat which simply wouldn't shift at £1.57. Many of these objects hang around for days but usually there is someone picking over the pile, so perhaps the managers know how very little they need to knock off.

The poorer old people do not go into the separate wines and spirits department except for a bottle of sweet sherry at Christmas or for very occasional other celebrations. Regular elderly customers there include professional men with purply-mottled cheeks and lost-looking widows picking up a half-bottle of gin. There are 'bargain' oddities here, too. Sainsbury's had on offer a bottle of Chablis, marked down because its main label had disappeared (stolen by someone who stuck it on a bottle of plonk?); its small back label was tattered. The price had been £6.89; it was now £6.64. A bottle of red Bordeaux, 1986, had been marked down from £10.99 to £10.79, presumably because its label was tattered. Are people who are prepared to spend almost £7 or even almost £11 for a bottle of wine going to be tempted to buy one without its pristine label, so prestigious-seeming to your guests, just so as to save 20 or 25p? Wouldn't that, with adjustments of scale, be almost like a willingness to do without the Silver Lady fronting your Rolls-Royce simply to save a few hundred pounds? Perhaps a solitary drinker would pick them up.

Those usual kinds of 'bargains' in the groceries department are distinct from and less advantageous than goods marked down, especially from the chiller cabinets, because they have reached their sell-by date. These are usually reduced to half their original price or even less and, if you acquire a sense of when they are most likely to be made available – the day and the time – you can save pounds and many old people do. Not only old people. I recently saw a well-dressed woman of about thirty-five buy twelve items of food, every one of which had been marked down to half or, in one or two instances, a third of the original price. I was the next customer and forgot to start unloading my own trolley because I was so busy calculating how much she had saved. Just over £17. It took a little time since each item had to be hand-entered; but at least she didn't then unload a bundle of bits of cut-out card each offering 10p off your next kitchen item, packet of cereal or fruit cordial. Most supermarkets take those as straightforward currency; and, again, I have seen a woman using them save two or three pounds in one visit.

The oddest basket of goods I have seen bought by old people contained half-a-dozen very large tins of the store's own brand of baked beans and half-a-dozen large tins of their prunes – a sort of dietetic cancelling-out or pre-emptive strike seemed to be implied – and there were some tins of cat food and four jars of marmalade; nothing else.

CHAPTER 4

OLD SKILLS AND NEW HABITS

My skill goes beyond the depths of a pond.
Martin Parker,
'When the King Enjoys his Own Again'

To one brought up in a virtually one-class, massively industrial, big-city district of about the same size as Farnham but less than a century old, a town like Farnham could hardly present more social, economic, cultural and occupational differences, novelties and complexities: mixed class, mixed crafts rather than mixed but related heavy industries, rural as much as urban, and with more than a thousand years of life.

The line of Farnham's skills up to the middle of this century is long and strong. Its huge oaks and its craft with timber brought it the commission, in 1395, to build the hammer-beam roof of Westminster Hall. That amazing structure took five years to set up: two hundred and thirty-nine feet long by eighty feet wide and with no supporting pillars.

The tradition ran through to Sturt's Wheelwright's Shop on East Street and that lasted until the internal combustion engine did for the trade. The building is now a car salesroom and the external plaque commemorating the link with Sturt has gone. But inside the salesroom, just behind the latest Saab (£24,000, the day I was there), is a faithful little exhibition on the wheelright's mystery. The Town Museum pays its dues too.

Then there was the wool trade and, even more, the wheat. Defoe said Farnham's was the greatest wheat market in England in the seventeenth century. Its location, on a key east–west route about halfway between London and Winchester, and not much further to the South Coast and Portsmouth, helped bring that about.

Most important of all was the hop trade. For almost four centuries Farnham was the greatest hop-ground in England, its white-bine grape-hops at one time among the most expensive in the world, treasured for their flavour and light colour. Malting lasted until 1946. Today you must go ten miles westwards, to Alton, to find the big breweries.

The only other and the most recent skill that knowledgeable locals will tell you about is Farnham's short flurry with motor-car production. A plaque on West Street recalls that in 1897 J. H. Knight designed (George Parfitt built it) the second petrol-driven car to run on English roads (some prefer to say the first two-seater). They also recall that Knight committed some of the earliest and oddest motoring offences, such as driving in pro-hibited hours. All this, of course, before the great amalgama-tions. But Farnham might just possibly have been a Cowley or a Coventry.

Today the town has no powerful single trade. Crosby's em-ployed a few hundred, mainly making doors; they moved west in 1991 after about a century in Farnham. There are the small trading estates. But generally there is a bittiness in industry and occupations. And in the composition of the citizens. If a town's population, seen as a whole, is like a cake which can be cut in several main ways, as I will continue trying to do, you will still be left – especially in Farnham – with pieces, smallish groups and individuals, which belong but don't easily fit; and will again have lost something, some texture and colour. Some of these other groups are marginal to the town's active working life and have largely unregarded but very complicated lives of their own – such as many among the Old Age Pensioners. Other groups are usually small and most are best looked at when popular recreations are described. And then there are peculiarly interesting individuals, some native in their activities to this town and this place, others odd-balls of a sort likely to occur anywhere. All interesting, like nuts and raisins or silver threepenny bits in the cake.

There is still a small group of people and trades which are local and well-rooted: a pottery over a hundred years old and hardly changed, an optician not part of a chain, a doctor come back to his home town to practise, a carpenter, a locksmith (now just gone), a blacksmith up a side lane and a glazier at the side of a short snicket – they will break off easily from whatever they have in hand to agree to do a small job for you, to fix a reasonable time when they will have it ready and not to overcharge. They employ themselves; they are decent craftsmen-tradesmen. The clock repairer can keep your things for quite a long time, but then he was for years busy as church organist also and seems one of the least financially ambitious of men. All of these appear to make at least a respectable living, to be able to take holidays of the kind they and their wives want and to be able to give their children a fair start in a chosen trade if they don't want to follow Father.

There is a substantial local building firm long established in one of the villages, which seems able in each generation to find and train men who will carry on an honest tradition; George Sturt again. There are among all these a few who will try to rip you off but usually neighbours can tell you of a reliable crafts-man and he is almost always a local. Neighbours will also tell you of a woman who will 'run up' curtains and chair-covers; no doubt others could name a dressmaker, 'a little woman who's marvellous with a needle'. The *Farnham Herald* lists many more, from 'House Clearance' specialists to those who will do your ironing for, in early 1992, '£3.50 up an hour'.

Some still live over the shop; others are a mile or so out in one of the private developments of semis with garden and garage and central-heating. That is where the short-back-and-sides barber lives. He still calls himself a barber. The title is so unusual now – 'unisex hairdresser' is more favoured – that you wonder whether the 'barber' is deliberately setting a yet newer fashion, where the old names come in again; just as 'Farnham Cobbler' and 'Aldershot Cobbler' and 'Guildford Cobbler' are likely to be used by branches of a national shoe-repairers' chain.

The barber doesn't seem that sort of man. Yet he moves with the times. He will tell you of his troubles in getting his new kitchen fitted properly – several thousand pounds worth of cupboards and shelving and electronic gear. Even more indicative: his daughter went from the sixth-form college to a big Redbrick university, took a good honours degree in one of the newer, consumer-related biological sciences and then, after a trip to China on the cheap with her boyfriend, had more than one job-offer; almost certainly the first of her family to enter the professional and from now on probably unrooted-professional class.

An old-style barber's shop is interesting above all as a centre for old-fashioned gossip, gossip whose points of reference, style and underlying attitudes have hardly changed over many decades: how the other local shops are faring, the increase in casual violence, a couple of deaths among the better-known local people or regular customers, the shortcomings of the Council, the ups-and-downs of newcomers among the tradespeople, the appalling increases in both rents and rates.

More difficult to understand is the interest shown by some other barbers in a violent by-pass of a hobby. One will be fascinated by militaria, the more manageable trappings of armies; another will have plastered his walls and ceiling with souvenirs from various air forces: models, badges, stickers, macho-mottoes. Yet another sells guns, pistols and lethal-looking catapults. The long-established side-trade in materials for that Trappist occupation, angling, is easy to understand since it is, like so much in the whole style of the barber's trade itself, a central feature of traditional English life; so are umbrella repairs and the now revived trade in French letters (but the ubiquitous machines for those offer strong competition). Yet what can explain the violent preoccupations? A reaction from the humdrum, body-servant, character of their work?

The most unusual person in this frieze is fairly difficult to describe without seeming trite. But the bare facts are enough. He is a friendly postman in, apparently, his mid-forties; he is also exceptionally soft-spoken and courteous. One day I happened to be at the front door when he arrived with the mail. 'I'm sorry to be missing some of your television programmes on Europe,' he said, 'but they overlap with Bryan Magee's series on philosophy and I've been following those from the beginning.'

The Open University most recently, as well as long established university and local authority provision, have proved that there is a considerable demand for adult education. But, for reasons easy to find, that demand has not been strong among working-class people. Still, I would have been less surprised by the postman's remark if he had said: 'I am doing a course on philosophy . . .'; but his seemed a purely personal announcement. Naturally some postmen, though their job itself doesn't normally call for much intellectual enquiry, have intellectual interests outside what would be the more common pursuits: the garden, doing things about the house, watching anything which happens to be on TV rather than following one of the more demanding series? This is all delicate and largely untrodden ground in discursive, non-specialist writing. That postman is unusual, is a kind of late twentieth-century Jude or Leonard Bast. I do not know why he did not go on to further education at sixteen; there were more chances even then than either Jude or Leonard had; perhaps his intellectual interests matured late; perhaps he had submerged talents which no teacher spotted; perhaps his home circumstances forced him to get a job as soon as possible; perhaps he simply likes the healthy life of a postman, a longish daily walking routine which allows him to think as he carries it out and ends early enough for him to turn to something else. He is a rebuke to the tendency to type-cast people too readily. He is probably slightly patronised by some householders, especially when they give him his Christmas-box; but he seems to have an exceptionally enquiring mind, which rises out of the usual habits of his group. It seemed natural, indigenous, Sturt-like, that the first time I saw him off-duty he was in the Palm Sunday procession going through the West door of the parish church.

He underlines another point which is worth making again and again. Jude and Leonard were straining principally against very plain hindrances, above all the lack of opportunity because of obvious social and financial constraints, to develop intellectual and imaginative interests. The postman's obstacles are less obvious but no less severe. In the late twentieth century, when even postmen have spare money at the end of the week and are commercially worth pursuing, those among them and those in similar occupations have, if they are to develop the intellectual interests they begin to feel emerging, to fight not the classes above them nor the lack of easily available intellectual sustenance but the whole culture of their time, and in particular of 'people like them', of what is expected of them and what not. They have to resist the voices which say all the time that the exciting things in life have nothing to do with intellectual enquiry, which is dry and dusty, but are objects, tastes, new and changing all the time, which you consume like candy-floss; and that if you step outside this ingratiatingly all-embracing circle you really are an odd-ball.

The first black postman on our round has now appeared. There are hardly any black people in Farnham. I do not know why. Perhaps the look and feel of the town puts them off. Asians, chiefly from the Indian sub-continent, regularly set up restaurants and some of them succeed; so do even more Chinese restaurateurs; they compete, as almost everywhere, with the hamburger joints, the pizza places and the Italian restaurants, a couple of wine bars with food, the pubs which announce home-made lunchtime meals (often delivered from a trading estate near London, microwaved on demand into a simulacrum of fresh life and then covered with dark-brown synthetic gravy – the English swamp-all); plus the inevitable Forte hotel and one other; and, surprisingly, two Austrian restaurants.

Asian shopkeepers already have a fairly firm foothold, running newspaper shops which are often also part of the Spar chain of independent local grocers, or pharmacies. Those, so far, are the two main occupations. One Asian family's grocery shop serves a medium-sized council housing estate; and serves it much more efficiently than did any of the earlier succession of British occupiers. Over a few years this family have changed a newspaper shop with only a few ancillaries into a small supermarket whose stock shows a responsiveness to local demand. You pay a few pence more for most things but save a trek into town and perhaps parking fees. Both the man and his wife are professionally qualified, the one – if I remember rightly – as a pharmacist, the other as a vet. They have added off-licence and video-rental sections; in season their forecourt is crowded with bedding plants and shrubs for sale. They assume that they will work long hours and are constantly pushing at the frontiers of the trade. They have become a main, if not the main, pivot of the estate.

Obviously, most of their customers are from the immediate area, and to watch them at different times of day is to have reactions more often disturbing than reassuring. Some of the houses have been bought by their previous tenants and are usually identifiable by their exterior changes – bottle-glass, carriage lamps, recent painting, decorative doorways, well-maintained gardens – those common results of pride in ownership and of the interplay of do-it-yourself willingness and the huge range of gear which the retail DIY warehouses on the outskirts now offer. Of course, some of the rented houses are not in bad shape and some of their gardens are very well kept. But all in all they reveal the difficulties local councils face in keeping their rented property in the way an owner-occupier would reach for; hence the waits by tenants for plumbing, electrical, carpentry and painting work. A pity so many Labour councils took a long time to see these points; they should have fought harder, once they had had to accept the buying of council houses, for the maintenance of an adequate and adequately serviced sector for renting. One disadvantage of mixed estates – part rented, part owner-occupied – is that in some areas a new division is appearing, with the poor, often one-parent, families inevitably in the rented part. To keep a home going on a reasonable keel is always a difficult financial and logistic task; 'To be poor and independent is very nearly an impossibility,' said Cobbett; it is harder, lonelier, if you are the only adult; the discrepancies show up even more. Soon the Hire Purchase and Loan sharks and the other con-men move in, and the mess becomes unmanageable.

Some of the revolving clientele of the Spar shop, and not only those managing on very little, would have shocked Cobbett, with his insistence on careful household economy and practice. It is clear that many ignore or do not see health warnings and dietetic advice. Before school the shop is busy with kids from five upwards, many of whom are given 20p to 30p each day for sweets; there is a range of particularly cheap sweets aimed exactly at them. How many have their teeth regularly examined, except at the schools' prompting?

They go to the nearest Local Authority maintained school. Luckily, the school is a good one, I would guess better than some of the private schools round about. But the point is that the children are sent there as a matter of habit, not judgement. In the last couple of years two successive Secretaries of State for Education have used the same argument and almost the same phrasing, when rejecting criticisms of their new policies, criticisms made on the grounds that those policies will put working-class people at even greater disadvantage. Won't, the first was asked, the opting-out of schools produce an even greater division between the opportunities provided for working-class children as compared with those for others? Lower-middle-class and middle-class parents will compare the opted-out schools with the others and send their children to the one most likely to do best educationally by them. Working-class parents rarely make such discriminations. The second of these Secretaries of State was similarly challenged when the ludicrously inadequate (as well as inaccurate) 'League Table' of schools' results in public examinations was published. Such moves are on a par with the proposal to 'privatise' the schools' Inspectorate. Her Majesty's – not a Government's – independent Inspectorate was another of those fine, nineteenth-century, Arnoldian inventions. ('Privatising' prisons is even worse; if ever there were a *society's* duty, a humane public duty on behalf of us all, it is in the proper conduct of prisons.)

Their critics were self-evidently right and the evidence is all around; most working-class people routinely but entirely understandably send their children to the local schools, to which they themselves probably also went. The two Secretaries of State made exactly the same rejoinder: 'I have more faith in the good judgment of ordinary people than you seem to have.' Nauseating contempt disguising itself as just and sympathetic judgment.

Later in the morning some young mothers will call in the shop for a couple of packets of cigarettes and odd bits of food. It is plain that some do not make regular visits to the supermarket – the nearest is half-a-mile away – that they shop hand to mouth and hence expensively. They go to the frozen and packeted food sections and pick up chips, burgers, fish-fingers, TV dinners. Even in their early twenties many of them are overweight and have that white, waxy complexion which indicates insufficient exercise and a misguided diet. Most seem to have one or two children already. It is as if they put out an allure from about fifteen until they marry and the first child appears, and then 'let themselves go'. None of this is new. The only surprise is that the pattern is so close to that of the thirties. For many the accommodation and facilities and the available money have changed for the better (we are not looking here, only or mainly, at one-parent families or families with no one in work); so, though much changes, many habits linger.

One girl of fifteen whom we got to know slightly went out, against her parents' greatly concerned advice, with a regularly convicted petty thief of about twenty. He insisted on unprotected sex if she didn't want him to chuck her; she didn't demur because she wanted to have a baby as soon as ever possible, and perhaps a baby would bring the man to marriage and family life; she quickly became pregnant. Her mother did not recognise her condition until she had a call from the local hospital to say the girl had walked in bleeding badly and had a miscarriage; at three months. The mother remonstrated with her, pointing out that their council house was already quite full. 'Oh, if I had a baby,' the girl said, 'and if you couldn't have me, the council would have to house me and give me the allowances. It's the law.'

This is a true report and the only such instance we know directly, but even as I tell it I can almost feel some friends resisting it uneasily. Playing into the hands of the Norman Tebbits and Peter Lilleys, and of the censorious, middle-class, Tory women. Not allowing for the inadequacy of the girl's background; or perhaps of her limited education. So, even if it is word for word true, you should not circulate it, is the argument. That is the thin edge of selective censorship, negative discrimination in word and thought.

I have no less a sense of the disadvantages of many people than those friends have. But by closing their minds to other than the purely social elements which prompted the girl's behaviour they – this looks like becoming a refrain – morally reduce her. She had a limited working-class background, it is true. But her mother, a hard-working woman who lived by good lights, had given her the best advice she could and the girl had ignored it. She was only fifteen and adolescence is a particularly self-involved time. She is now married, to a different boy, and is a devoted mother. It is too soon to say whether she will become, through peer-group pressures, like some of the young mothers on the estate I have described above, or whether she will take after others in her generation whose ways are like her own mother's. Given that family background, I would bet on the second result.

What about the young men who make their girlfriends pregnant, often at an early age? In these days many are out of work; and, in work or not, some would make a poor fist of being reliable husbands and fathers at this stage in their own lives. But the worst aspect of all – which you may verify any evening from listening to conversations in pubs and clubs – is that much in the culture of young working-class males is crudely macho, imprisoned in a universe of beer and sex in which girls are there to be poked; and if they become pregnant, 'That's their fucking look-out.' I am not implying that habits among young middle-class men and women are different in kind; but they do have more safety-nets when there's trouble.

Another true incident will fall just as unhappily on ears which equate sympathy for working-class people with justification of any failings among them on social not individual grounds (a justification rarely extended to young middle-class people who have picked up rapacious entrepreneurial habits from their particular backgrounds). A local garage-owner trusted for honest servicing lost his two best mechanics when they set up on their own. He appointed two young men from nearby and gave them good training on the job. But they failed to turn up between Christmas and the New Year, though they had promised to do so. Meanwhile, complaints about the servicing had begun to come in. He looked carefully at some of their work and found they had claimed to have done jobs which they had not done, had failed to tighten important nuts and bolts, and generally carried out all their work only sketchily – some of those omissions could have had dangerous results – and that they had carelessly damaged some expensive power-tools in the workshop. When they did turn up he gave them their cards, which was expensive in legally required paying-off charges, but probably less expensive than making them work out their time, and probably damage yet more equipment. They didn't mind, they said; they could go elsewhere and meanwhile live off the dole and their mothers. One of them took his former employer to a tribunal but did not turn up for the hearing, so the case dropped.

Yes, there have been complaints like that about the bad habits of idle apprentices for centuries; and yes, many bosses are up to every fiddle they can get away with and push their employees into fiddling for them. But the styles change. Sturt, talking about young country workmen at the turn of the century, could not say the lazy ones could fall back on the dole and a household which could absorb them at least for a while if they were sacked. He says they could be inefficient and lazy, 'shy' (an odd word today, though it probably survives in 'work-shy') and 'lubberly' (an even odder word but well worth reinstating for its right purposes). He recognises the nasty tricks of some farmers to get more than their due from their hired hands. But in general, he finds the 'honest day's work' tradition strong among the labourers; in and around Farnham today that remains more true than not among craftsmen and the firms who employ them.

Thirty years ago Auden, looking at and listening to the crowd in a Birmingham pub on a Friday night, said he now understood why he did not like the entry of the masses into society; they were noisy and obstreperous. Naturally, I demurred on the best democratic grounds and would have done so today. We cannot regret the loss of deference. We can object to the snobbish manners, towards others lower down the scale, of those middle-class women I have spent so much time on. It would be evasive not to regret also the sight of drunken young men on the train having no hesitation, assuming it entirely their right in public, to 'fuck-and-blind' and harass the young woman on the other side of the carriage. Or to dislike, as much as one dislikes the snobberies of those elderly ladies, a man in his twenties, in The Borough, whose way through for his truck has been blocked by a thoughtless driver of a saloon, not hesitating to lean out and scream obscene abuse.

There is, in Farnham as elsewhere, a steeply rising number of crimes. So much so that the town has recently been put in a higher-risk area by insurance companies. There are serious crimes right up the scale to the ram-raiding of jewellers' windows, but those are professional jobs by crooks who get quickly away down the motorways. Many, perhaps most, petty and often deeply unpleasant crimes are carried out by locals: vandalising of shop-fronts and cars (if you leave your car long after dark in the station car-park, you will be lucky to find the windscreen intact), stealing of electronic equipment and mountain bikes, unprovoked assaults on passers-by, distracting the attention of old women living alone so that your accomplice can steal her savings or petty cash. These are not all carried out by drunken lads from the council estates or the soldiers from Aldershot. Middle-class youths and their girlfriends are as likely to be involved, if under the influence of drugs and seeking more money to buy them. All this is transforming the streets at night of Farnham as of many such small country towns.

To come back to the nervousness of some colleagues on the Left when they hear any critical remark at all about working-class people. That is why I said above that such tenderness reduces the right of working-class people to be responsible for their own weaknesses. It is a deep-seated disinclination and, in my own direct experience, goes back to at least 1957.

In that year I published *The Uses of Literacy*. Among other things it attempted to describe working-class life as I had known it when a boy. And it described changes going on in working-class life at mid-century, particularly under the ever-growing pressure from the media of mass-persuasion. The book was written roughly between 1950 and 1955.

Most people on the Left liked the book and approved of its criticisms of some major elements of modern consumer capitalism as they were then emerging. But one passage many were irritated by: no passage of mine has been more often challenged. I had at the time a Workers' Educational Association evening class in Goole, a dreary industrial small town well up the Humber from Hull. To a visitor it seemed Chekhovian in its lost air; one could imagine some of the inhabitants so bored that they stood at the town-centre level-crossing to watch the occasional trains go by. Obviously it wasn't as boring as it seemed; and my class was a rewarding one. Still, the town was dull – itself, its landscape and what it offered; especially to young people at that time.

Occasionally I had a cup of tea before the class. This was, remember, about 1950. The only handy place was a milk bar, all cheap plastic, battered tubular chairs and one of the early jukeboxes, stacked with records from the USA, British pop music not having flowered by then. There was always (this would be between early to mid-evening) a group of young working-class teenagers in there, tapping to the juke-box, making a milk-shake – or more likely, since it was cheaper, a cup of tea – last a long time, now and again joshing each other or the young woman behind the counter. I never heard them carry on what might be called a conversation. Such talk as they had showed they were barely literate, or literate at a very low level. They did not look interested or happy. They seemed bored without knowing they were bored since so much in their life was boring anyway, lacked interest or sparkle and suggested nothing more engaging. It may be that Goole had at that time a youth club; if so, it evidently did not attract young men like those (there were very few young women in the milk bar).

Had it come to no more than this for these young people, I wondered, this apparent lack of inner resources, of things which might interest them, of enthusiasms, 'hobbies' (a cycling club, a soccer team, a swimming group), which would fill the evenings instead of this daily hanging around – I use the phrase deliberately – this neon-lighted shabby space?

I wrote five pages about 'The Juke-Box Boys' and, being depressed by it all, became linguistically melodramatic: 'Compared with the pub around the corner, this is all a peculiarly thin and pallid form of dissipation, a sort of spiritual dry-rot amid the odour of boiled milk.' Extravagant; understandably, some people felt that particular sentence was rhetorically and imaginatively excessive.

There followed two pages of an attempt to understand and explain why they passed their spare time like that: the boredom of their jobs, their lack of internal living-space, room for manoeuvre, the constant barrage of those early and mechanical forms of pop culture.

I have just re-read those pages and, apart from toning down the rhetoric, would not wish to alter them. I owed it to the young men, and to my own direct experience of the limitations of a background such as theirs until I got to grammar school, to try to see and tell things as they were. Not a happy thing to write about but I was not belittling them; sad but charitable; angry also, on their behalf, at the different opportunities open to different ranks of people and at the easy way most of us put up with others' deprivations.

The objections had two main thrusts, one factually off-balance, the other subtler. The first group lost a decade or two and spoke warmly of discos they had known, the Beatles and much else in popular culture at that time. But they were talking about the sixties and seventies, I of the early fifties before discos had appeared, at least not in smaller provincial towns. They were talking about hi-fi systems which had an ample supply of new and often inventive British pop music. Most were too young to have known places like the Goole Milk Bar, year of 1950. Or a slight memory of it had been erased by the excitements of sixties-and-after discos.

I stand by my picture of that milk bar at that time especially when, in 1992, a thirty-seven-year-old insisted that I got it wrong because I had not noticed the richness of the culture of those young men of Goole, seen and described when he had not yet been born. That was the second objection; that, even if the physical description of the milk bar was correct, I lacked an inward understanding of what really made up the lives of those young men. If I had had that understanding I would have realised that even their disjointed speech had a complexity and effectiveness of its own, that their responses to the lives offered them could be very sophisticated, critically sophisticated; that I was at best an Arnoldian do-gooder who wanted a single-culture society of articulate people all earnestly reaching for the best that has been thought and said.

This general approach has produced a number of interesting, stimulating and often corrective books since the seventies. They start no earlier than the sixties, with the discos, the Beatles, as ever, and go on to motor-cycle gangs and many another partial rather than representative sub-culture of young people. They make good points, some of them; but most drop into what I have called elsewhere the 'stay as sweet as you are' attitude towards those they are writing about. Don't swallow bourgeois cultural assumptions or Arnoldian aspirations; your culture is as good as theirs, in its own way as rich. The sociolinguist William Labov's fecund and fascinating studies of New York gangs are often their over-extended model.

Most of them overplay their hands even in their descriptions of group styles – lively and inventive as some have been – among young people in the sixties and onwards. They are once again allowing their critically observant edge to be blunted by a disinclination to make a judgment on aspects of the way of life of young people from depressed homes and areas; so they are, yet again, unwittingly belittling those people by reducing their responsibility for their own actions or by, sometimes quite subtly, glamorising their ways. They are blunting also the edge of right and necessary anger – at the exploitation of so many and the humbug with which it is justified; today as in the fifties. They are allowing preconceptions and good-will to get in the way of true judgment; and, again, of just anger. So much about the results of this culture is appalling; but it has become almost a sin – insofar as the concept of sin is still recognised – to say so.

In spite of the always intriguing differences between the styles of different types and classes of people in a town such as Farnham, isn't what is often said true: that we are now if only gradually becoming classless in several ways, in how and what we eat, in recreations and holidays and above all – the great blurrer – in our clothing and general sense of ourselves and our place? This is one of the trickiest areas in the whole business of trying to identify and place groups of people; these and related questions will continue to be raised as we go along. Just now, since we have been thinking of the streets and shops and how we present ourselves in them, we could look at manners and clothing.

Clothing for all ages, both sexes and all social groups, is indeed more colourful and cheerful than one could have predicted thirty years ago; in that sense it has acquired common qualities; but that does not make it classless, a leveller.

Whatever their clothing, teenage middle-class girls are almost always and immediately recognisable. By their current hair-style most strikingly; a slightly off-centre parting, and a full soft wave on either side, with the larger wave falling towards one eye, usually the left. In the centre the hair is drawn back to show a surprising height of forehead and at the top, in some, a tiny bump on each side; at the back, the hair is layered to the neck; a very attractive style which may eventually pass on to working-class girls, but probably will not. It has an assured casualness which is not often part of the 'feel' of life for working-class teenagers. It goes with, at the least, Benetton or even 'designer' clothing, private schools, horses owned or more often hired; and with unquestioned young-middle-class attitudes, about their own adolescence and their aspirations; attitudes distinctly different from those of working-class teenagers, even of most of those who work in Boots. Miss Joan Hunter-Dunn lived in Aldershot; her descendants are all around us today; they rarely wear shell-suits.

Though they do not walk from the hips, boldly, in the way Italian young women do, they have a casualness in their stride which is rarely found in the English working-class; young working-class women tend to walk from the knees, trottily. Incidentally, the English middle-class stride is also different from the American. Well-built American teenagers hold their breasts up and out, bouncily but not erotically, pleased and proud, as though they have just been presented with them after an Evangelical Fun Run. Early middle-aged American professional women stride too but in a purposeful, well-spread way which suggests space and wide-horizoned expectations, not alleys, snickets, ginnels, short side streets, physical and psychological.

Middle-class girls here are likely to become – twenty years on (as do girls of most classes, and boys in relation to their fathers) – like their mothers, who favour those Burberry hats in tartan check. We have seen that those are both a uniform and a signal, especially if worn with an aggressive tilt to one side.

But, as we also saw, Barbour jackets, green wellies, flat racing-style clipped-neb caps, even cavalry twill trousers are bought by people from all parts of society now; you can't tell what part of society they come from – can you? Yes, you can, if you get to a yard or even a bit more from them. I was hailed on Castle Street one morning not long ago by an elderly man in a flat cap, wearing a waxed jacket, cavalry twill trousers, solid brown shoes and carrying a stick. From ten yards, asked to guess, I would have said: 'retired officer'. 'Remember me?' he asked, as we drew close. 'I used to be on the counter at so-and-so's' (a shop which employed three or four staff). He was enjoying retirement very much, went for long walks with his dog and – this was new – had joined the local golf-club. Perhaps the outfit was his disguise there. Close-up, it was clear that the cap was from a chain-store, the waxed jacket either from a Saturday market or through mail-order, the trouser material not heavy and close-woven (the mark of quality in cavalry twill) and, with the shoes, also from a department store. It was all a reaching towards or purposeful disguise. Our clothing is not making us classless; it is taking over class fashions or seeking class-blurrings or even a sort-of-classlessness which pleases a lot of people who aspire but do not wish to seem to, to aspire and not to aspire; it does not worry the secure middle-class who can tell an expensive cloth and cut from much more than a yard off.

Farnham's golden girls and boys are secure too; their schools together with their family backgrounds have seen to that. Their world is limited – to this bit of Surrey and their kind of people within that bit; to their favoured holiday haunts and discos and out-of-town inns; to the Conservative Club, to the right kind of tennis-club, perhaps to a drug-pusher whom the group (and groups from other classes) all know, to the right kind of suburban district before and after marriage, the right kind of car.

The cultural differences of these young men and women from working-class and even lower-middle-class people of their own age almost amount to ethnic differences. Their expectations differ enormously from those of people they recognise immediately as just below them. They expect a good salary and a good pension at the end, and much help from Daddy – especially from the girl's Daddy – with the first house and car. They are likely to live longer than people less plushily secure, and likely to be freer of ill-health at least until a fairly advanced age. But this is partly because, more than middle-class people, many working-class people as we have noted tend to feed themselves unwisely, to smoke more and take less exercise.

By their dress shall ye know and divide them. In the ways we present ourselves publicly, in the ways we dress as well as in vocabulary and accent we can still be easily distinguished. True, young working-class men and women on the town on Saturday nights are not quite so easily distinguished as they used to be – clogs and shawls, we might say, are out. Working-class young people have spare money; they use a lot of it on, for example, expensive haircuts and in this imitate not the middle-class but popular idols. If they do branch out into middle-class-favoured styles, especially under the influence of TV and other advertising, the difference is still recognisable without much difficulty, in the outfits themselves and in the ways they are carried off.

CHAPTER 5

SERVICES AND INSTITUTIONS: PRIVATE, PUBLIC – AND HARDLY ABSORBED

It's more than a game, it's an institution.
Thomas Hughes, *Tom Brown's Schooldays*

So Farnham is substantially a servicing rather than a manufacturing town; and to a lesser degree a dormitory and retirement centre. The little trading estates, like those outside most British and West European towns, are labour-intensive: tyre and exhaust fitting, photographic services, quick printing, electronics. Now the thrust by the large supermarket chains to follow the French pattern and move into gargantuan hypermarkets is beginning to encroach on the outer and larger of the trading estates, displacing some of the smaller firms there; by the nineties many of those non-residential areas on the outskirts of most towns have become too handy, too near main roads and motorways, to be left alone.

Farnham's hinterland of settlements is several miles deep. It has to have an extensive range of commercial and professional and public services: of solicitors, surveyors, architects, accountants, estate agents; some locally owned, some members of national chains since, over almost all professions, trades and general services, this is the pattern nowadays. The chains grow all the time, the locals dwindle.

We do not attract, as larger places such as Guildford and, massively, Croydon do, the regional or chief headquarters of national bodies. But our rents and rates, cheaper than those in Central London – though still very dear – the good road, rail and air services and housing, have brought at least the headquarters of the National Licensed Victuallers Association; very apt, that, in view of Farnham's notoriously boozy past. They have an attractive early nineteenth-century house at the bottom of Downing Street. I have never seen anyone go in or out. Perhaps they use the beer-off entrance, the back.

And there are banks; too many of them. In less than a hundred yards on one side of The Borough are branches of three of the main clearing banks; the fourth is a few yards up Castle Street, at right angles to the others. They are generally disliked, as they seem to be over much of the country. For one thing, they can behave cavalierly and unhelpfully; not at all 'Listening Banks'. An obvious example: they load the rates for buying and selling foreign currency, with slight, arcane differences from bank to bank, but always very much in their favour. Travel agencies are less fuss and building societies more helpful.

Much more homely, whether they are parts of national chains or locally owned, are the chemists and the opticians. The opticians, in particular, now face sharp competition as regulations are loosened. If you are a local optician and see on your TV a famous personality saying how pleased he is to get his bi-focals virtually over the counter and probably for less than he would have paid locally, you would be foolish to delay in increasing your own competitiveness. Most chemists, it seems, are reasonably well-cushioned by the combination of National Health prescriptions and beauty aids plus mixed ancillaries. With W. H. Smith's and the like, they must thank Heaven for that ever-widening range of ancillaries.

*

His head,
Not yet by time completely silver'd o'er,
Bespoke him past the bounds of freakish youth,
But strong for service still, and unimpair'd.
William Cowper, 'The Task', Book ii

Of the public services, properly so called, the Town, Borough and County Councils must come first, and have already been described to some extent. Briefly, they are not bad and most seem nowadays, in their approaches to their Council Tax payers, reasonably civil. They do not seem to have different manners for different grades of people, as they had in Leeds in the thirties. Even if they retained those scales today I might not notice, being, once I speak, recognisably educated, and so to be treated cautiously by the would-be snooty. But there does seem to have been a general gain; those who at any time and in any circumstances would have been polite remain polite; the incipient bullies have been at least partly tamed; and the dreadfully superior petty functionaries – because they assume they are one rung up the social ladder from many clients, customers or citizens, and cling to that distinction and division – are often less evident and less confident in that style.

Local authorities are more responsive to new ideas than they used to be. They establish bottle banks, aluminium banks, waste-paper banks, old clothes banks. If Farnham is a good guide, their refuse-collecting services are efficient and rarely bloody-minded. The road engineers are fairly quick at getting to the repair of pot-holes and displaced flag-stones. As we shall see, the policy on parking charges is misguided; it has become geared to profit. That recalls the spokesman for a recently nationalised public service who was asked on television why he refused to provide for an outlying hamlet. It would cost too much, he said, and 'my first duty is to my shareholders'. There is the authentic, dire voice of the eighties and nineties, the voice which has not heard of public service and of equality in major services no matter where you live or how wealthy you are.

Question: if the postal service were established today and obviously as a private concern, would charges be the same for delivery all over the country? Would the public service idea in broadcasting have been conceived, maintained by a uniform modest licence fee? Would free public libraries have been set up? Or public parks with no entry charge – and museums – and art galleries? And very cheap allotments? And what chance of being born, as a place of relatively cheap access, would an Open University have? Still, Farnham's admirable sports centre would have been unthinkable in the thirties, so we move a little. In public services, in the idea of public service, that movement has been one step forward, two back in this last decade and a half.

As to schools, Farnham is typical but with knobs on for a town of its size; it is prosperous enough, middle-class enough, Tory-voting enough to keep several private preparatory schools going. One occasionally bites the dust because rent and rates have gone up too much or rolls fallen, or both. Some are too small to have a good range of well-trained teachers, and over-reliant on part-timers who share their ethos; but desperate to get as many pupils as possible equipped for entry to a public school; any public school, sometimes.

Hence the rain of advertisements in the local papers; never so many hurrah and buzz and PR and uplifted Newboltian words:

> caring – friendly – parental involvement – excellence in sport – realising full potential – successful preparation for entrance to senior schools – superb facilities – lively, caring community – developing leadership – emphasis on manners, conduct, leadership – stimulating, friendly ethos – highly qualified and well-motivated staff – stretching – high standard of pastoral care – disciplined and caring – all-round character building to uphold values and standards – a very positive attitude to life – full and rounded education – shooting-range and assault course – leadership training – Christian tradition and environment – a broad academic and sporting curriculum – family atmosphere, firm and kindly discipline – semi-military discipline – self-discipline – upholding traditional values – innovation with tradition – purposeful – heart and soul and mind can grow – structured and disciplined.

Such, such were the joys!

What a revealing, sad, hilarious essay could be written on those repetitive, gesturing, imprisoned themes; or threnodies.

West Street just before nine in the morning is full, as Castle Street is busy with school-buses, of the usual station-wagons, BMW's, Volvos and all the rest of the indicative carriages, disgorging the pupils in those odd tigerish blazers and comical peaked caps which so intrigued T. S. Eliot when he met them on visits to his mother-in-law in a 'better-off' part of Leeds. One looks at the mothers and thinks of the inescapably high fees and of the effort by the teachers to keep up-to-date and maintain some sort of reasonable academic standard, and thinks: you poor, mistaken women (and your husbands), wasting your money for an education probably no better in many instances than your children would have in the cheerful, good, maintained school two hundred yards away.

But that misses the point. However much they might protest, these parents – unless, because of special circumstances, they have no choice – are spending a lot of money for reasons of simple, uncomplicated, but hardly eradicable snobbery; they are keeping their children away from common children, trying to ensure that they will have the right accents and manners to move in middle-class schools and middle-class society. In protesting against such a judgment they are not being humbugs. Humbug is conscious misleading of others. Theirs is unconscious misleading of themselves. All this is still strong in the nineties; the English learn very slowly; they would sooner drop their pants in public than drop their aitches, since that would indicate more of a social drop; this is the most depressing single phenomenon in a town such as Farnham.

How did they react, one wonders, to the news in 1992 that one of the numerous public schools around Farnham, an expensive one – indeed, they all are, have to be – had just been shown to be, as to GCE results, in the bottom 5 per cent of schools of its kind across the country? No doubt they were then told and told themselves that grubbing for marks was less important than good manners, good bearing, good address, good connections, a healthy mind in a healthy body. As to the speech-manners-contacts pattern they may be right: it can get jobs; of certain kinds.

What I have seen and heard of the maintained schools in Farnham is largely to their credit, right up to the sixth-form college (as almost always, based on a several-centuries-old grammar school), which is clearly better academically than some, perhaps most, public schools round about. Shrewd parents have spotted that and acted on it. Under the new regime parents will be encouraged to shop around even among the maintained and opted-out schools; and some will, choosing on academic grounds above all. As we know, perhaps most working-class parents will continue to send their children to the nearest maintained school.

The Butler Act of half-a-century ago was a magnificent docu-
ment, second only in vision to the National Health Service. It has
done more than any other single Act to improve education in
schools. But the great divide is still substantially there, even –
well, particularly – in a town like Farnham: the combination of,
the unconscious complicity between, a succession of governments that will not recognise that some working-class parents
are their own children's worst enemies here (middle-class parents may be educational enemies to their children, in a reverse
way), and the resistance of those many working-class parents to
the idea of education after sixteen – these two forces are making
parts of the school system more retrograde now even than they
were before Butler. We are still a badly under-educated nation;
we waste the brains to be found in large parts of society as
though they grew on untended trees, and we need only leave
aside the masses of windfalls.

Meanwhile, to come back to one of my favourite arguments,
most of the mass-media tell those ill-informed parents that they
are right; intelligence, training, imagination do not matter. As a
result many bright working-class children have to fight against
their home, their street culture, the trashier aspects of television
and the trashy papers. They have to fight once they begin to
suspect that life need not be as low-level as virtually all around
them seems to suggest. They may have to fight even harder than
our generation did.

As to major public services, I am, being a Socialist, slightly
chagrined to have to say that some of the services of British
Telecom have improved since it was nationalised, except for
some pistol-at-the-head excessive charges, meanly presented, so
that it is difficult to see just how high the hourly rate now
is. Whether the improvements have emerged because BT has
become leaner – made many redundant but given the rest higher
wages and bonuses – I do not know.

Gas services are more reliable now, too, and their annual
servicing system very good and not given to counting every
minute, like BT. One engineer had to spend far longer on a job
than he or we expected, and we sympathised with him. 'Well, I
don't like to leave a job until I'm satisfied it's been properly
done,' he said, not at all sententiously. So far as we are concerned,

the Electricity Board provides a more or less silent service. The Water Board, even more than the banks, is widely disliked and not only for cutting people off. They are given to large, sudden and inadequately explained increases in charges.

The dead too are disposed of with smooth efficiency, commercially or Council-managed. The Yellow Book no longer records 'Undertakers' but refers you to 'Funeral Directors', most of whom have their own 'Chapels of Rest'. Farnham Cemetery is just at the bottom of our road but I have never caught sight of a burial there. The crematorium lies between Farnham and Aldershot and is much like those you begin, at our age, to know all over the country: for me, among others, Hunslet, Leeds, where Aunt Annie was taken; South-East London, for two colleagues from Goldsmiths'; Norwich for a relative by marriage; and Grantham for my brother Tom.

By and large they are as alike as the branches of a national dry-cleaners: a bit of surrounding garden, a parking-circle, probably an arcade of plaques commemorating those cremated there, a small chapel, canned soft melancholy mood music, a duty clergyman who may or may not know or have taken the trouble to learn something about the dead person. Sometimes the curtains slide across as the brief service ends so that the mourners are shuffling out as the coffin goes unseen to the flames; sometimes the coffin is left exposed until the mourners have had the opportunity to go up and touch it before leaving. Our crematorium is much like the rest but is still rather subtly different from Hunslet's; lower-middle-class; and helpfully accustomed to letting you use the office phone if you are running late for an appointment.

We have already seen that the police occupy a rather obscure space, at least for other than young people, that we do not think of them as part of the community, our group of local bobbies, that they are regarded as County officials. During the 1968 student troubles the Surrey police acquired a bad reputation for their handling of the Guildford College of Art sit-in. Not much of that seems to have spread across to Farnham; but Farnham has not had that level of provocation. It has instead that regular vandalism and violence of drunken young men on a weekend spree; those – and the visits from the professional heavy men in the robbery business – are certainly enough to be going on with.

Motor-cycle police from the County squad appear now and again, often inhabiting that insentient, macho world of their own, fond of accosting young motor-cyclists but, as is the way nowadays, disbursing their casual but studiedly provocative rudeness to anyone they think they can pick on. It may be a sign of enhanced democracy that policemen seem to have lost their in-built scales of deference in response to assumed differences in social status as those are indicated by clothing, accent and bearing. A pity more of them could not find a middle way in their encounters, though, instead of offering to everyone they suspect of the slightest infringement the insulting brusqueness from the bottom end of their scale, that which was formerly reserved for young men from the council estates. Arnold Bennett's Edwin Clayhanger, responding to his first sight of a smug middle-class town, Brighton, sounds as if from a very distant age:

> Edwin had only seen the pleasure cities of the poor and of the middling, such as Blackpool and Llandudno. He had not conceived what wealth would do when it organised itself for the purpose of distraction . . . And the enormous policemen, respectfully bland, confident in the system which had chosen them and fattened them, gave as it were to the scene an official benediction.

Ah well, better the 1990s than that aspect of late nineteenth-century England.

Two events affecting the local police in the eighties gave modest pleasure to the citizens, who have the usual mistrust of officiousness. One was an IRA scare which caused the town to be sealed off for some hours. It proved to have been set-off by a young policeman who was off-duty at the time and rather the worse for wear. And there was the raid on a suspected brothel in Firgrove Hill, a respectable lower-middle-class area. The police visited, satisfied themselves that the services openly offered could be widely extended for payment, made their excuses and left. The magistrates were not satisfied and threw the case out. Whether they were unconvinced that a brothel was operating or dismissed the case because – though there may have been a brothel – the prosecution presentation was unconvincing, I do not know. We quite liked either possibility.

Thoughts about the police and their role recall Joseph Conrad.
As so often Conrad, being of Polish origin and used to dangerous
societies, put his finger on something we simply take for granted,
as self-evident. It is self-evident but not in the way we assume.
We *know* or think we know that the social ground is firm
beneath our feet. Conrad knew it was not and that it only came
to seem so by a continuous act of will by many people to whom
we have given that task. As in the opening to *Heart of Darkness*:
'. . . lights began to appear along the shore. The Chapman light-
house, a three-legged thing erect on a mud-flat, shone strongly . . .
"And this also," said Marlow suddenly, "has been one of the
dark places of the earth" . . . "What saves us is efficiency, the
devotion to efficiency." '

The ground is not firm beneath our feet but paper-thin; order
could soon collapse; we almost walk on the water every day.
Imagine what would happen if all police-services were removed
from towns such as Farnham and if we knew they would not
come back: within two hours, looting (one hour in the big cities),
within a month, murder, battery, rape, burglary on a huge scale,
random shootings to protect homes, citizens' gun-happy vigi-
lante groups. The big cities would become no-go areas. The
power of the police is less in the actual crimes they follow up (let
alone clear up), more in the inhibiting force they exercise simply
by being there; so that great numbers of crimes are not committed at all. If all the incipient villains were not thus inhibited
the police, unarmed, in the numbers we at present have them,
would be quickly overwhelmed.

So we come to one of the most commonly used public services, the Post Office. Deliveries and collections are, in general,
excellent, probably among the best in the world. The only
blot, but a bad one, is a tendency to clear the boxes ahead of
time. But the general demeanour of the postmen is friendly and
helpful. The Post Office itself is much changed and becoming
more changed by the month. As in the corralling within metal
railings so that no one shall jump the queue, and that is fair; nor
do you have to wait long, usually. But whilst thus penned you
are treated to a VDU display with running commentary on the
virtues of this or that new Post Office service, or of someone's

photo-processing, or someone else's cure for a few common ailments – backache in bed, say. Formerly nationalised services which have now been privatised, or made into executive agencies which have been ordered to act as if privatised and to develop aggressive commercial habits, drop their old sobriety and do promotional high-kicks – like a teetotaller who has been urged to take to the bottle for therapeutic purposes. By comparison, some of the shrewder large commercial concerns begin to look like church-wardens.

Still, some – a few – of the Post Office cashiers, nearly all women, are not professionally or commercially reconstituted; they are true descendants of their great-aunts in the thirties. They tend to have an unwelcoming air which suggests: 'I am only doing this because I have to, until I find something better / because there's a respectable pension at the end / until I get married / until I can leave my elderly parents / until my husband earns enough to keep us both in the style we like. But I don't have to be pleasant to you, in fact I don't like the look of you, and I'll bridle if you question any of my calculations.' You wish them no harm but in some ways would feel better about some aspects of lower-middle-class public manners and about these ladies' deep-down individual characters if it transpired that they had some secret sorrow they could not shake off, one which made it very difficult for them to put a brave or at least a cheerful face on life. The more disaffected, as you are finally at the front of the queue and see a position vacant, will close their window just as you arrive there.

It is, of course, in many ways a boring and routine job and one can sympathise greatly with those who have taken it up and now feel trapped. So the most bemusing day of the year in the Post Office is Christmas Eve, when the staff have had a little drink and wear funny hats as they serve you. You wish them a happy Christmas, fervently; and just as fervently but silently hope that they have a happy family life and an engrossing hobby.

The public service of which we are all most aware is indisputably the National Health Service. Most of those old enough to have welcomed and wondered at its introduction in 1948 still think of it as the greatest domestic achievement of the immediate post-war years – this in spite of the setbacks of the intervening four and a half decades and especially of the last decade.

I am thinking chiefly of the medical and surgical rather than the dental side. If Farnham is a guide here (and there is no reason to doubt it) the Dental Service, always regarded as socially inferior to medicine, is in a mess; but it has been for much of its life. There are in Farnham as in similar towns a number of purely NHS dentists (though the number began to dwindle in the early nineties because of a dispute with the Department of Health) and a few who work privately. Those who did mixed, NHS and private, work are, again, dwindling.

NHS dental practice can vary from the conscientious to the sloppy. The sloppy ones tend to skimp, to neglect restorative and preservative work, to exploit the system. In some practices you are likely to find a new, and often newly qualified, practitioner at each six-monthly check-up. There is a pervading sense of haste, of chalking up the various permitted charges as fast as can be, of equipment not frequently renewed. The atmosphere in the waiting-room is more thirties than nineties; you feel you are on charity. I know there are better NHS dentists in or near the town but hear more about a sort of rapacity than of work well done. Neither payments by piece-work nor by capitation fees always sit well with fully professional care. Latterly the increases in charges to the patient have discouraged many of those who most need dental care from seeking it.

After a small item of bad bridge-work which he seemed unable or disinclined to put right, I switched from the NHS dentist to a practice where they handled both NHS and private work, and enrolled for the NHS side. The difference was striking, in care, in advice and in available equipment. This, you felt, was what the NHS was meant to be like.

Medical and surgical issues are inherently much more complex, and made more complex by the way the NHS has developed – in particular on the consultant and specialist side. In Farnham almost all medical services which people use normally are excellent. The GPs are conscientious and hard-working. Like most practices, ours has now an appointment system; no more peering round the door, seeing a large resigned crowd and deciding to come back earlier tomorrow; now you may expect, on most occasions, to wait about fifteen minutes. Each doctor can call up your file on his VDU and will, unless he sees a problem, issue repeat prescriptions by post. All no more than patients have a right to expect but not to be taken for granted until recently; or everywhere, even now.

The other elements of the Health Service we are likely to see fairly often, or at least to be aware of, are all of good repute. The small local hospital may have you in for a day or two and, if it is late when you arrive, offer you a couple of slices of Marmite on toast and a cup of tea, to 'put you on'. The physiotherapy staff are cheerful and talkative in the new manner, except for the very occasional unredeemed sergeant-major. Here as everywhere, the acid-test – my own recurrent acid-test – is how they treat nervous and outfaced old women; they do that well.

Microbuses trundle through the town all day, loaded with patients of one sort or another. When those are fully occupied saloon cars are added, their own cars driven by pensioners (up to seventy-five years old) who are glad to be doing a bit of good and to have the mileage allowance. The conversation in the cars is more continuous and informed but I marginally prefer the buses; they hold a range of local invalids – from young people who have had an accident at sport or on the road through to the very old and senile whose heads droop and nod and who do not speak. They are going for one of their whole-day sessions at the Day Care Centre where they can be attended to in small and large ways (suppurations dressed, toe-nails cut), fed, amused a little – and so that those at home can have a rest from constant servicing. The microbuses' big brothers are the ambulances, especially the Paramedic Ambulances; they wail through town so often that you are bound to wonder that so many people in Farnham seem so often at death's door; still, help is obviously always near.

One of the brewers, Trimmer, gave Farnham a Cottage Hospital in 1935. It is now the Phyllis Tuckwell Memorial Hospice and, though always hard up, manages to create a loving domestic atmosphere for the terminally ill. The growth of the Hospice movement over the last few decades is one of the best proofs that imaginative charity is still alive in Britain.

Our local Casualty Department is over in Aldershot, at the Cambridge Military Hospital. My wife had a broken ankle fixed there; exceptionally expertly, since the Parachute Regiment is nearby. Below the level of actual and assured medical and surgical treatment the Cambridge gives an impression of a mixture of formality and casual amiability; which proves nostalgically that the British Army hasn't changed much since the last war. Almost everyone has a rank, and uniform accoutrements to go with it. In their big black boots, corporal-clerks clank down the corridors as regularly as ever, batch of papers importantly in hand. The food owes more to freezer purchases in bulk than to culinary imagination. (What did many hospitals and schools and other canteens do before the arrival of fish-fingers and burgers? And why are fish-fingers even more clung to, more favoured, than burgers?) The nicely brought-up young ladies – for the time being, below the ranking level – who come round and sweetly ask you to choose your meals for tomorrow from the choices offered, get the orders wrong quite often; but no one would dream of complaining.

My own experiences with the big County Hospital – the Royal Surrey at Guildford – have not been so winning. They began with a visit to the local GP whose list we joined on leaving London (he is now retired). I told him I had had a bad knock on a knee, three or four years before, that the pain from it was becoming a nuisance and I would be glad for it to have attention. He said I needed an examination with a photographic needle; and he would ask for this to be done at the Royal Surrey.

We had lived in France for the previous five years and had not, in that time or before in England, needed much medical attention, apart from the usual children's ailments. Nor had we lived in so prosperous a town as Farnham. I had not therefore heard the question, put as the GP's ball-pen still hovered over his note to request consultant services: 'BUPA or National Health?' Startled and shocked, I answered: 'National Health,' as crustily as a Kiplingesque OR might answer a question about his patriotism. Thus it was recorded. Then I waited for the small attention. For thirty-four months. At that point I wrote to Guildford pointing out the delay. A reply snootily asked me the medical equivalent of the once familiar, surly and evasive, question: 'Don't you know there's a war on?' – meaning in this case: didn't I know that medical services were under-funded? I said I knew that but had the feeling that if I had been with BUPA or some such fund the wait would not have been anything like thirty-four months. No direct reply, but fairly soon a cyclostyled call to attend for the treatment arrived; for only six weeks hence.

We know it is the duty of the middle- and professional-classes to use public services critically, to keep them up to the mark. The received wisdom is that the better habits thus encouraged filter down or across to patients of all kinds. I no longer believe that. Those medicos who are inclined to be casual with NHS patients are not likely to change, short of a Hippocratic conversion. But they are usually quick on their feet and will pipe off dissent, accommodate the articulate complainer.

They didn't show me the photographs, said nothing of the knock I had received and pronounced that I had arthritis; from then on it was pills all the way. A year or two later I developed a trapped nerve in the other leg. More common among women than men, they said, and – yes – very painful, like constant toothache. A small op. would be needed to release the nerve. Another long wait; another letter protesting the delay; another fairly early appointment – to have the operation as a day patient; and about that one cannot complain, if it helps clear the backlog.

But it was a pity that the nurse in charge of that nearly empty ward was an old-fashioned tyrant. After an hour of what became a three-hour wait, I had drawn a chair up to the bed and was using the bed itself as a desk to work on college papers. She swam up and said I could not move a chair from its accustomed position against the far wall. Why? Because the doctor might trip over it. All of them being extremely short-sighted, apparently. The day-room is for that kind of thing, she insisted. The day-room was loud with the sound of television and of elderly ladies talking. That nurse was simply exercising the love of nay-saying for its own sake which pleases some civilian NCO's; the petty despotism of petty functionaries again; and again one remembers timid old women or men who would meekly do as they are told.

After the operation I was put to bed to get over the anaesthetic and to wait to be collected as soon after five as possible. No cup of tea, no biscuit, no word. Some time before five the two other nurses, plainly married women anxious to get home and prepare tea for the family, put on their coats. I was the only patient left in the ward. Would I mind lying there until my wife arrived? Off they went; I was alone.

I was called ten days later and pointed out to the young surgeon that there was still a slight leak from the incision. He said it was of no importance and that a nurse would put on a piece of something like Elastoplast. After all these years, I still find myself – our children entirely lack this feeling – slightly deferential towards GP's and even more to consultants: I went over to the nurse.

Two days later I had a meeting in Strasbourg. The leaking hadn't stopped and by the time I reached the hotel I felt groggy. That night, after the meeting, we were all taken to a restaurant in town. Halfway through the meal I fainted at the table. By some miraculous intervention a senior Strasbourg surgeon was eating there. He took one look at the incision and said I was infected; blood poison had set in. To the hospital! A quarter of an hour later I was in bed there, on a drip and penicillin; and stayed there a week. The French were entirely helpful but surprised that the wound had been left with only sticky plaster for protection (and that I would not move to a private ward). I had my E111 and so was only due for the proportion of costs which a French citizen would have had to pay for attention in a public ward; about £250. I sent the bill to the Royal Surrey Hospital.

There began a sequence of letters with The Administration in which they denied all liability. In the end they passed the file on to the lawyers in London whom they entrusted with tricky claims. The lawyers sent me a big bow-wow letter full of the jargon of their cult but thrashing around for a good argument. In the end they said – this is still difficult to credit – that in their view the fault was mine because I had failed to tell the surgeon who discharged me that I was going to Strasbourg two days later. If I had offered that information perhaps he would have said: 'Well, as I say, you are clear'; or: 'Oh dear'; or: 'How interesting!', and perhaps ordered that a further piece of Elastoplast be stuck on.

To me the saddest aspect of this sorry tale bears directly on my respect for the whole conception of a National Health Service. I had been innocent, before this, of the self-evident fact that even the NHS would find it terrifying to admit an error and would use the toughest legal operators to avoid that possibility.

What the Royal Surrey had described as simply arthritis on the right leg continued to plague me. I asked for more X-rays and finally they were made; but not shown to me. I was then called in to meet a surgeon; as always, one I had not met before.

Here I shall, and with judgment aforethought, come up against some anti-racists and proponents of linguistic political correctness. Not the majority, perhaps, but those among them who, to quote Goffman again, 'confront everyone else with too much morality'; or with misapplied morality. It would be silly, in a book which has been very critical of many English habits, to refuse to criticise, to refuse to say anything but good about, anyone who is not English.

The surgeon, and this does matter as will be seen, was Asian, perhaps Indian. He was casual and extremely *de haut en bas*. Self-evidently, he was of a high caste and a well-to-do family. Hence, I imagine, the superior manner. But it was an open expression of superiority, to a degree which is less common than it used to be among English surgeons; and it had a special, ineffably superior air to it which I had not met in England anyway. Why do I mention this? Partly because it is true to the nature of the encounter, a part of the picture; and also because it is culturally interesting and important; it has texture; it tells you something about the different forms and styles of class-superiority – assumed class-superiority – among different societies (and, yes, I have heard since that working-class people do not like being treated by this particular man because of the unaccustomed nature of his superior manner).

He wasn't very helpful, that surgeon. He said: 'You've got arthritis there, that's all.' So what's to be done? 'Well, from now on just take it easy. Don't go upstairs more than you have to, for example.' All in a hardly concealed tone of impatience. You are saying, then, that there is nothing to be done except live with it and take pain-killers? Then his sense of superiority came right to the front. 'Do you understand plain English?' he asked.

That was and will remain the total of my relationships with the Royal Surrey. Others report somewhat similar experiences. Do they, the medicos and the managers, not know that they create these impressions, that in some departments people feel they are being treated as second-class citizens if they are not private patients; that some tones of voice, some social assumptions evident in the way they treat people – whatever the consultants' origins – are now not acceptable? The contrast between their fine, new, big premises and the feel of the place, so far as I met it, is depressing. How can such criticisms be made to influence those consultants who live well in the more expensive parts of Guildford and its surroundings? This division, between those who will pay handsomely even if some who do so can hardly afford to, and those who either simply cannot pay or are unwilling to subvert what should have been the moral unity of the NHS, this chasm is a disgrace to a group of specialised professions and to this democracy, the one real failure of, the fault running through, Bevan's otherwise splendid social architecture; and one, it is said, he himself greatly regretted agreeing to but finally accepted so as to get the rest built.

I have since heard of a Trust Hospital which suddenly called in a large number of startled patients for one-night-stand minor cosmetic surgery – so as to improve the look of their waiting lists. The emerging mood is also captured by the growing gap between the Trust Hospitals and the National Health Hospitals. In late-1993 a North London Trust Hospital refused to accept a very old and, it proved, dying NHS patient because, as the Chief Executive explained: 'If we admit that sort of patient we lose money'. The dire voice of the 1980s and 1990s again.

It is often said, even by people disappointed as I am by some particular aspects of the NHS today, that the service rises magnificently to emergencies. I know that to be true from personal experience, from the life-threatening illness of one of our children. He was treated very rapidly on the NHS by an eminent London surgeon and has continued to be kept under surveillance. It may very well be that the Royal Surrey County Hospital would have behaved in much the same way.

My own medical story, so far, has a happy ending. After over a dozen years of increasingly severe knee-pain (some of this trouble may have been brought on by a bad burning of the legs during the war), alleviated by the maximum number of pain-killers and anti-inflammatory pills allowed each day, I asked if surgery was possible. By then one of the Tory government's better ideas was in force. Our group of GPs had not taken over their own budget; but one might now, under certain conditions including agreement from the Area Health Authority, go outside that Authority for treatment. Did I have any preferences? I knew that Guy's in London had a good reputation for orthopaedic work and suggested they be approached.

Guy's saw me within a couple of months and showed me the X-ray. There's arthritis there, certainly, but your main trouble is that the cartilage on your right knee has gone. Presumably that was set off when I had that awful knock on just that point; as happens to footballers. No wonder you were in pain, they added; the bones were grating together. Hearing that I had had twelve years of waiting, they fitted me in six months later, for a replacement cartilage (it works beautifully).

That became a compressed introduction to a better aspect of the NHS, 1992-style. The large, male and female, ward was a world of its own, a barque becalmed just off-shore from the bustle of London Bridge Station. Its life was a slightly distorted microcosm of much in working-class society today. You could tell straightaway that it was a very good-natured place. And devoted to Christian names. 'There you go, Richard', as they handed you a urine bottle; 'Cheers, Richard', each time they left you.

There was the usual linguistic gentility, meant to reduce embarrassment in the inhibited and to soften the indignity of being dependent on others to carry out the most intimate bodily functions: 'How are the waterworks today, Mrs Smith?' 'Has the tummy stopped playing up, Mr Jones?' (The 'the' instead of 'your' has its distancing use also. So does the embracing-plural: 'How are we today, Mrs Robinson?') A friend of ours, a congenital donnish wit, resisted the bland wrappings and insisted on saying, extremely politely: 'Nurse, I wish to micturate, please.' They enjoyed that.

In twelve days I heard only two expressions of impatience from the nurses; and they were understandable. A cluster of four beds near mine should have been called 'The Bus Lane'. In succession and overlapping, an Irishman, a Scotsman and a cockney came in and went. They'd all been hit by London buses, two of them certainly, the other probably, when under the influence. The Irishman told me he was his own worst enemy and plainly that was true enough; but he was a charmer. The second sat on the bed, making a cardboard Valentine one foot by two for his girlfriend. He had to wait until the evening on the day of his discharge for her to collect him. She had had to wait for release from Holloway, whither she'd been consigned for three weeks for assaulting a policewoman after a family party in a pub.

The nurses treated them as they did the rest of us, and that was a special triumph with the third, since he could not utter a clause (not a sentence – any clause) without inserting 'fucking' into it. That would have been easy to ignore; his violent abusing of the nurses was not. They said they were used to worse on Saturday nights, after the broken-beer-glasses-and-knife fights. You were advised not to bring in alcohol, but it was clear that some did. One had his Scotch in a couple of medicine bottles. 'We turn a blind eye unless it looks likely to be really harmful,' a nurse said. You could have the radio and TV on whenever you wanted but were asked to use an earpiece so that others weren't disturbed. Few did.

I talked about these changes to one of the nurses. 'Yes,' she said, 'it's all different now. And we don't have to wear our caps any longer.' Touching that that particular relaxation was re-membered first. Today's overall principle is that so far as ever possible they simply don't bother you, moither you, regiment you. But when you were just up from the operating theatre they came to your bedside, quietly, every few minutes. So, near-permissiveness ruled. Two visitors at a time from two to eight, the notice said, or as the senior nurse approved. In a single room at the end of the main axis of the ward a man was strung up on Heath Robinson wires and pulleys. One night ten people were round his bed till nearly ten o'clock. It sounded like a wake. In a way it was. 'He's a Millwall supporter [or player],' the nurse said, 'and they've just lost.'

The overwhelming preoccupier, from early morning to late at night, was TV; one in three or four had those, their own or rather wonky hospital sets. A visual and oral pacifier, it almost always stayed on when visitors arrived; and most visitors, after a short exchange, fell into silent watching too.

It brought out sharply the habitual and taken-for-granted self-indulgence of many working-class men, the now often out-of-date but not always discredited assumption that because the man is the bread-winner he has to be cosseted at home. One evening a man watched his colour TV continually, the sound loud, and even well after the main lights were switched off just after eleven. The light from colour TV is remarkably diffusive and intrusive; this one set illuminated half of our large arm of the ward.

On leaving, I decided against giving yet another box of Cadbury's Roses and asked if they would like instead something useful for the ward. They would, very much. Handing over the cheque, I suggested that some of it might perhaps go on earpieces for radio and TV. The senior nurse thought that was very funny indeed and gave me a kiss. All nicely in keeping.

Among most towns' institutions, psychological separations are trickier and more interesting than the largely geographic. Institutions which townspeople in general and by mostly silent agreement can 'take to' will be accepted, others ignored, not assimilated.

Farnham has two such not-quite-absorbed institutions. The West Surrey College of Art and Design lies only two hundred yards or so back from the centre, on the edge of the old hop-fields. It was once smaller than Guildford's Art College but has now more or less absorbed it, Guildford's having blown up during the 1968 disturbances; it is said that the leader of the Council then declared that the Guildford School would get no more growth money and that that is why Farnham has flourished and Guildford dwindled to a rump. Certainly Farnham had at the crucial time a forceful Principal. It now claims to be for some disciplines one of the best arts schools in the South, and grows rapidly.

The Safeway supermarket is a hundred yards away, between the school and Castle Street, so one can see much of the students, especially at lunchtime buying sandwiches and soft drinks and in the early evening getting together the elements for supper. Most are like arts students anywhere, 'going with themselves', trying to live up to their own mental image, the young women often in long, unironed, Charity Shop cast-off dresses and skirts, the boys still given to very long hair and even fonder than the girls of paint-bespattered overalls. One afternoon two of the young men minced arm-in-arm down Castle Street – heavily made-up, Oxfam dresses and tattered Ascot hats, high-heels. Whether it was a dare or an attempt to prove a general sociological or specific homosexual point I do not know. If one or both of the latter, then they proved that Farnham phlegm is not to be disturbed by what would be regarded as 'antics like that'. Of the passers-by, one in three gave a rather longer than usual look but didn't break tread. Another looked round as if for the television cameras.

The local newspaper consistently does its best to nourish the idea that the College is an integral part of the town, perhaps even an adornment. It publishes any news to the College's credit. It also has to publish, more often, less creditable news, such as the students' habit of having very noisy, very late-night parties. Or that the College has once again been broken into and expensive equipment, students' wallets and bicycles stolen.

Such items apart, Farnham as a whole, as a group of families and individuals, does not much think about, is not much aware of, the College of Art from one year-end to another. Unlike a university of five thousand students and upwards, it does not employ a great many townsfolk at several different levels of work. Some people will take in students as lodgers but the College's lodgings officer always has a hard fight to find enough accommodation, especially now they are expanding. There is a Board of Governors, but those who are town residents seem not to succeed in making their gubernatorial duties publicly interesting or even known. I expect the Director (the title has now changed, to suggest a more managerial job) is very willing to talk to a Rotary luncheon and such-like, but have not noticed reports of that kind of thing in the local paper. Some staff live in town, but tend to cluster with their kind, and there are suitable houses nearby.

Farnham is not interested in a college of art and if it thinks about such an institution will be slightly suspicious of it, since even now we all know that 'artists' are often no better than they should be, at the least untidy and not sufficiently often washed. Would the citizens be more aware of, more accommodating and welcoming to, a technical college? Perhaps, so long as its style and subjects were not too outré. Towns no larger than Farnham have accommodated medium-sized universities. Could Farnham? Not without great physical upheavals and, even more, because of mental indigestion, difficult psychological adjustments. Whatever the College of Art may have attempted in public relations initiatives, in trying to become better known and respected, it will remain, in this middle-class, medium-sized, conventionally minded town, on the fringes, a bit stuck in the craw, not an entity which can be absorbed easily or willingly. Perhaps the College should have an annual 'Rag' for local charities; but a well-behaved Rag.

Then there is the Castle, looking splendid up on the hill: 'The most important mediaeval domestic building in Surrey,' Pevsner said. The early histories make much of the importance of the Bishop up there; a presence the town was greatly aware of, in default of a hereditary, land-owning duke or earl to look up to.

For the last four decades the Castle, deserted by the Bishops (eight hundred years of Winchester, thirty years of Guildford), has been the Centre for International Briefing. That began as a Church of England initiative but has been secularised. It runs courses for those going to work overseas (in oil, banking and the like), especially in the former Empire and Commonwealth; and for similar professionals coming from overseas and thought likely to gain from an induction course. The setting is lovely, the bedrooms have been improved, the food is better than might have been expected. The intellectual calibre of the courses, in the time I saw the work quite closely, needed sharpening, and the air of middle-class gentility reducing. A group of ladies who help the visiting students socially used to be known as 'hostesses', but a modern shift in language is said to have made that unacceptably ambiguous.

What does the Castle mean to the town today, in its new socio/educational role? Little. Friends of the Castle do the usual valiant British work of welcoming foreign visitors into their own homes and making them feel cherished; and no doubt the visitors appreciate that. The staff of the Castle at all levels are too few to have much influence in making the place known. It can be visited on one half-day a week, and some musical and other 'occasions' are held there.

The College of Art and the Castle and its doings are two institutions, therefore, which are more or less outside both the main physical and the psychological nodes and rabbit-tracks of today's town; one seems out-of-date, antique, and now engaged in activities most people neither know much about nor would find very interesting; the other is new and insufficiently assimilated because mildly alien. Other assumptions, other ways of life, freer interests, less respect for church and social status, and the usual English uninformed lack of interest or respect before art and intellect, now rule. Social points of reference are more varied and complex than they used to be because less formally prescribed and defined; they give one of the best sets of indications of how the English have changed, are, and see themselves today.

CHAPTER 6

BIG SHOPS, CHAIN-SHOPS
AND LITTLE ONES
IN-BETWEEN

Today you're unhappy? Can't figure it out?
What is the salvation? Go shopping.
                                    Arthur Miller, *The Price*

The revolution in food provision of the last quarter-century, which has made three or four supermarket chains dominant, has affected all of us except hermits and a few ideological resisters. There are also odd academics, especially, who can claim never to have set foot in such a place; their partners do all the shopping – they are kin to those who still cannot drive a car or prefer not to and are chauffeured by their partners. There are some who feel towards entering a supermarket an antipathy similar to that felt by those with a fear of flying, for whom to start climbing an aircraft's steps is to feel claustrophobically sick in anticipation.

And there are those who have never quite got over the Bisto Kid feeling, and so take special pleasure in being not on the outside looking in but on the inside with money in the pocket; and feel even more pleasure from realising that so little seems tempting, no matter how winningly it is promoted.

Supermarkets are interesting because they have become a sub-sub-culture of their own. My most vicariously regal moment was to be in our branch of Safeway's when it had just opened. A state visit was being paid by one who seemed *the* top man – to judge by his entourage and its deference, the senior subordinate at his side, two others in step a pace behind; and to judge by his own elegance which suggested at least a middle-range public

school plus the higher reaches of the City rather than a large
chain-grocer's. I have only once before seen that style, that group
walk, that group deference; in 1942, when the Major-General
came round the Battery.

What do people eat in this district as compared with another
district twenty miles away? What changes can be seen over a
couple of decades? Are there class-divisions between what is on
offer? Can these be identified also by their placing in the aisles?
And by the time of day? What new habits in shopping have they
induced – especially among the recognisable regulars?

There are class-divisions and class-overlappings: on the shelves,
the display-counters, the freezer-cabinets; in the ready-meals, the
frozen fast-foods, the delicatessen, the packeted vegetables, the
more expensive 'traditionally prepared' foods, the more sugary
children's drinks. Most can be made to fit existing tastes by class
or across class; some aim to broaden tastes, cautiously and from
a known base.

In Sainsbury's, Farnham's largest supermarket but in national
terms only medium-sized, you can see, at the correct early times
towards the weekend, retired professionals taking orders from
their wives at the trolleys as they, shopping lists in hand, des-
patch the men on a sequence of precise errands.

Listings-and-despatchings – another supermarket innovation –
recalls the short, broad, driven man who scoots round Sainsbury's at weekends with a long piece of paper and the largest size
of trolley. He moves so quickly that strangers might wonder
whether he has been in a promotional competition and won
the right to have, free, all the commodities – except spirits – he
can put in his basket within five minutes. He is really more like
a Sergeant-Major-by-accelerated-promotion or a Scout master
since he usually has one or more children on hand, glances
pulsatingly like an urgent cock-robin at his list and sends the
children in different directions. As they return he just as urgently
ticks off what they have brought to the mobile nest and sets them
off again. Himself, he gives a new edge to the definition of
'scurry', is like a pointer beset by too many falling partridges,
reins up like a mail-pony at each display – a special offer here, a
new something or other being promoted near or at the check-out
– and grabs for each item as though we are at war and supplies

running out. He must be the supermarket's ideal customer, responsive to every offering. If we did have to resort to rationing again it would be important to get into the shop ahead of him or, if that weren't possible, to look out for his flying trolley and extensible arm.

Some old ladies, in particular, are Grand Mistresses at various forms of delay and queue-jumping. They will regularly fail to notice that this check-out will take baskets only, or a dozen items only or no cheques. The cashiers seem to have been told not to make a fuss and never do. Nor, this being England, do the customers being held up. Instead, they exercise the English skill at raising their eyes to heaven, saying something like 'She knows a trick or two' in a low mutter whilst giving that slight heave-and-turn of the shoulder which indicates that they know when they have been out-smarted but will of course put up with it. The nicer or perhaps more cunning or simply confused old ladies leave with an apologetic nervous smile; especially if they have added to the irritation behind them by opening a purse and counting out and checking three times every single item of coinage. (But in this they are easily outclassed by elderly French housewives. The French coinage seems to lend itself to being collected in the smallest denominations at the bottom of deep purses. Tipped out on to the check-out, their owners' haruspex-inspection can keep you waiting for several unexpected minutes.) Or, and this is the final stalling-motion in British supermarkets, though they may glance at the total now shown above the cash register, some customers will then pack their bags, item by item, as carefully as for an Everest expedition, before turning to their purses and preparing to pay. Again, the cashiers seem to be under instructions not to demur.

So one could go on. The pros and cons of supermarket life are lengthy. They will suddenly acquire a particularly good brand of ice-cream with some inventive flavours. A few weeks later, when the computer scrutinisers have been at work, you find the range offered reduced to three – say, strawberry, chocolate and vanilla, because those shift from the shelves quicker; if you like maple brittle, tough luck. You should move to Chelsea or Hampstead, or go to a hypermarket with fifty-odd check-outs. If you don't, you could in some things have less choice than you had with the corner-grocer; at least he would stock particular items for particular customers.

In other things they try to be helpful. As for example in giving advice on a card above exotic vegetables, on the way they should be cooked. A chasm of near-disbelief opened the day we saw such an instruction over a heap of fresh peas in the pod. Something like this: 'Preparation: first open each pod so as to release the peas. Discard the empty pods . . . etc.' Could it have been a joke? I hope so but suspect not.

It is, after all, usual to stand behind a young wife and mother and see the ready-meals and the packeted oven-ready chips and the packeted desserts being piled on the check-out counter – and to know that she is paying at least twice as much for all that as they would cost if she bought fresh minced meat and raw potatoes and knocked up a bread-and-butter or rice pudding.

The influence of the supermarkets has run in two directions. The rather more sophisticated customers have had their increasingly sophisticated tastes more and more catered for; discoveries made on their foreign travels soon find their way on to certain of the supermarkets' shelves. At a large mark-up. Compare only the price of extra-virgin olive oil in a French hypermarket and a British supermarket. At those prices you could almost bring it over by special messenger and still make a profit.

Less sophisticated people, especially those most pressed for time, have had their tastes not so much widened as switched, from the foods you prepare at home to the packeted ones on the shelf. Here the key is not only that such things are indeed 'convenience foods', take little preparing and so do save the time of a wife who is out at work all day. Much more important is that they hit, if they are to be successful, the dead-centre of traditional majority taste; they are indeed 'tasty'. If you know how to season a stew of quite cheap meat and fresh vegetables the result is mouth-wateringly 'tasty'. To make that stew is more of a fuss and does take longer than is needed to open a packet and put it into the microwave. The packet provides also a substitute tastiness, often induced by chemicals; funny, though, that the food often manages also to be bland.

Here we come face-to-face with two current myths about English feeding: that we all eat better nowadays and that we are to some degree becoming classless in our diet. One could argue in exactly the opposite sense: that some families eat worse than the generation before them did and that the class-division in feeding has widened. Most working-class women once knew how to make nourishing food out of very cheap raw materials; social workers in the poorer council estates nowadays will tell you that some young wives nowadays have little idea of how to make a stew, even though their mothers knew. We eat better at the top, but sometimes worse further down.

So this is one point where we have to modify the absorption-by-adaptation argument put forward earlier. Working-class people may not use television, videos, motor-cars in the way the persuaders expected and wish; they resist, modify, adapt to their own traditions, especially when what is newly offered bears directly on entertainment. Where there is no, or no longer, such a strong traditional pull – as in feeding habits – the advertisers score, flow through the weaker parts of the tradition; they can persuade people to change their patterns of eating in just the ways they, the persuaders, want.

Most of this has been about Sainsbury's, the front-runner among supermarkets in our area and most other places. They are to groceries what Marks and Spencer are to clothing (Marks and Spencer's food departments are another and loftier affair altogether). Sainsbury's have an aura which suggests fair trading, respectable value, cleanliness, the very acme of that area where the British mid-middle-class meets the lower-middle-class and the very respectable working-class. By comparison, Tesco have to live down their barrow-boy image and slogan: 'Pile 'em high: sell 'em cheap'. They are trying now to 'lift their image', especially through organic, healthy, diet-worthy foods; they are making some headway elsewhere, but not much around Farnham.

Though we have no Tesco's we do have the Safeway store. Tricky to fit in, that; not quite the cachet of Sainsbury's but certainly not 'down-market' in the way Tesco's used to be and to some extent still is thought to be. Sort of lower-middle-class to working-class and putting up a spirited battle. There is unavoidable overlapping in all these categorisations.

The most interesting identity of all, because the most firm and yet elusive, is that of Waitrose. Waitrose has silently come to occupy the position of supermarket to the professional, the executive, sometimes slightly the intellectual middle-class. It is hard to see how that face emerged from the aboriginal fog of its beginnings. Some of its prepared foods are exotic in the way which appeals to people who take holidays in Marrakesh not the Costa Brava, who know where Chiantishire is and what pesto and extra-virgin olive oil and specialist funghi are; or who, when the children are young, go to Eurocamps. Did that sort of thing begin to establish the image? Or did it arrive after the image had indicated that such items would be acceptable? Did the very name of John Lewis (the owners) give it an initial push? Our nearest Waitrose branch is in Fleet, about five miles away, and some Farnham people wish it were here. A very large Tesco's has opened on the edge of Aldershot, still much occupied by soldiers and their families even after the cuts of the turn into the nineties – and so very suitable there, surely, some people feel.

In spite of and partly because of all these fine gradings in the presumed status of shops, Farnham and Aldershot are symbiotically bound. Because Aldershot caters for 'the cheaper end of the market' Farnham doesn't attract those sorts of shops; its middle-class character is protected. A bit of the *Boule de Suif* syndrome. On the other hand, the shrewder Farnham citizens know that if they go to Aldershot for many household goods and routine services they will pay a good deal less.

The gains from the appearance of the supermarkets are obvious; if you know how to use them properly. If not, not. If you are old and not able to afford to use the few remaining specialist provision merchants you may be in difficulties unless your neighbours rally; delivery to the home – of the sort offered here by Mac Fisheries and Cullens not much more than a decade ago – survives only in the more expensive specialist grocers and greengrocers.

Farnham has recently seen a small rebirth of individual butchers. And there are three private greengrocers, two of which have weathered all the storms, and a new one. Of the older couple, one is of the 'purveyor to the middle-classes and local restaurants' type, rather expensive but reliable and good. The other is that fruit-and-vegetable stall at the bottom of Castle Street. The third, new, one has rapidly established its role, especially by some imaginative undercutting. The last two almost always beat the supermarkets on price.

The story about fishmongers and bread-and-cake shops is less happy. The supermarkets have chilled as well as frozen cabinets for fish. But they are limited and unimaginative. A stall with fresh fish, rather expensive, arrives in Castle Street only a few days a week. Thirty miles from the South Coast. As I write, a young man has taken over the shop vacated by a failed butcher and started a wet-fish shop there. He'll be lucky!

There is no local bread-and-confectionery shop. Such shops as there are belong to chains and have fancy names – 'Ye Crusty Baker'; something like that. The breads are indifferent – but one of the supermarkets, though with a hiccup from time to time as it wonders whether it could use the shelf-space more profitably, offers expensive but good specialist breads from London. As to pastries the situation is poor; it would make a housewife in a small French village militant to see that what is available is from entirely industrialised or semi-industrialised production, even though some of it pretends to have originated in Aunt Flossie's or Grandma Perkins's kitchens rather than on electronic ovens using industrialised doughs, at the back of the store, or on an industrial estate miles away. You cannot find a good fresh piece of pastry, made with the very best of fresh ingredients, above the homely Women's Institute level, in the whole of Farnham.

We have, of course, many of what are known as the major national multiples. Guildford has the rest: Marks and Spencer, Habitat, Heals, and – less middle-class but useful – BHS. It seems odd at first but is typical and explicable that some Farnham working-class people will go double the distance in the other direction, to Basingstoke rather than Guildford, for occasional largeish shopping, such as the pre-Christmas expedition. They feel more at home in new-town Basingstoke's great, mixed-class, shopping precincts. Guildford, handsome, old-established, smells of money and status and style. And Aldershot? Well, if you're going the four or five miles there by bus you'd just as soon get the Basingstoke bus for a much wider range of choice in the sort of shops you like; and it makes a bit of an outing.

So Farnham has Currys and Rumbelows for electrical goods; W. H. Smith's for newspapers, journals, stationery, books which move easily off the shelves, greetings cards and the always growing range of fancy goods; Halfords for anything to do with cars, motor-bikes and cycles; and Boots – like W. H. Smith's, another mass-multiple with a long-established base, in this instance pharmaceuticals; and also a constantly growing and wider range: beauty preparations, photographic affairs, opticals, picture frames.

The dominant nationalising trend has been long at work also in hotels, which their PR people like to call 'hostelries'. Inescapably, our one remaining hotel with a history as a coach-and-horses place has been taken over by Trust House Forte. We only once took guests for a meal there. The restaurant's poetic prose was not a good guide to its cooking; or perhaps one tasteless floridity could be said to match the other. The plate yielded a respectably sized if not generous portion of beef, near-cold roast potatoes, tepid and flaccid Yorkshire pud, gravy from the same stable: a loveless meal.

Later I had breakfast in one of their hostelries over in East Anglia. In spite of the fact that the Wilhelmina Stitch menu called it something like 'The Great British Breakfast Experience' it was excellent. But then, as Somerset Maugham said, breakfast is the one meal British chefs can't ruin. On that East Anglian occasion the secret of success was soon revealed. It was early and the kitchen manned by a middle-aged local woman who couldn't have ill-cooked her bacon and eggs if she'd tried.

We are left with Woolworth's, a nodal point in the childhood of most working-class people but, as we have noted, charmless now, uncharismatic. The process is easy to understand and, it could be and no doubt is argued, extremely hard to resist once the experts have done their complicated mathematics about the cost of shelf-space, the profit margins on various types of merchandise and the speed at which they are sold. The allure, and that word is not excessive, of the old-style Woollies lay in both its sense of being an Arabian bazaar and in its psychological accessibility. It didn't frighten you; it belonged to your class; you hardly ever had to ask for things since they were all laid out in open troughs, and clearly priced. Even after they had dropped the 'Threepence and sixpence only' tag it was cheap, 'pence cheaper', as we used to say when pence mattered, than anywhere else.

Above all, it kept things they knew we wanted even though some of them might not move quickly and, being small and cheap, produced minute profit margins. Perhaps today such things would be called 'loss leaders', items sold deliberately cheaply, even at a loss and no matter if slowly, so as to tempt you into the shop. They didn't feel like that then. You took it for granted that they would stock such things. If pushed to think about it, though you never were, you would probably have said that of course Woollies ought to stock small packets of this or that handy little thing for the home.

I have by now lost count of the useful things Woolworth's no longer stocks. Typical was the day I asked a senior assistant to direct me to the household polishes and the like. 'Oh, we've stopped stocking those,' she said with an accustomed resigned and slightly sad air. 'And a few other things like them, too.' Another told me with the same air that shaving cream is 'one of the items being phased out'. Woolworth's not stocking household polishes and shaving cream! It's against nature. Still, in many branches, their gardening and DIY sections remain valuable and competitive.

They went through a bad patch some years ago and new talents were brought in to 'turn it round'. Perhaps they have been, in their terms, successful. So we have to adjust, drop the old homely feeling and note their new areas of concentration: cheap children's clothing, toys, audio-visual software, small electronics, beauty aids and other 'Toiletries'. And all shifted relentlessly around, expanded, reduced, with the seasons. No stillness, no sense that you will always find this kind of product halfway down that particular aisle; a bland and yet hectic marketing operation throughout. Theirs is now a faceless world, a world which does not attract affection or attachment; or even much interest. Compared with it, Boots and Smith's have each a firm style of their own, the equivalent of the assured, semi-detached home-owners as against an uprooted and dispossessed working-class.

Luckily, one shop which belongs to a medium-size Southern Counties chain but manages to feel local fills something of Woolworth's former role. A biggish central hardware store, it probably makes much of its profit from electrical goods, garden furniture and household products with a rapid turnover, such as kitchen-ware and cleaning materials (its mark-up on some of those is high). But it keeps upstairs an exceptionally varied collection of household odds-and-ends. Most are displayed in removable rigid plastic containers, open and cut-away at the front to make their contents easy to get at – nails of all sizes from 5p for ten, washers of different materials from about 3p each, split pins also sold singly and in different sizes, keys for bleeding radiators, brass rings, prickers for gas-jet holes, a multitude of screws and other such things. You pick up your three or four odds and ends and the assistant hands them over in a little paper bag, screwed up as bags for sweets used to be. The firm cannot possibly recoup the costs of detailed attention, detailed service such as this, let alone make a profit from it. No doubt some day an accountant specially qualified in such calculations will point this out to them. We have to hope that on that day the owners will reply that it is worth while as a service which increases good-will; and that any-way he's glad to provide it for its own sake.

That shop is one of a type which I had not greatly noticed before living in Farnham, a type which slots in between the national chains and the individually owned, single, shops. These are the small regional chains – men's outfitters, health-food stores, pottery shops – with half-a-dozen branches scattered over this part of Southern England. We have several. At their best, and the hardware store leads for us, they combine something of the good qualities, in range and buying power, of the larger multiples, and in addition the sense of local service and know-ledge more often found in privately owned shops.

We have seen to how great an extent Farnham has had in the last decade and a half a floating population of golden-hand-shaked commercial-chance-takers, many of whom have had a very short life for their 'designer' offerings (but bankruptcies were common in Edwardian Farnham also). For their time here the gamblers live alongside a large number of old names among the town's tradespeople – names, and I am not trying to be comprehensive, such as Langham, Pullinger, Robins, Goodridge, Rose, Stevens, Patrick, Wilcox, Eggar, Swain and Jones, Barnett and Small and Elphick. Such a list has to be set against the list of the departed: Cullens and Mac Fisheries we have already noted;

there was also Home and Colonial and Dewhurst's, and Worsam's the bakers which recently closed after almost two hundred years. Some of those were parts of chains but had a bit of a local feel. Worsam's and Smyth's, a women's outfitters with a disposition towards the needs of the older and the larger woman, were truly local.

Only a few of the remaining locally owned enterprises now have their particular pitch to themselves. Almost all are competing with national chains: the opticians, the stationers, the booksellers, including two good modern versions (second-hand and remaindered-book sellers have recently fought back, with mixed success), men's outfitters (a long-established cut-price shop also fights back, and so does one which somehow holds its status as tailor to such gentry as we have; they spot non-gentry at once and are suitably toffee-nosed; a much pleasanter men's outfitters still seems successful in providing reliable middle-range clothing without pretensions). Young men lose their savings regularly in setting up outlets for other young men with striking tastes like their own; this happens slightly less in women's outfitting, perhaps because the national chains in women's clothes are more highly organised, harder to break into. You have to be very clever to fight Benetton and the like; as you do if you take on the big chains in women's shoes.

The local garden-and-pet shops can survive against the garden centres because you do not want to drive out four or five miles every day of the week; so do locally owned flower shops and electrical and camera shops, because they can give a knowledgeable personal service; the newspaper shops scattered around the town have a firm base in their daily deliveries. The dairies deliver milk to the doorstep every day too but are almost all in conglomerates by now. We can support two well-stocked and suitably expensive delicatessens. The weekly Women's Institute market has a crowd outside before the chapel doors open each Friday; we may not have a good pâtisserie but know good home baking when we see it: Victoria sponge, treacle tart, Madeira cake, fairy buns or drops, flapjacks, rock cake, ginger cake, lemon curd cake and chocolate fudge cake.

There remain oddities. Why do we have two very reliable but expensive jewellers and a third, smaller but still trustworthy one? Because Farnham has people who will pay their prices. But why have none of the mass-chain jewellers broken in? And is there no national chain of kitchen-equipment providers? Perhaps there is no call for one; our individual shops of that sort seem to go bankrupt regularly. And the sewing-machine repair shop closed. Yet why do we have those three shops offering to frame pictures; and a fourth very upper-middle-class one selling prints as well? Are Farnham people constantly reframing their pictures? More likely, young people from a College of Art and with some access to money may queue up to take this sort of chance at niche-retailing.

Meanwhile, in all this shifting sand, the charity shops survive and multiply, beneficent ticks on the sick part of the trading body. So does our only department store, Elphick's; modest as department stores go, but it expands, puts in another escalator and some new departments; and the owners live just down the road. It is a triumph of local enterprise in a branch of commerce where buying-out and concentration dominate nationally. Elphick's too recognise the need to provide for odds-and-ends interests; their haberdashery department is devoted to the full range of homely pursuits in sewing and stitching and embroidering. Things on cards, and not dear. Their coffee bar should be preserved as a sort of lower-middle-class cultural monument. (Why are the English so addicted to sausage rolls? And why are those rolls, waxy, puff-pastry casing and all, so lacking in taste – surprising in a culture which gives so high a rating to 'tastiness'?) Elphick's men's outfitting department seems frozen in the sixties; not at all expensive but not interesting.

The owners of individually owned shops are under constant and increasing pressure and most are anxious. In some this produces a nervous deference which neither they nor you like; in others it can induce a kind of short-tempered, take it or leave it, attitude; as though they are all the time near the end of their tether, under threat, living on margins and ready if pushed to explode, whatever the consequences.

You can also identify new kinds of shops and services; types which would not have existed or existed only rarely a quarter of a century ago. Laundromats or launderettes are the most obvious of early examples. In the last fifteen years these kinds of

enterprise have sprouted and withered like mushrooms, egged on
by the Tory government's praise of the entrepreneur, the self-
made millionaire. Sharks did for some; the recession of the early
nineties has picked off very many of the others. You had to be
very tough indeed to survive as, one has to say yet again, the
constant succession of newly empty premises in Farnham and
towns like it indicate.

The franchise system has been imported from the USA –
whereby hopeful would-be shopkeepers pay to use the name, the
process, the materials of a particular national service; a brand of
fast-food, new printing technologies and their ancillaries. Some
franchisees, as presumably they are called, survive and prosper;
others fail, so there goes one more lump sum put out at a
venture. It seems unlikely that the franchiser will lose; he has not
risked capital in sites all over the country.

Related but not quite the same is the system whereby small
grocers, to counter the threat from the supermarkets, pay to
band together and so get the benefits of mass-buying power;
'Spar' and its silly slogan, 'Open 8 Till Late', is the most common
name here.

Two main forces, changes in the culture, explain the nature
and style of most of the new enterprises: increased prosperity
and the pressure towards endless successive consumption (of
goods, habits, styles, notions) and the new technologies, especially the technologies of communication if that word is used in
its widest sense – to include everything from cam-corders to
mass travel. Taken together, these make the most powerful joint
drive in late twentieth-century open commercial democracies,
across Western Europe and the rest of the highly developed
world. Their chief exponents are able to thrust ahead and gobble
all before them, like powerful salmon in their fish-farm enclosures; and to be able to ignore those who sink to the bottom,
unable to compete or take part; like the detritus which piles up
at the bottom of the salmon enclosures.

So we have more than one glossy tit-and-tat shop selling cards
of all possible kinds and an ever-widening range of 'collectibles',
most from Taiwan or China; toy shops of increasing glamour
and expensiveness; wine merchants hoping they have found a
new angle; bigger and bigger independent or national chain-shops

to provide objects car-owners need or can be persuaded they need; shops which specialise in fancy fully-fitted bedrooms or fully-fitted kitchens (usually, like the massive carpet retailers, having a constant 'Sale' and knocking up to 75 per cent off what must have been very notional original prices), or specialist bathrooms with a twist to them – cast-iron Victorian-style, say; and the inevitable, ubiquitous double-glazing – very useful, but what a hard sell they employ.

The quickest trades/professions to move in when a prime site becomes vacant are travel agents, usually from a national chain, and building societies. The style and the offerings of the different large travel agents are worth an essay in themselves. Add those who trade only by post and you would have a very large essay on different and changing cultural assumptions. The tyre-and-exhaust specialists are worth a look, too, though a shorter one. Two or three national chains are in fierce competition and the atmosphere at their outlets a mixture of the frantic, the spivvy and the blokeish as each possible corner is shaved. But they prosper because they are much cheaper than the larger garages; the mark-ups there were bound sooner or later to attract sharp competitive attention. Even so the British tyre-and-exhaust places charge far more than the French.

Shops which remain empty for a longish time attract short-term-rental operators – very cheap clothing, sportswear with illicit famous brand names, blown-together furniture and – most surprising – framed prints of woodland scenes. Against those last one can set the branches of Christie's Contemporary Art. We have one, and wonder by what alchemy it can pay the high rent and rates charged in one of the best locations in town. Even in Farnham and district, how many Christie prints can you sell in a month? Cards in good artistic taste might do well but you would need to sell a lot of those to meet the rent alone. Still, almost any price seems possible for the things some people want, in a district where a garden centre can offer Koi fish at £2000 each.

As if in reaction from all these increasing and often increasingly sedentary pleasures, there have come the sports and fitness shops (exercise bikes up to £1000 each), the health centres and the health shops; all those different and successive slimming and keep-fit routines, to specially selected piped music, in con-

verted chapels and the first-floors of redundant warehouses. All
that procession of magic potions and unguents, ginseng, Evening
Primrose tablets, oil of this and that. One sports equipment shop
has just closed, leaving a note in the window blaming Mr Major.

Money, money, money; sometimes towns such as this seem, in
parts at least, to have an excess of it and to think of little else. So
we have yet another new breed, the Financial Advisors. Some are
surely reliable and some, we know from the newspapers, are not.

Among those shops which are a direct result of new technologies the casualty rate is often very high. Video-hire shops come
and go every few months here as elsewhere; most of all the
individually owned. More stable, especially if they are parts of
chains, are shops selling audio and visual electronic equipment;
so are record, cassette and CD shops, and TV rental agencies;
and stores selling food for freezers in sizes between retail and
wholesale. Farnham manages to support at present three printing shops which will also design, duplicate and handle faxes;
sophisticated descendants of the old jobbing printer up one of
those back alleys. There are also three or four firms which
specialise in fitting the new, 'lifelike' gas fires; some work on the
Milkman Principle of 'charge according to what the customer
looks worth milking for'; so you can be quoted from £200 to
£500 for exactly the same type of fire.

But one of the happier by-products of the communications
revolution – at least when you are a reader rather than a writer
– comes from the upheavals in the publishing trade which have
caused remainders to reach the market early and in quantity.
Our own remaindered bookshop is intelligently run and almost
always has something of interest at a price you could not initially
afford.

One off-putting development is the unprompted attempt to sell
by phone. Ours is usually a young-sounding woman with an
assured telephone voice which suggests she was once a secretary
but may now be married and, after answering an ad. in the local
paper, is earning pin-money by doing this sort of work from
home for an hour or so a day. She introduces herself cheerfully
by first name: 'Hello, this is Heather' – or Carol or Valerie – 'I'm
sure you would be interested in our special offer this week of a
family photograph for . . .'; she names a price high enough, her

bosses guess and hope, for a district such as Farnham to bear, whilst being willing to believe they are getting a bargain. Once or twice I have suggested, always with sustained politeness since you can't know what led them to this kind of work, that there must be better ways of using their spare time than, uninvited, interrupting people at their work or leisure (they usually call from about seven in the evening). They seem to have been coached neither to defend nor to excuse themselves. A curious little way to earn money but not as depressing, to judge from accounts in the papers, as those women in another by-way of modern communications technology, those who sit in booths all day 'talking dirty' to men who phone in for that service; at premium rate.

As in so much, the leader over the past few years, the bench-mark national chain, in all this interaction between the growth of consumer spending, the new types of goods which we con-sumers buy, and the applications to all this of electronic techno-logy, is Argos. The crowd at Argos on a Saturday morning before Christmas cuts across all classes, is large and yet almost silent as half of those in the concourse-like spaces before the counter peruse the coloured catalogues and most carefully try to get the catalogue numbers right, and the other half stand at the tiny whirr of the computers whilst the assistants look at the VDUs and say: 'Walking Talking Mutant Teddy Bear at thirty-five ninety-nine. Right? How will you pay? Credit card? Fine.' Argos has been a marker-beacon of the eighties – and into the nineties: of the consumer-driven, mass-communications-techno-logy-serviced-and-partly-technology-inspired, society; it may be just past its peak, as new points-of-sale appear.

Thirty women's outfitters (some extremely expensive), ten men's outfitters, nine estate agents, seven shoe shops, most of them women's or women-centred, thirteen beauty salons, nine dent-ists, six travel agents, too many banks too close together . . . and so on. And in most the two-hourly tea-ceremony, whereby the most junior assistant brings mugs of tea to those on the desks and counters. The visible tea-ceremony belongs to the old, small shop, world, not to that of the supermarkets. Above all, the supermarkets are the main in-town meeting-places today. It is there that most encounters take place, either through a quick nod and a passing of the time of day or through a more extended talk which nearly blocks the aisles. The talk in the supermarkets, the sequences of different kinds of meeting there, remind you that more and more we live in nuclear families and that many of us most often leave them – apart from journeys to and from work and in spite of our 'leisure pursuits' – chiefly to foray into the shops, above all the supermarkets. Talk there is the modern equivalent of talk at the communal washplace, or oven or pump; or corner-shop or Co-op. It is of a different order from talk in clubs and societies. Talk in those places is closer and more intense since the talkers are united by a common enthusiasm. Talk in the supermarkets is truer to the dominant character of the end of the century; it is narrow and two-dimensional in many ways but has more texture where, as is general, it is nuclear-family and near-neighbourhood-based; and there is much of that. Its roots do not go down much further than family and neighbourhood; it is one of the sequence of spiders'-webs we noted earlier, swinging gently in space, multiple and, all in all, of great tensile strength.

Such encounters sometimes have a melancholy, universally human, aspect also. You catch sight after a long gap of a face you remember only as that of another customer. That face has changed far more than the passage of time since you last saw him or her would suggest. And you think: 'Ah, advanced cancer'; so the sense of mortality fills you again – all the more sharply in that place so dedicated to the pursuit of the pleasures of appetite.

It is clear that I am in many ways and for much of the time fascinated by shops and shopping – partly because so much in changing cultural styles is on show in such places.

Supermarkets are for many of us at the very heart of modern urban living, fascinating parades of a town's human variety, sharp indicators of change by age and class and of changes in taste, trend-setters, clean, air-conditioned and hence smell-less – a deodorised grocer's, God wot! – unless there is an 'In-store Bakery', and then the smell of fresh bread and cakes is surprisingly – deliberately – pervasive; well-lighted, glossy, like air-terminals or the newer type of railway station, temples to levels and varieties of consumption most customers could not have foreseen only thirty years ago.

It is an odd realisation too if, after all this talk of shops and shopping, one proves to have not a trace of the entrepreneurial commercial spirit, that it does not matter to me if I never sell anyone anything, that I would much rather give away even fairly expensive surplus things than sell them, that I like trying to write – 'make' – a book even if it brings little or no profit, but could not settle down to making an object specifically and only for sale. In Farnham, not with any feeling of superiority, I heard this gap between types of people vividly illustrated when listening to the rapid patter of an early-middle-aged woman, with the most vividly hennaed hair which itself seemed to be saying something. She was trying to sell me a piece of reproduction furniture. Her lingo was entirely entrepreneurial, as much an inner-world lingo as that of the turf or computer-buffs. One phrase typified them all. How much is that small table, please? 'That will see you sixty-five.'

Yet I sometimes feel fed up with the whole over-creaturely business and busyness of shops and shopping. At those times it seems as if the whole town – the whole island – is preoccupied with buying and selling things, new, old, good, trash, from and to each other. Then I remember Browning in one of his more sententious moods:

> *Because a man has shop to mind*
> *In time and place, since flesh must live,*
> *Needs spirit lack all life behind,*
> *All stray thoughts, fancies fugitive,*
> *All loves except what trade can give?*

CHAPTER 7

SETTINGS LARGELY SYLVAN

*From [Hungry Hill] I knew that I should look down into the
beautiful and fertile Vale of Farnham.*
                    Cobbett, returning to the town in his fifties, in 1815

*Thou waterest her furrows, thou sendest rain into the little
valleys thereof.*
                    Book of Common Prayer, Psalms LXV: 11

*One sees great things from the valley; only small things from the
peak.*
                    G. K. Chesterton, *The Hammer of God*

Time for a breath of more countryfied air. As we saw at the start,
Farnham lies low and easy along the banks of the small and
leisurely Wey as it pushes towards Godalming and Guildford
and so to Weybridge, where it joins the Thames – all a strange
contrast with Andernach on the Rhine, with which it is twinned
(it should be twinned with Romorantin-Lanthenay, naturally).

To the West Alton, which, though it took some of the big
breweries, is still a Hampshire country town and, though now
home also to some small, labour-intensive and technologically
advanced industries, remains an attractive semi-rural shopping
centre, especially around its crooked market place. The space
between Farnham and Alton is almost entirely agricultural.
There is a little bungaloid ribbon development in one or two
hamlets fronting the road, but not enough to suburbanise the
countryside. Slightly larger, well-established villages just off the
main road, the A31 for Winchester, are virtually untouched. We
have learned something in the last thirty years.

To the north and east lie Aldershot, Farnborough and straggly, undistinguished or often ruined places such as Ash, Frimley, Fleet. Aldershot was set up in the mid-nineteenth century because it offered miles of heathland for barracks, parade-grounds and training areas. One cannot object to that; it was needed. It still has some interesting Victorian buildings. But inevitably it cast its shadow on the area. George Sturt noted its effect – Ash, he said, was a mean and ugly settlement under the Aldershot blight. Recently, years of delay in building the Blackwater Valley Road have added planning blight. The road will soon be finished and the environment much improved. Sturt's uncle farmed in Farnborough and he writes with affection about that unremarkable but at that time deeply rural landscape. You can still today pass the pubs at which his uncle's carters stopped on their way up or down from London. Steak houses now, as likely as not.

Frimley has one of the large area hospitals; at some point the local authorities of both Frimley and Fleet threw in their hands and let ex-urbanite development ride. You wonder whether some of the new inhabitants mistake their way into their own homes as they wander, tired, from the station each night. But no; that isn't likely; the distinguishing touches in gardens or on façades will prevent it. Small sneers like that come too easily. There can be an attraction about these Avenues and Closes and Courts which asks us to get below the obvious jokes to what is being expressed, sought after:

> If it form the one landscape that we, the inconstant ones
> Are consistently homesick for this is chiefly because it dissolves
>   in water . . .
> . . . Dear, I know nothing of either
> But when I try to imagine a faultless love, or the life to come
> What I hear is the murmur of underground streams
> What I see is a limestone landscape.

That respect for what we tend merely to dismiss as 'the suburban dream' comes more effectively from the homosexual, domestically hardly house-trained, Auden than from most of us.

Another Hampshire military settlement, Bordon, a few miles south of Farnham, straggles along the Petersfield/Portsmouth road, blocks of married quarters like something from the back-end of Bermondsey – do Ministry of Defence architects ever step outside their London offices? – and a central shopping bit which has strayed from a 1910 industrial township in a duller part of the Midlands. Fortuitous-looking, cheap and nasty, depressed and depressing. A trail, a spore or slime, like a snail's; a place which looks always ready to be left precipitately, deserted, as the troops leave for somewhere overseas and as many wives as can go back to their mothers with the kids, for the time being.

Such blots apart the countryside, especially to the west, is at Farnham's doorstep; the small, busy and for centuries tightly circumscribed little town defined both itself and its hinterland very exactly. Sturt's villagers apprehended it as an almost moated entity, or as set in a tight bowl. But nearby are Alice Holt Forest where the Christmas trees come from and there are miles of wooded walks; the Frensham Ponds – one originally the Bishop's fishing pond; in the late seventeenth century, incident-ally, Isaak Walton was steward to Bishop Morley – with broad sandy walks between and around them; Waverley Abbey on one side of the Wey and Moor Park roughly opposite on the same set of bends. Swift was amanuensis to Sir William Temple there and made to feel his subordinate place. But he also met Esther Johnson (Stella) there, so that made up for a lot. Between 1939 and 1940, before being called up, I wrote my Master of Arts thesis on Swift and his circle of friends and by the end thought I knew a lot about the relationship with Stella. But either I was an inept research worker or the censoring of books even in scholar-ly libraries was tighter than I had known. It was only decades later that I came across one of Swift's letters to her, written on a very cold winter's day, with a sentence running like this: 'I wish I had my hand on the warmest place about you.' That puts you in touch with two human beings far more effectively than any of the usual public declarations of affection. Moor Park is now an expensive finishing school for young ladies; who would be dis-couraged, one assumes, from letting penniless young clerics put a hand on their warmest parts.

A little further out are some of the loveliest villages in Southern England: Tilford, its large and irregular green and cricket pitch, the pub, the yeoman's houses, the bridges over the two arms of the Wey, the Lutyens Village Hall. (It is said that the villagers have detachable TV aerials so that they can, for payment, remove them when commercials are being filmed there.) And Thursley, much quieter, more straggly but even more evocative of eighteenth-century England.

Surrey, we all know in the cliché-pocket of our minds as we all know that Essex is tattily suburban and dull, is fairly well-to-do suburban merging into ex-urban. In fact, much of West Surrey is still agricultural, as agricultural as its neighbours to east, west and south, Sussex and Hampshire. The vernacular architecture and vernacular speech have common bases and the rhythm of the year is no different; not for most the rhythms of the executive life. Conventional substitutes for wisdom see all Surrey as extensions of Croydon, Kingston, Surbiton.

Conventional wisdom therefore misses the true interest of West Surrey. It is, in part, not suburban but ex-urban, certainly; but going down its still narrow and heavily overhung lanes you might well fail to notice its strange, hidden character. The sensible attractions – the good piney air, the dry sandy soil, the early railway lines into London – long ago brought in not only Victorian and Edwardian tycoons but also writers, intellectuals, artists; the Webbs and other Fabians (George Bernard Shaw is said to have walked one Sunday from Farnham station the three miles to a meeting at Tilford, that village which is the essence of the old, near-gentry, West Surrey settlements).

The lambent qualities of that air, the gentle hills and over-arching sense of rural amiability – so long as you could accommodate the knowledge of the hard life of the country labourers – brought a large number of celebrities to a circle with a radius of about ten miles from Farnham. Tennyson had a special reason; he came courting Emily Sellwood at Hale Place, only a mile out (staying at a hotel where Argos now stands: 'let the great wheels run for ever/Down the ringing grooves of change'!), James Barrie, Charles Kingsley, Edward Thomas, J. H. Hudson, E. M. Forster, G. Lowes Dickinson, Edna Lyell, Lloyd George, Baden-Powell and the newspaper tycoon Pearson all had homes or connections nearby. The jewels in that lovely irregular crown round Farnham are Gilbert White's Selborne and Jane

Austen's Chawton, both of them by some extraordinary good fortune much as they were a couple of hundred years ago; and, a little south, is Edward Thomas's Steep and its 'hangers' – wooded hills.

Just south, like a looping pendant, is one of the most unspoilt and wonderfully varied of British trunk-roads; the A 272, running almost horizontally between Stockbridge and Haywards Heath, via Winchester, Petersfield, Midhurst, Petworth, Cowfold and Cuckfield and several lively villages; a particular favourite with Dutch visitors who have nothing to compare with it; and a tribute to the regulations against ribbon development and the like.

Coming back from such places in the early evening through the pale grey wood-smoke and the sour-sweet smell of slurry, after showing weekend visitors around, is all the more poignant because there are, once you are off the main road and still a few miles out of Farnham, some small-holdings of a type found all over England. They harbour broken-down cars and trucks, tacky, ramshackle bungalows, mongrel dogs and scruffy cats, scrawled signs saying that logs, manure and turkeys are for sale; all the detritus of people who are semi-living off the semi-countryside, not doing very well.

Over the decades the landscape has also come to contain two main kinds of institution: housed in large premises taken over when the wealthy owner died or retreated. Expensive homes for groups of well-to-do old people can be glimpsed through the trees at roughly half-mile intervals. Usually further back from the road are prep schools and a few minor public schools. So healthy, all that upland air around Hindhead. Auden's prep school, St Edmund's, is still to be found at Grayshot.

We have seen that many of the tycoons are still there – big bankers, stockbrokers, chairmen of oil firms or of the new electronic giants. Their homes – whether enormously mock-Tudor or West Surrey manor-houses or small mansions – are almost always removed from the road or lane. There will be a discreet doorway and an equally discreet rustic name-plate, usually showing that Sussex/Surrey predilection for plurals or possessives in place-names as in shops: Chowdrys, Hunters, Mumbles, Plimsolls, Ratlins. Say a word like that and it conjures up some of the peculiar assurances of the Southern Counties' semi-rural comfortable middle-class; put up in Yorkshire, such a house-name would be as out of place as a Sloane Ranger.

Pevsner's descriptions of these big houses behind trees – 'a high-class suburb' – is not quite right, misses the differences between them and even the highest class of suburb. Ian Nairn, who prepared the second edition of Pevsner's *Surrey*, was even wider of the mark: 'Like Southern California, Surrey is entirely directed to serving urban man . . . in the Green Belt as much as anywhere else.' It is easy to see the points of similarity, the places where the similarities just fit. But to do so is to blur far more important cultural differences. Ex-urbanite West Surrey breathes honour, a conventional honour to be sure, to well-established English mercantile middle-class *lares et penates*; to long-established trees, finely mown lawns, the expectation of regular rain, a clutch of horses and the pair of Labradors, tea on the lawn or in the drawing-room, accents and manners which may have come down through at least a couple of centuries or been picked up quick. By contrast, Southern California is explicitly, philosophically, impermanent, unsettled, unrooted, open, two-dimensional; hugely interesting in its own way but not a near-neighbour of West Surrey.

Farnham, fifteen to twenty miles further out than, say, Woking and Esher, is not a commuter town in the sense that they are; nor is it a country town in the sense that Alton still is. A bit of all these, it still manages not to be neatly typecast as 'country' or 'commuter-land'. One could not claim that it is at ease in this betwixt-and-between condition. It is, its citizens are, neither unhappy nor happy in that state; they are hardly aware of it as most are hardly aware of the town's history. To repeat: many of them will hardly have heard of Cobbett, though the pub's name gives a good hint, or know why the town started where it did, or what its great trading days were; or, for that matter, how it fits into the present-day life of the South-Eastern Counties. Or that, if you climb Firgrove Hill and look across Surrey to the south and east, you can still see the blue haze of Hindhead across the great heath – a view Sturt loved – its middle-range villas now softened to a pink amid the blue.

Orwell called these landscapes 'sleek' and in some ways that fits; but the judgment is a little on the surface, seen from outside.

Parts of Surrey are slightly battered, over-lived-in; and too much breathed over; the air, like the tap-water, greatly recycled. We came to live here for inescapable family reasons and do not regret it. And the Tennysonian cosiness has its charm, even the lukewarm-bath feeling. You feel as though you are at the warmer bottom end of the tight little island; you are. But sometimes we miss the sharp, cold, harsh, chill air of Yorkshire and the Pennines, the feeling that the air has not just been going round and round but has been a long way away and come back purified and sharpened, from mid-Atlantic or the Urals.

The vegetation is different from that of the North, lusher; it all 'comes on sooner'. By early September you can't give away the apples even to good causes, but the local lads still find them worth shinning over a hedge for. The old countryside persists and, paradoxically, parts of it more and more encroach. The urbanisation of wildlife can be seen increasing almost month on month. The traditional birds and beasts are still there, the sparrows, thrushes, starlings, blackbirds, wrens, tits, finches, robins, odd rabbits, field mice. But more and more birds which used to be shy pop up in the gardens: jays, magpies, big fat woodpigeons, Great Spotted woodpeckers, collared doves (they reached here in the mid-fifties, from East and Central Europe), field-fares, missel-thrushes, rooks and crows. Foxes have been urbanised for two or three decades, and squirrels too; now we have small deer which eat all the rose and tulip buds in the early dawn, leap high fences and gates, and occasionally in the evening step delicately across our house front, with a quick glance in the windows. Recently the first hare was sighted in a suburban garden two hundred yards from West Street. Perhaps in twenty years we will walk in gardens populated by deer, foxes, hares, woodpeckers, missel-thrushes; strolling as in a scene from a child's colour book, clothed in leaves and branches.

PART TWO

PARTICULAR AND
PECULIAR LIVES

CHAPTER 8

WHO REALLY RUNS SUCH TOWNS?

We will also graunte for us and our successors for ever that the said burgesses and their heires for ever shall have all lyberties and free customs hereunder written, as heretofore they have had.
                                        Farnham Town Charter, 1249 AD

There, too, full many an Aldermanic nose
Roll'd its loud diapason after dinner.
                  R. H. Barham, *The Ingoldsby Legends: The Ghost*

Who runs places such as Farnham? Who are 'the authorities', 'Them'? In one sense, the official, the answer seems simple; but even there it soon becomes murky. At the unofficial level, which may in the end be the more important, it is even murkier.

We have seen that this burghers' town, without a lord of the manor in the usual sense or local aristocracy, nevertheless had a Bishop – of Winchester – up in the Castle from the seventh century until 1927; then the Bishop of Guildford was there until 1956, when he left for more manageable and warmer accommodation. In the early centuries the Bishop acted as, informally, but seriously took the place of, a lord of the manor, overlooking the town in two senses; and the burghers paid him due homage. (But, especially in the early eighteenth century, the common people of Farnham more often fought the Bishop and poached his deer. The 'Black Act' was vigorously opposed in these parts.) As recently as 1906 the local Council, true to form, resolved to 'tender congratulations' to Edward Ryle, the son of Bishop Ryle, 'upon his attaining his majority on 1 October, and to enquire whether it would be agreeable to him to receive a deputation at the Castle?' They clubbed together to present a silver ink-stand. They sent loyal addresses to a new Bishop when he arrived and fervent good wishes when he went. The son of the incumbent during the First World War was killed in action and 'the town' sent a moving message of condolence to the top of the hill.

The Castle could be from time to time the centre of more intellect and imagination than a typical aristocrat might have nourished; there were several distinguished scholarly bishops and major Lords of the Church. Still, the harvest is not large and was by its nature restricted in its interests; an intellectual or artistic peer or two might have done better.

Nowadays there is a Town Council, re-instituted in the mid-eighties after a gap; and hence a Mayor. The local paper does its best to make us aware of the Council's business and the Mayor's public doings; but most of us would not recognise a Mayor or past Mayor if he or she walked past us in The Borough, swinging the chain of office; and offered us a 'personalised' lapel-badge bearing Farnham's coat-of-arms. The only former Mayor I can recognise is a large, jovial-seeming man who runs a hire-car business and can often be seen bearing a placard – 'His Excellency Dr Subawaya', say – at the exit from the down-platform as the train carrying some of the participants for the Castle's latest course swishes in.

That we should have a Town Council is straightforward, even though its powers are few; almost forty thousand far-West citizens of Surrey have the right to such a body. Of course, some people would like us to be swallowed by Hampshire; that is still a rural and a horsy county, not suburban or much ex-urban. Aldershot and Farnborough are exceptions to this dominant Hampshire character, and the first is considered by many as rather common. One doesn't really think of it as part of Hampshire but as a plonked-down national base for the soldiery. Even its Marks and Spencer's is one of the lower-graded branches.

Surrey housing is in almost all parts expensive but if we were transferred to Hampshire prices would probably rise – just as house prices differ between the opposite sides of some streets in London, at points where the postal codes change in the middle of the road and the social ratings of those codes differ.

None of that is as important as the effect on Farnham of the Local Government boundary revisions of 1974. We are now part of the Borough of Waverley and that confuses newcomers. But if you have to invent new names for new conglomerations this is better than some which were dreamed up twenty years ago. 'Mountains divide, rivers unite.' Not in East Yorkshire, not across several miles of water. 'North Humberside' still enrages people in and around Hull, and they look forward to its early demolition. One of the oddest concoctions is Selnec, which appropriately sounds like a cut of tripe: 'Half a pound of chitterlings, a pound of black pudding, three faggots, a mug of peas, a quarter of thick seam and two ounces of selnec, please.' South-East Lancashire, North-East Cheshire, it means. Against such as that, 'Waverley' is graceful; it recognises that on a bend of the Wey within its boundaries lies Waverley Abbey, the earliest Cistercian Abbey in England and the inspiration for Scott's novel.

The problem is elsewhere, lying in the fact that the Borough Headquarters are in Godalming, a dozen miles away. Godalming is a handsome and lively West Surrey town with some fine old buildings. But it has no easy natural or man-made connections with Farnham, except for this relatively new administrative linking. We are separated by hills and heath; the roads between us are minor; there is no railway connection; we each go, for largeish regional shopping and from different directions, to Guildford. So it is with connections with London; road and rail do not interconnect. Our postal services are run from Guildford, our telephone services from Aldershot, our gas services from Basingstoke and electricity from near Southampton; our Health Service area is East Hants and West Surrey and we look to the large hospital in Frimley, Surrey, as much as we look to Guildford's. There is a Borough Locality Office in Farnham (oddly abstract name, that; for years I had used my own unconsciously invented name, which might have seemed more apt, at least as an indication of aim – the Borough Amenity Office). Godalming is in another world; the divisions marked by those hills almost remind you of such divisions in Hardy's Wessex a century ago; we do not think of Godalming except when the Council Charge assessment notice arrives. The occasional *Waverley News* drops on every doorstep; it does its best to suggest a sort of unity but still reads and looks like a subsidised parish magazine in a small new town.

'Waverley' exhibits a pattern of strengths and weaknesses, as one supposes all boroughs do. They are a particular product of the voluntary character and to some degree the amateurishness of elected British local governments. The pattern of pros and cons will differ from authority to authority, according to geography, history, industry, commerce and population make-up; but pattern there will be.

Waverley's main or at least most irritating fault to its citizens is in its handling of car-parking, at least in Farnham (so perhaps Farnham Town Council should take some of the blame). Farnham, as we have seen more than once, is a shopping centre for communities from several miles around since there is no adequate bus-service; cars are almost essential for those living outside and especially for the large number of retired people, many of them not sprightly. Yet Waverley's parking policy gives the impression that it would like to keep motorists as far away as possible and, if that proves impossible, milk them as much as possible. Until recently they imposed charges earlier in the day than Central London and retained them longer. Their hourly rates are higher than most places round about. When it was proposed that a half-hourly charge be instituted since many people do not need a full hour every time they go into town, the proposal was rejected. So, if we use much less than the time we have paid for, we ignore the cheeky 'Not transferable' on the ticket and give it to someone just arriving. The rejection of the short-time charge revealed a major error in local government financing. The fair treatment of individuals was sacrificed to the Council's funding needs. It was announced, as a justification, that parking charges were a very substantial part of their regular income and they were not willing to do much to reduce that element. Parking charges were not to be seen as a self-balancing service but as a major source of income. The disinclination to alter this was no doubt helped, in Farnham at least, by one councillor who seemed to hate the motor-car and wished to banish it from the town altogether. We recalled then the bearded man who rides a tricycle about town, rucksack on back, and takes to and uses the whole width of the pavement so as to run against the traffic flow when the one-way system incommodes him. The thought of platoons of elderly, arthritic men and women tricycling up and down those narrow winding lanes to shop in Farnham is so eccentric and Edwardian as almost to be encouraged.

But again it is part of the British pattern that a blind eye on one side may be compensated for, or at least might slightly balance our judgment on the way things are done, by good performance on another. Here in Farnham, the rewarding practice is in the provision made for old people. There are good service flats and maisonettes, sheltered housing and complexes which look like three-star hotels and are in some ways equipped like them but also contain fully independent suites – sitting-room, bedroom, bathroom and kitchen. One of my wife's very elderly spinster aunts had finally to go into an Old People's Home, twenty-odd years ago, in the North-East. It was unrelievedly unimaginative in physical provision – more than one person to most bedrooms, a horrid thought to most old and easily embarrassed people; a common television-room with pre-ordained seating to avoid quarrels; and with niggling rules for every eventuality. By contrast, our provision is imaginative and not penny-pinching. It helps people to keep their self-respect and dignity.

Add the work of the Citizens' Advice Bureau, the Women's Royal Voluntary Service (formerly WVS), Farnham Old People's Welfare co-operating with Age Concern, the Drop-in Centre for old people and the Day Care Therapy scheme. It is not sufficient and never will be, and there is no ground for satisfaction with this level of provision in a society as comfortable as this. Some slip through the net. But it all does very good work with a lot of old people, especially those who are alone and lonely, very much more and better work than was done before the war. Passing along the snicket from the Sports Centre to the Theatre you can see them through the windows of the Drop-in Centre, warm and being fed by the industrious battalions of middle-aged volunteers. Few contrasts highlight more clearly the differences between the developed and the Third World than a sight such as that on one hand and on the other the streets of São Paulo, Delhi and many another disordered ant-heap of a city; thin and diseased old people lying in the gutters and holding out scrawny arms for aid.

It would be interesting to analyse how a particular council comes to be deaf to one particular need but responsive to another. Is it through the persuasive power of one or a group of elected representatives? Or of an official with a mission? Or of a combination of the two? Or through a push from central government? Or a change in the social climate which has been promoted through the mass-media, seminars and pressure groups until it reaches councillors and council officers?

The procession through the Magistrates Court is sad and sub-fuse. Small-scale street-traders who slip into a local shop and steal something pocketable; shabby-looking couples who obviously can't cope with family or finances and have slid into the spiral of debt and petty fiddling; a young and quite smart-looking flasher. The atmosphere is complicated and contradictory; a veneer of traditional acts of slight theatrical dignity, an initial holy hush, standing up on the entry of the members of the Bench, bows all round, black-gowned ushers, whispered solemn conferring between the JPs before the judgment is announced. On the other hand the Clerk to the Court rattles off the detail on each case at a speed which must leave most of the accused bewildered; between cases all is smiles and quick bits of continuing gossip ('apparently he took all his clothes off'); the most severe-looking JP, who makes great play of looking over his half-moon spectacles, turns out to be the Bench's wit. Like that of the hospitals, this routine is more relaxed and informal than its predecessors of thirty or forty years ago; and more thoughtful, better prepared and practised.

Most councillors, of Town or Borough, are admirably conscientious and hard-working. My own experience suggests that the women are more conscientious than the men though my sample may be too small. But at least there has been a change; for decades women were hardly represented on the local Council. Now a woman, a Liberal-Democrat, leads Waverley Borough Council; very effectively.

In a semi-rural town nowadays you do not usually meet the all-powerful rule of particular party cabals; if they look like appearing then sensible would-be councillors tend to register themselves as Independents or, nowadays, as Liberal Democrats. Waverley is at present in their hands; by the narrowest of margins, but still that would have been hardly credible a few years ago. In massed urban centres each ward is likely to be inalienably Tory or Labour; if the Ward Committee takes you on as a candidate, you are in. So long as no one looked at the candidate before polling day – he or she could be said to be on the way home from an important foreign assignment – they could elect a horse; which Dean Swift would have regarded as preferable to some of the humans who would be likely to offer themselves. In Farnham the councillors are more independent, more their own men and women.

All that is on the sunnier side of local voluntary political action. There are less attractive aspects, naturally – an odd nutter, usually insistent for some single-minded cause or another; and, more typical of English local government generally, there are the confidently loud-mouthed, 'I call a spade a bloody shovel' ignoramuses. A few miles away, in the grounds of the Abbey at Farnborough, Napoleon III's Empress, Eugénie, is buried. A pathetic thought, that she should lie in that by now nondescript residential and shopping area. Recently there was some suggestion from France that she might be re-interred over there, so the local Council had to debate it. One councillor said that the request should be agreed to; after all, he said, we didn't need Frogs around the place, or words to that effect.

Until not very long ago the clergy were prominent and influential figures; once the Bishop had gone, the Rector had to take on much of his public role. Nowadays, though the Rector will appear at the more and more infrequent Town Occasions – with the Nonconformist ministers, of course, the Mayor, members of the Council, perhaps the British Legion, the Scouts and Sea Scouts and female equivalents and the chief local policeman – the senior clergyman is not much more than a merely formally noticed figure.

There is, and this is a late twentieth-century phenomenon and owes much to the regional activities of the Arts Council and the Regional Arts Boards, a set of fairly influential cultural groups. Not a Mafia; they are too much in separate groups for that, though there is overlapping membership within the groups. There

is the Maltings' governing body and those for the Redgrave
Theatre (in 1993 it ran a 'Rally for the Redgrave' to reduce its
large debt) and the Farnham Society; and local presences on the
Boards of the Castle, the College of Art and a few smaller outfits.

How do they recruit? Presumably by word of mouth. What is
their predominant style? At a guess, reasonably cultivated middle-
class. Is one aware of them as influential figures in the town?
Not really. Does the Board of the Redgrave Theatre have meetings as hilariously under-informed as those at, say, the Birmingham Rep. thirty years ago? I hope not; hilarity can be too dearly
bought. Is the Maltings Committee dynamic? Well, it is very
active and on the whole effective at keeping the ship afloat.

Below the managerial level the volunteer genteel ladies (mixed
respectable working-class and lower-middle-class) take over and
it is them the public mostly sees. There they are on Saturday
mornings in the open kitchen behind the snack bar, buttering the
baps, asserting that a vegetable substitute is real cream for the
rather thin coffee, chopping the boiled eggs and making triangles
of shoulder ham. They all look fresh, the volunteers I mean, and
fresh from their fresh-looking semis. But for a dozen years there
was no single item of change in what they offered in their baps
at the Saturday Market. Obviously, brown or white baps with
chopped egg or boiled ham are the pinnacle or archetype of
public sandwich-making. Perhaps some day, long after we have
gone, one of the ladies will come back from a holiday in France
and ask: 'Why don't we try a nice pâté de campagne?' – and
they'll discuss it; and probably carry on as usual. Still, recently
someone persuaded them to try tuna. But now the snack-bar
catering has been contracted out.

Surveyed in this way, the local cultural managers seem to have
surprisingly little 'presence' in the town. Farnham, towns like
Farnham, does not feel it has many cultural problems to engage
with. Most people do not oppose the Theatre and such things –
though the inevitable few inevitably argue that the money could
be better spent on more policing. Most hardly think of the
Theatre; only a small and loyal core do that, the Board members
and the regular buyers of tickets. Compare them in numbers,
though, with the audiences of sixty years ago; compare the
building and its equipment; compare the acting with that of the

tired Rep. companies of the thirties and you see some gains. Still largely middle-class but now also more lower-middle-class than it used to be. Like the universities, only marginally more open to working-class people. It's an achingly slow movement but it does just exist; the large creature that is British society sometimes shifts in the warmish straw.

Outside the officially elected bodies and the cultural and other committees, all with different kinds and degrees of influence in deciding how the town shall be, and shall be run, are less official bodies of influence. Of these, the most important is the local newspaper, the *Farnham Herald*. Politically the *Herald* is, not surprisingly, more Right than Left. But it does not push its politics too much and what there is is not aggressive, not rammed down the readers' throats. The *Herald* is confident that it is going the way the world is going so need not overstress such things. I have come, surprisingly, to enjoy looking at it. It implies – asserts, imagines – a strong sense of community; it assumes a structured community, with its group or groups of well-motivated local citizens doing their best at considerable personal cost on behalf of us all; it takes care to keep in mind all the surrounding villages; it is a paper of record to a degree which any national paper now feels increasing difficulty in being; it records births, deaths, in memoriams, eighteenth birthdays, twenty-first birthdays, Silver and Golden and Diamond weddings, thanks from the family after funerals or for surprise celebratory meals, and congratulations on holes-in-one. Much, quite often, is in off-the-peg, sentimental rhyming couplets or quatrains. It all adds up to an attempt at a formidable, social-cementing operation week after week. The coverage of highway and building proposals and of applications for permission to build hypermarkets just outside town are important examples of that role in action. So is the coverage of crime. Whether the level of violence and assorted crime, as shown in the *Herald*, is higher now than it was in the mid-nineteenth century seems, proportionately by population, unlikely; but there is enough of all kinds to destroy the dream of Farnham as a town which can be rosily portrayed.

The local 'freebie', the *Surrey and Hants News* – 'Surrey's oldest newspaper' – is now owned by the same group as the *Herald*. It was for many years a full-scale, normal provincial

newspaper and well-regarded by many for its more radical stance
than that of the *Herald*. So there is some loss, less diversity of
published opinion. Yet it does still try to be rather more than
an advertising vehicle. It has a crabby, opinionated, enjoyable
columnist who knows how to stroke local prejudices but also is
willing to move out on his own and utter what he knows to be
un-Farnham-like sentiments. Its advertising features on the pleasures of the district's restaurants are instant period pieces, well
outpacing the local estate agents' prose. After this manner: 'I
chose the succulent and delicately glazed spare ribs whilst my
lady companion – who had been the recipient of a rose on
entering – partook of a most generously proportioned seafood
crêpe. Both were beautifully presented, in keeping with the eleg-
ant décor and ambience.' This paper presents a world slightly
below that of the more confidently established and comfortable
Herald.

We have to come to the question: is there, behind all the formal
ranks and positions and authorities, a shadowy inner group
which really runs Farnham? Who, what kind of people, if any,
take the place of the prominent brewers of two or three centuries
ago? Do those long-established names in the commercial and
professional life of Farnham still have a hidden influence? I think
not. Does the Conservative Club have a role, intervene occasionally, to a degree few of us recognise? And the Masons? The
Lions? The Chamber of Commerce? The professional group who
frequent the Bush Hotel's best bar? Do they indeed still meet, or
meet there? That bar is now transformed and probably made
unattractive to such a group: there are two pin-tables, one very
large and offering a game with or about the Addams Family –
rather an up-market pin-table, that, so perhaps welcomed by
some even in that group.
    Is there palm-greasing through any of these collectives? Are
there dinner parties at well-to-do houses at which many of the
town's issues are sorted out, hidden from any record? I would
guess not, or not much and not very effectively. We do not
interconnect enough, at any level, for that. More important:
members of the local authorities, elected or employed, give the
impression of being 'clean', not bent.

We do not have much sense of a 'Them' outside who govern us. Most Farnham people do not have much residual deference. We do not feel governed – certainly not in the old way of Eastern Europe. Or even in the way of France. Years ago my wife and I were driving through France to a conference in Italy. Somewhere south of the Massif Central we ran into a dispute which had closed the petrol stations in several contiguous départements. The Mayor of a small town gave me a note asking any petrol station within his mayoralty to give us a tankful so that we could drive clear of the affected départements. The man at the first station I found looked at the note, said 'Fuck the Mayor' and refused. The important differences from England were two: that the Mayor assumed his note would move the citizen; and that the citizen, even though he refused, was fully aware of the Mayor's assumed presence and power, of what he was deliberately saying 'Fuck you' to. We wouldn't be likely publicly to recognise the one assumption, or to think it worth while to express the other attitude.

CHAPTER 9

THE DOOMSDAY BOOK OF ENGLISH LEISURE

The English take their pleasures sadly, in the manner of their country.
Maximilian de Béthune, Duc de Sully, *Memoirs*

The Englishman never enjoys himself except for a noble purpose.
A. P. Herbert, *Uncommon Law*

England is the paradise of individuality, eccentricity, heresy, anomalies, hobbies and humours.
George Santayana, *Soliloquies in England*

'Hobbies', we often used to call them; now we say they are 'Recreational Pursuits'; and they are not all as sad or solemn as the above judgments suggest, though there is a little truth in each.

Some time in 1963 I was talking to the Secretary-General of the Arts Council, the great cultural maverick W. E. Williams; he was due to retire a few weeks later. I asked him what he would do with himself when he left that command-post of an office in St James's Square. 'Write the Doomsday Book of English Leisure,' he replied without hesitation. At this distance in years I can't vouch for his exact next words but remember they went something like this: 'Throw a brick in the main street of an English [or British] town on Saturday afternoon and you'll hit two amateur-operatic singers, a couple of straight actors, a member of the Townswomen's Guild and one of the St John's Ambulance Brigade, a folk-dancer and several collectors for charities.' No nation, he went on, is so devoted to amateur, voluntary activities; and it should all be recorded. I think he did not finish the job and do not know if he even began it, though he lived for fourteen years after retiring. It would be well worth doing – something with much more flesh on it than the usual statistical compendiums produced mainly for the advertising market. The idea kept recurring whenever a relevant incident brought it to the front of memory, and that was surprisingly often.

I remembered that conversation when house-hunting in a middle-class but unsmart district of Birmingham. With a flourish different owners displayed the huge size of their built-in bedroom wardrobes and out would tumble costumes for amateur dramatics, voluntary bodies, Country and Western singing, pantomime outfits, US Civil War uniforms.

So when, about twenty years later, an independent television producer asked me to mull over ideas for programmes, I suggested one on the Doomsday Book of English Leisure. He was interested and we drew up a short outline. A senior producer in one of the commercial companies liked the idea too and commissioned a fuller draft. We had to find a town big enough to have a good range of leisure activities but not so big that it, and so some of those activities, were divided into distinct geographical areas; the tracks had to be clear and fairly compact. My brother in Grantham, a retired headmaster, was much involved in several voluntary activities. At about thirty thousand, Grantham's size suited. Tom, my brother, soon identified getting on for two hundred activities, from the great staples – fishing and gardening – to collectors' clubs of several kinds, sports-clubs, bodies committed to 'doing good works' and others which offered exotic escapes from Lincolnshire reality.

All went well in the senior producer's office as he received and made a quick first reading of the expanded pilot script. Then he looked again and the word 'Grantham' seemed to come up and hit him. This was in the mid-eighties. 'Grantham,' he said, 'Mrs Thatcher . . . and you. We can't do this; least of all with the franchise coming up for renewal.' I saw his point once I had as it were seen his point of view. The fact that Mrs Thatcher had been brought up in Grantham had simply never entered our minds as we prepared the draft. Nor had a fragment of floating gossip of the time, which had prompted the senior producer's 'and you', occurred to us. It was sometimes said in those years that

Mrs Thatcher, whom I have never met, had referred to me
(though I can't have been alone) as 'that man who criticises
me and my government'. An understandable if small-minded
remark: at that point I began to feel that late-eighties Britain was
like a reformatory run by a vengeful Directrice. She had managed
to make even senior television producers pre-emptively behave
more royally than the political Queen. The programme, still a
very good idea, has never been made.

Hutchison and Feist's *Amateur Arts in the UK* records that
in 1989–90 there were 66,000 performances of amateur opera
and drama in Britain, that 1.8 million people were involved in
staging them and that they had audiences of 12 million. The
Institute of Policy Studies' 1991 review calculated that 3 million
people were amateur exponents of textile and other craft skills.

W. E. Williams's subject and mine is practitioners' not spec-
tators' pursuits, what people do not what they watch. They do not
include football, rugby, cricket, insofar as people go to see those.
Nor will such sports figure as participant pursuits since I have
little experience of them. And 'hobbies' are little written about,
whereas there are shelves of books on cricket and football.

As to Farnham, we will see later the wide range of activities at,
particularly, the Sports Centre and the Maltings. Those are the
big ones; there are dozens of others. The husband of the couple
from whom we bought our house (very middle-class) was a
beagler. On his own though that may have been because the
marriage was breaking up. Many retired people prefer outdoor
activities they can practise together, of course.

Outside the Post Office one day there was an, obviously retired, ex-officer: the usual outfit – Barbour jacket (genuine), flat
sandy-coloured cap, very pale well-washed fawn cord trousers,
large and well-trimmed moustache, heavy brogues. His wife – he
stayed silent – was somewhat younger, slim, even willowy; she
was talking to an acquaintance, making a restless 'T' with her
feet like a ballet dancer. She recalled Kilvert's wonderful and
yearning: 'The women of Clyro walk like storks.' 'Yes,' she said,
affectionately, 'George and I' – George scraped the pavement in
circles with his blackthorn – 'went fishing *thare* last week. Very
bad indeed it was.' Other couples share a love of 'twitching',
bird-watching. Golfers are of course everywhere, singly and in

pairs; and devoted gardeners; plus the musical and dramatic society activists.

Reports and advertisements in the local paper are the best quick guide. Here is a large but not altogether comprehensive list: the Tennis Club, Archery, Fishing, Athletics, Roller Hockey, Roller Skating, the Spiritual Healing Centre, Dancing Classes for adults or children, Friends of the Earth, Flower Arranging, the Inter-Varsity Club, the Carers' Group ('Practical Neighbourly Help'), a Swimming Academy, Farnham Visitors' Council ('Making Farnham a better-known place'), the Sequence Dance Club, the Workshop for the Retired, the New Age Group, the Citizens' Advice Bureau, Saturday Markets, the County's Adult Education and Recreational programme, Militaria interests, the Women's Institute and especially its Country Markets, the Townswomen's Guild, Bird Watchers, The Farnham Society, the Farnham Voluntary Service Council, Jumble Sales, Car-boot Sales, Garage Sales, Table Top Sales, 'Draws', Raffles and Bingo, Fun Runs, the Jazz Club and other similar outlets, the Live Music Society, the Film Society, the Music Club, the Choral Society, the Waverley Singers, the Inner Wheel, the Scottish Country Dancing Class, the Film Society, the Film and Video Makers' Society, the Workers' Educational Association, the Philatelic Society, the Camera Club, the Family History Society, Amnesty (particularly strong), the Muscular Dystrophy Group, Total Initiatives [what?], the Bridge Club, Riding for the Disabled, the Astronomical Society, the Model Railway Society, the Steam Preservation Society, the Hard of Hearing Group, the Toddlers Club, the Writers' Circle, the Winemaking Society, Weightwatchers, the Art Society, the Blind Club, the Sea Cadets, the Army Cadets, the Air Training Corps, the Civil Service Retirement Fellowship, Homemakers, the Federation of Business and Professional Women, the Allotments and Gardens Association, and the peripheral activities connected with the churches and chapels. The urge to join, to mix and to do is phenomenal.

Think, then, of the great numbers involved, many in more than one activity, and of the huge amounts of time they collectively give to them. There can be few in such a town, except the determined recluses, who do not take part in one or several of these. I used to think and to some extent still do that one of the most

boring and unrewarding of jobs must be that of a ticket-office
clerk at a railway station – all that issuing of tickets for other
people's travel, plus the hassle from those being held up and in
danger of missing their trains because someone in front is booking for two adults, two children and two dogs to John o'Groats
for a fortnight hence, using a variety of discount cards and
wanting on-the-spot answers to a series of questions such as:
'Will there be a taxi at John o'Groats when we arrive there at
eleven p.m. on the Sunday?' I now think it likely that most clerks
can work well without getting a high temperature because they
have, in that nice French phrase, a 'violon d'Ingres', a spare-time
activity entirely apart from their bread-winning job.

You could divide all such activities by the average age of their
participants and by the decades of British history over which
they have been practised. Fishing (which has 4 million adherents
in Britain) would then figure early; and so would gardening; and
among all classes. Few things surprise first-time foreign visitors
as much as a drive through a typical English, un-grand, suburb;
they tell more about English life than the Changing of the Guard
or a look through the railings of Buckingham Palace: the continuing evidence of elaborate care over lawns (most foreign
lawns, especially those of North America, look coarse-grained),
the deep green (part due to rain, part chemically induced), the
careful massing and disposing of shrubs, perennials and annuals
to produce equally carefully worked-out patterns of colour; the
intense weeding and hoeing. All that is much more important
and indicative than the gnomes in red conical hats eternally and
immobilely fishing over the pocket-handkerchief-sized concrete
ponds. Or, rather, the gnomes tell us about something else; not
so much about leisure activities as about that suburban dream
we glanced at when thinking of Fleet, Frimley and such places.

Then animals, especially horses and dogs. The Volvos and
Range-Rovers swing into Sainsbury's car-park with stickers on
the back-screen telling us that: 'The horse was on our roads
before the car.' A bit wonky, that, historically; the car brought
the roads. The Capris and even the Granadas as well as the
Novas and Nissans prefer to announce that 'Surfers do it standing
up' and all the variants on that silly and by now tired *double-
entendre*. Neurotic young parents, who see all other drivers as

potentially murderous road-hogs likely to slaughter their loved little one unless sternly warned off, favour 'Back off. Baby on board.' No doubt someone will eventually produce 'No child on board. Feel free to bash me.'

The urge for large dogs affects all classes, not just those living a little out of town with room for exercising the animals (most often seen by townees shifting and rootling endlessly in their rear cages in the car-parks). Many big dogs clearly live in small semis, belting the china-cabinets and hostess-trolleys with their tails as they wander restlessly around. A small-scale sample unsurprisingly suggests that childless young couples are more likely to have one and often two large dogs than do those who have started a family. The dogs' shit is almost as big as human shit, but it would apparently still be thought by some people an intrusion on personal liberty to require them at least to pull the dogs off the pavement and into the gutter to perform. Recently those of us making for the dry-cleaner's in The Borough were required ourselves to step off the pavement so that an Afghan hound could squat. One assumes the dogs are house-trained; their owners are rarely pavement-trained on their behalf. We saw one young woman let her hound shit on the pleasant sandy beach of Frensham Great Pond, that nearby weekend air-hole especially liked by families. Noticing our surprise she carefully shoved a thin coating of sand over the pile so as just to conceal it . . . from, for instance, any child disposed to sit down exactly there. In comparison with all this, cats, who are probably more numerous than dogs overall, are noiselessly well-behaved; better behaved out of doors than most dogs and many dog-owners.

It is a cherished and self-flattering myth that the British are the world's greatest lovers of dogs, as widely accepted as the less flattering myth that the British are the world's greatest consumers of chips-with-everything. Both are easily refuted. To go no further than straight over the Channel: the Belgians are much greater consumers of chips – and better chips – than we are. On the approach to the long outdoor stairway up the man-made hill which leads to the view-point over the battlefield of Waterloo, there is a sign: 'Do not take your chips up the monument.' Not even in England would the assumption be that many people habitually clutch a bag of *frites* when on outdoor visits. And the

French are at least as besotted with dogs as we are, often big dogs kept in small Paris flats.

Some of the more home-bound and minutely demanding hobbies – that is still the exact, evocative word, defined by the Oxford dictionary as 'an individual pursuit to which a person is unduly devoted' – are fading, perhaps because they need at least a table-top and close attention, and in many homes the television would now be a major distraction. The Houses of Parliament built in match-sticks was the usual way to symbolise all this range; it captured the huge amount of time, the care, the obsessiveness, often the historic nostalgia of this kind of hobby.

Then there are or were the putting together of soldiers for famous battles, ship and aeroplane kits and, especially for those with plenty of space, model-railway outfits. One of our neighbours, long retired, took up a whole large attic with an elaborate, electronically controlled railway system.

Of all the hobbies, odd pursuits, crazes, obsessions of the British (this is one I share to a high degree), the most widely spread is the love of hunting a bargain, something remarkably cheap that 'might come in handy', 'a real find'. Jumble sales are the long-established precedents, jumble sales arranged by the local church or chapel, the Boy Scouts or Girl Guides, or many another voluntary body; jumble sales patronised by almost everyone at some time or another but haunted always by women who are 'dead keen' on a bargain and often come back home with extraordinary objects rescued from attics and, quite often, put back into another jumble sale not long after.

Car-boot sales are their natural successors and have put jumble sales into a subordinate place. They have quickly become professionalised; and, for many, a tax-dodge; car-boots nowadays by no means always contain the odds and ends, the white elephants, which any household amasses; they contain stuff fallen off the backs of lorries or produced with sweated labour somewhere in the Far East or discarded as sub-standard by the manufacturer. A mixture of the tattily genuine and the tacky imported. The latest trick is that the sharp ones arrive early, snap up the many bargains at about a pound each from amateur owners who have undervalued them, and then set up their own car-boot displays with those goods marked at two pounds and upwards. They are descendants of those at Hunslet jumble sales of whom it used to be said: 'Ooh, I do hate them right *keen* ones.'

A sub-branch of this consuming interest has given rise to the small, fat, illustrated catalogues sent by post, often from a trading estate in Swindon, the archetype of post-modernist towns, or pushed inside the Sunday papers. They claim that many of their offerings are 'spin-offs' from space technology and almost all technologically advanced: a tiny electronic pill-box with its own water supply, a small machine for cutting perfect edges in paper, a desk-top shredder (paranoia in the suburbs), a reducer of stomach flab; tanning pills, hair-removers, security devices of many kinds, Chinese Food Kits, instant crease-removers; what fears, what hang-ups, what obsessions, what endless hunts for the latest fashion in tastes of all sorts.

At the peak of each season – high summer, before Christmas, the other Bank Holiday periods – the local paper announces several fairs, or 'Fayres', in the nearby villages; in local halls, cowboy and fly-by-night operators offer at unbelievably low prices (except that a lot of people do seem to believe in them) electrical or sports goods or carpets. Farnham's Maltings has a very large indoor and outdoor Maltings Market on the first Saturday of every month and is crowded. Some stalls remind you, if ever you need reminding, that the English have a crazy, surrealist love of concocting the weirdest objects out of the weirdest materials: lampshades from cemented and varnished sea-shells – the caramelised profiteroles of domestic lighting – are at the less exotic end of the range. But they are bought. Many shufflers move from the Maltings to the Chapel Market a quarter of a mile away. That also operates alone, on the third Saturday of each month, and is altogether a cheaper affair where you can still pick up an odd something you suddenly realise you are in need of – such as a wooden tie-rack. The Chapel Market has a stall of a newish kind – where surplus Public-Relations-Encouraging objects made to be given away by large firms to their favoured customers, from ball-pens to quartz alarm-clocks to golf umbrellas to leather wallets – all go for a fraction of their shop prices. You may have to put up with a would-be-dignified fancy gold monogram or corporation logo, though.

The Maltings is a more exact and sensitive barometer than the Chapel Market of changes in taste and in varieties in spending power. Over no more than six months you may see second-hand book stalls rise or fall, and, a new feature, the remaindered-books stalls take the spaces vacated. Very occasionally I see old or remaindered copies of books by me. I always buy them, feeling like a father recovering a lost child. You will certainly see the steady rise of rather expensive bric-à-brac stalls or of those for antiques in furniture and much else. In between are a few charity stalls, displays of home-made jams and cakes, health-food stands, brass and copper, jewellery which looks as though it has been made at the back of an old mill by two renegades from an art college, and a thirties stall.

As in all things English, there is a pecking order among bargain-hunting places. On the whole middle-class people, except the exceptionally keen or very curious among them, do not go to jumble sales or to the Chapel Market. They will go when the same hall is housing an antiquarian-books sale. People from all parts of the town's society visit the Maltings Market but working-class people will not go to a genuine antiques fair. Those are for the middle-class and especially for people whose setting up of a home has begun with a few 'choice' or 'nice' pieces given by Mother or a fond aunt. Much the same is true of the riotously chintzy National Trust shops – Mrs What-not's home-made marmalade with its chintz cover, at very high prices – as it is true of membership of the National Trust itself.

Of all such places within striking distance of Farnham the most huge, disordered and noisily working-class is the Sunday market at Blackbushe airport. The car-park alone covers a good few acres and needs a large posse of marshals. As you approach, you not only hear the sustained high hum; you smell from three hundred yards away the hamburgers, the hot-dogs and above all the frying onions. It is Bartholomew Fair, 1990s-style, on an arterial road about twenty-five miles from the boundary of London and drawing custom from miles around. You can get bargains there if you look very carefully indeed. But your heart sinks when you see couples obviously just setting up a home lugging almost unmanageable cartons containing very cheap, polyester-hollow-fibre-filled duvets, or knocked-together, gaudily varnished, four-foot high barometers-cum-grandfather clocks, or tawdry floral pottery in large boxes, or cheap video cassettes, or huge packs of frozen meat (it is taken for granted that virtually all families have freezers, microwave cookers and video-recorders), or enormous pink nylon teddy-bears whose filling hardly bears thinking about.

But it is all fascinating and the crowds who push down the aisles obviously love it. It is very much bigger than anything I knew in the thirties, in the North, and is culturally different. Not because it is predominantly working-class; physically and in dress the Northern and Southern working-class do not greatly differ today. The main difference is that the crowd is now part-white, part-Asian and part-Caribbean. West Indians love a crowded open-air market at least as much as the English. But, and this is the main cultural difference at Blackbushe, the Asians have now moved in as stall-keepers to a considerable degree – especially in leather clothing, in colourful fabrics and in shoes. There is hardly a West Indian-managed stall to be seen; in fact, on many visits I have seen one solitary West Indian helping to man a stall; he was working with white people. The Asians manage many of the stalls, the West Indians love walking round them.

Of the newer leisure occupations, much the most time-consuming, and one which needs no more than briefly mentioning, is watching television. It may be that Farnham's record here is somewhat askew of the national overall average since it has more than the national average of middle-class inhabitants, and middle-class people view a good many hours fewer each week than working-class people. Whether their patterns of viewing or the intensity with which they view differ I do not know. I know of no study made in Farnham. It would be reasonable to guess that working-class viewing here and middle-class viewing too respectively reflect the national averages and patterns. And, like most places in Britain, Farnham will be slow to realise that one of the things done well in this century, the establishment of broadcasting in the public service, has now been put at serious risk. As to the national newspapers, Farnham will reflect its middle-class weighting in readership of the populars and of what it has recently become the fashion to call, with an attempt at neutrality, the 'broadsheets'.

The greatest area of growth just outside town is in places which make use of almost universal private transport, prosperity, the avoidance of high rents and what we used to call 'rates' in town and their need for lots of land; plus for the customers the convenience of ample and free parking and of being able to shop on Sundays, especially for couples both of whom go out to work.

Here, the main nodes are the garden centres. They are predominantly lower-middle-class to middle-class in clientele and on the whole expensive. Most of them expand all the time, so clearly the customers are increasing. There is not much of a price-war between them so far; saturation-point in demand and supply appears not to have been reached. They are bright, attractive, often have good cafeterias and are generally very tempting. Few of the weekend staff know much about plants and flowers, or conservatories or garden ponds or koi fish – but they will usually find someone who does. Like Argos, these places are centrally of the shiny late-eighties, one of their more acceptable faces. Between them, thriving Blackbushe and a thriving garden centre bracket a whole range of the modern English social world, outlook, habits. In not much more than a one-mile stretch down the Petersfield Road south out of Farnham there is a large garden centre, a large country market with pick-your-own acres attached and a big, weekly car-boot sale, Birdworld (a successful bird-park) and the Alice Holt Forest and Recreation Area.

Next in size and growth to the garden centres among new leisure-time institutions are the vast DIY hangars. They are centrally working-class to lower-middle-class and more competitive with one another than the garden centres; less attractive, too, and more market-led. Presumably their expansion has been set off by at least two new trends: that as mass-produced major domestic equipment becomes relatively cheaper year after year (compare only the improvements in the specifications and prices of television sets over the last twenty-five years), so hiring the labour of actual hands becomes dearer. Second, to recall an earlier point, the increase in home-ownership among the respectable working-class and in particular among those who have now bought their council-estate houses again increases the wish, the need, to do it yourself. The supply has risen to meet these needs and to extend them; the competition is cut-throat; the new aids, tools, equipment, materials on offer are always increasing and always improving. There is even – well, predictably – a ranking-order, by price and quality and to some extent according to different strengths, among the DIY places, with Texas, MFI and B&Q in the lower area and Sainsbury's Homebase and Smith's Do It All in the upper. Around them all cluster those huge stores which inhabit a world of perpetual-but-never-to-be-repeated special offers on carpets and kitchens, the car spare-parts emporia and the fast-food chains.

Smaller recreational initiatives include the fitness centres, with gear which looks like torture equipment, the haunts of young women and of not-quite-so-young young mothers determined to defeat flab; lower-middle to professional-middle-class again; places more than usually likely to go out of business as one too many opens in town.

My own favourite, a major node, is the Sports Centre, an uninspired building but with a vivid internal life. Open a hundred hours a week for hundreds of visitors a day; twenty clubs meet there and sixteen schools. Before I began to swim there on most weekdays I assumed it was a sort of tarted-up public baths; but that phrase belongs to the old world, like 'Slipper Baths', where poor people could get a hot bath for a few pence.

There is a very large pool, of course. Special sessions are set aside for school parties and also, sensibly, there are open sessions for the general public when school groups are not allowed in. School groups make the place sound like an over-crowded aviary; adult groups sound like cultivated carp at feeding time; they do not mix well.

There is a session for disabled people and groups of children with Down's Syndrome are brought from time to time. Sometimes a section is roped off for the local Sub-Aqua Club. (Who gave them that favoured name, instead of 'Underwater'?) Piped music radiates from the sun-room at the side, where you can get a pre-holiday tan or hang on to one when you are back. There is now a sauna. The strangest of all this enclosed island's various sweet noises is the music which swirls around the great arc when the Formation Swimming Group is in session. The instructor knows as surely as a popular disc-jockey what music 'goes with' formation swimming; or perhaps there are suppliers of the right kind of theme music; it is languorous, swooping, all curves and sustained sweeping movements; big-band stuff; like music for aerobics in slow motion.

Nodes by their nature form societies of their own, shifting or fixed, indoors or out; and are always taking us by surprise through what they throw up in their compositions and habits, like flower-beds which have seeded themselves. The Sports Centre is the focus for many of the particularly athletic and generally unmarried young people. Recently some of the young women have revealed engaging little tattoos, romantic or sentimental – blue-birds, butterflies, hearts – on their right buttocks. There is to a certain degree a good-natured classless quality. All is consistently cheerful. The attendant young men and women, in green, short-sleeved, jersey-cotton shirts and dark-blue shorts, have thighs like tree-trunks, all being fine swimmers.

The general, open, non-school-group sessions at midday attract older people. One or two forty-odd-year-olds have left their offices and, bullet-headed caps and blank-looking goggles on, snort menacingly up the lane reserved for those doing proper lengths. My sort take things easy, doing leisurely breast strokes. Some seem to have waterproof hearing-aids. Most talk all the time or almost all the time. After an initial greetings chat, a group of elderly ladies slip cautiously into the water at the near-end and float along like lazy porpoises. They time their strokes to match the conversation, which hardly ever stops. At the far end they pause for a more workmanlike talk. The more determinedly social do one-third swimming, two-thirds talk: about the local food shops, especially the delicatessens and how reliable they are for parties, and about 'how I make my stews . . . or flans'; or the more worriedly personal: 'So I said to her, "I know I've no right to speak where my grandchildren are concerned. But –" ' To that and all such assertions of injured right-mindedness there is always silent or murmured agreement. The day a listener says even as much as: 'Still, I do see their point of view,' a basic rule will have been shattered. But this is Farnham and you may just as likely hear them discussing the latest M. J. Farrell. One handsome middle-aged lady is fond of complaining that her agent always phones when she is at the baths and has forgotten to switch on the answering machine.

Elderly men, some in small groups, appear regularly. One of them sometimes paddles up to a group of early-middle-aged women and makes jokes which are obviously slightly risqué, to judge by the delighted screams of laughter and the 'Well, I nevers.' He knows the rules and boundaries exactly, how not by insinuation or by particular words to put the hearers off. He couldn't say 'knickers' or 'She's got a rare chest – or bum – on her' or they'd silently move away. I have heard him say, cautiously, 'dirty weekend'; that is probably his understood limit.

One man, not a swimmer, is curiously interesting. He arrives in a modest but smart car with a neat logo on its side. He takes a cardboard box out of the boot, carries it to the big machine in the foyer and replenishes the crisps, biscuits, chocolate. The puzzle is this; it seems strange that such a job can keep a man in that sort of modest but certainly not shabby style, with a company saloon, simply on the replenishment of vending-machines. In the thirties he would have been shabbily dressed and gone round in an old van. Also, does he never get bored with his round? Perhaps his job is more difficult than at first appears; perhaps he can mend the machines if they fall foul of bent and illicit coins, and is known as a Service Engineer, which might increase his satisfaction; he doesn't look unhappy (perhaps, like so many people, he too has substantial outside interests).

We could try some other ways of sorting out patterns of play. By sex, for instance, but that doesn't get us far, not interestingly far. Obviously, there are the Townswomen's Guild and the Women's Institute; and those clubs such as the Masons and, to a modified extent, Rotary, which are male enclaves. Few men, presumably, attend needlework or flower-arranging classes; quite a number take up cookery, as some women do carpentry. But many occupations attract both wives and husbands, from bridge to helping at the Maltings, from old-style dancing to collecting for charity on Saturdays.

Divisions by age, then? Yes, again obviously, and we have

already touched on them. For young or youngish people, from the
tennis clubs through all the athletic occupations to the drugs-and-
drink raves. I would guess that a count would show that boozing
in pubs, especially fairly well down the social scale, was the
favourite. Almost as intuitively as starlings heading for their group-
congregating places as night falls, young drinkers know which pubs
are in, which out; and that sort of allure doesn't entirely depend on
the landlords' inducements to get them in, such as different pop
groups at weekends or even night after night. There are other
favoured places out of town for weekend congregating right up to
the acid-house parties the local press makes much of.

A man in a barber's uttered an outsider's nostalgic view on all
this. He was heavily early-middle-aged, had a shop and employed two or three young women. In a voice which carried more
of a sense of leching than he realised, and which carried also a
Larkinesque feeling of being born out of due time, of opportunities sadly missed, he described to the barber his staff's
weekend habits. Down the pub in couples or threes, knickers left
at home. Buy them a few drinks, get them outside in the angle of
two walls, your hand up quick and it's all yours.

Recreational divisions by class, much as many people hate this
to be said nowadays, remain the most distinctive and important.
The main, voluntary, local achievements in leisure provision are
solidly middle-class initiatives: the Redgrave Theatre from 1973,
the rescuing of the Castle (it receives course members from all
over Britain and abroad, but was pushed on at the start and is
still buttressed by the town's middle-class), the very successful
revival in 1947 of the Farnham Society, and the Farnham Buildings Preservation Trust (to their great credit, not groups of
Nimbys), and above all the buying from the brewers in 1968,
against the threat of its demolition for subsequent 'development', of the magnificent brick Maltings and the successful
turning of it into a many-sided leisure centre. In 1992, and apart
from the Maltings own variety of activities, more than forty
clubs and groups met there regularly; and a third of a million
people went through its doors.

All these recall the strength of that very English, but not
uniquely English, formulation 'The Friends of This and That';
we very much like to adopt that, in Farnham. How far people

enrol as Friends because of their conviction of the worthwhile-
ness of the enterprise, how far as yet another indication that they
have 'arrived', and how far as a sign that they seek to arrive, I do
not know; the usual inextricable mixture, I would guess.

Some even more interestingly class-defined recreational habits
are so much taken for granted, almost as facts of British life,
that they are hardly noticed. These are the differences in weekend habits of families with young or youngish children. Lower-
middle-class, middle-class and professional families feel it is
important to go for walks at weekends, to get the kids a breath
of fresh air, to have a blow, a little trip out, to stretch their legs;
so they go off to Frensham, Alice Holt, or to one of the National
Trust properties with big grounds a few miles off; or to a large
or largeish private garden thrown open on certain summer weekends – all proceeds to a charity, of course. That's a neat combin-
ing of three very English things: a near-universal hobby,
class-ranking and the doing of good works.

Much the same set of assumptions applies also to the planning
of the annual holiday. Self-evidently, differences between social
groups here are partly to do with how much money is available;
but not most importantly. Eurocamps, walking tours in the
Lakes or even in Austria belong to a quite different part of the
general culture from English holiday camps or the Balearics.

Even more sharply marked as a form of differentiation is that
hoary old institution, the Sunday Dinner. That still stands, an
assertion of family stability and of a reasonable degree of security and ability to manage, from the respectable working-class to
that point in the professional middle-class at which you prefer
and can now afford without calculation to go out to a pub for a
few mid-morning drinks with acquaintances and then a good
Sunday dinner in the adjoining dining-room.

For families in difficulties the collapse can be severe. A Church
of England vicar talked about how greatly affected he now is by
the ways of less secure, poorer, families within his parish. Some
battle on (as our own mother did in the twenties, on a pound a
week plus some grocery coupons for the four of us), but it is not
surprising if some are ground down. Forty or fifty years ago, the
vicar went on, almost every family would have thought it
important to aim at a Sunday Dinner (Argentine beef at a shilling

a pound, Yorkshire pudding, a lot of potatoes and carrots, plus rich gravy followed by rice pudding with jam or an apple pie); but some families nowadays (40 per cent, he estimated, in the worst affected area), he had found, rarely have a home-cooked meal at any time in the week. In the kitchen there will be some commercially prepared food from the shop up the road, to eat whilst watching television with the others in your – it might be one-parent – family. All this is a pity for even more than nutritional reasons: Sunday dinner, the smell of it beforehand, sitting down and feeling eager as the joint appears, the sense of an occasion, of the family together at a sort of celebration and that for more than merely so as to eat heartily . . . all this can make one meal in the week more than an indulgent event; even in the most agnostic or atheistical of families, it has a touch of almost religious communality.

Such a division within working-class people (though there may be something similar among the middle-class), marked by the presence or absence of a proper, home-cooked meal at Sunday midday or thereabouts, also marks, like the new division between home-owners and tenants (though the overlap is not complete, of course), the change in the composition of working-class groups, especially on council estates, since the war. Such districts in the thirties had a few one-parent families, as well as some 'shiftless' who would hardly ever cook a full meal. But to repeat: the nineties are different, the divisions sharper and the two kinds of people less unevenly balanced in numbers. The combination of ready-cooked meals and the constant attention to television have speeded up the process but are not the main causes. In Hunslet and such places before the war, if you walked round the streets on mid-Sunday morning, you met the smell of roast beef from almost every house. When more homes than before have only one parent, she – it is usually a woman – is likely to be tired almost all the time, the children clamour for those TV meals, it is easier to sit and watch TV than to spend time in the kitchen preparing food – when all these things come together (and self-evidently they influence other than one-parent families), then the smell of roast beef in the streets on Sundays, with all that can signify, becomes only intermittent.

*

We could also trace 'patterns of play' as they change with the seasons. A town map of the sort described much earlier, marked in different colours according to these seasonal changes, would show the pattern of the year, changing within itself, but not much from year to year; summer and winter pursuits being shaded into and out of autumn and spring. On that you could superimpose the great public markers of the year's revolving: the traditional main Bank Holidays, Harvest Festival for church and chapelgoers, Bonfire Night, Christmas and New Year, Easter, what we used to call Whitsuntide, now submerged in the first of the new Spring and Summer Bank Holidays; and the great County and lesser Shows.

The annual Surrey County Show at Guildford on Whit Monday is all that a very prosperous, part-agricultural, part-urban county should stage: marquees full of vegetables, flowers or animals, stalls selling clothing and country crafts of all kinds, agricultural machinery, suitable saloon cars, displays of horsemanship (that's a very powerful sub-culture, full of strapping girls and lean men with hard hats), the Red Arrows or the Red Devils, special tents where after banking your proceeds you may drink spirits free with your friendly manager, and a variety of stalls for eating. No Blackbushe burgers here. Instead, shrimp and smoked-salmon sandwiches, roast beef and roast pork baps, strawberries and cream and Loseley's Jersey ice-cream. I marginally prefer somewhat smaller fairs; not the smallest – they hardly get off the ground – but the middle-range such as Alton's; less spectacular, less out-facing, more genuinely countryfied but large enough to occupy you very happily for an hour or two.

That same seasonal-change map should also show how much the same people appear doing different things in different seasons; criss-crossing and overlapping routes, often involving changes of clothing, of uniform; that is the most impressive visual indication of the British addiction to its Doomsday Book of Leisure occupations.

The reference to changing clothes recalls the love of 'dressing-up' and not just for the demands of amateur drama and opera, though that is part of their attraction. Obviously, one dresses in a special way also for many sports, especially team-sports such as cricket and football. Then there are the Scouts and Guides and

Sea Scouts and Boys' Brigade and Church Lads Brigade – not so
much the children's uniforms as the dress of the adults who lead the
processions. And the ubiquitous and much respected St John's
Ambulance Brigade. At any relevant Farnham occasion you may
play Spot the Neighbour through the SJAB uniforms. I met this love
of service-with-uniforms early, up in Leeds. My professor of philosophy in 1937 was a gentle Quaker who hummed to himself when
thinking: Professor Harvey. On Saturday nights he could be found,
humming and patrolling the main commercial and entertainment
artery, Briggate, in the uniform of a Special Constable. He was
inspired by his Quaker concept of service; but he also loved wearing the uniform, like a delighted boy. A great many English women
secretly want to look like Florence Nightingale – or Carmen; a
great many Englishmen wouldn't mind looking like that too.

Cowboys of the Far West, musket bearers of the Sealed Knot –
in all this is the wish to strike histrionic gestures and to throw
your voice over vast spaces, outdoors or in; as in the 'pantos'.
Which leads to the taste for sex-change outfits. Of which the
main historic instances are to be found in the pantomimes, and
few towns would be without their own amateur form of those.
The panto – transvestism with songs – is rooted, more than any
other popular art-form, in the rock-bottom elements of the
English sense of slightly naughty fun: bums and tits. We remember first the Principal Boy, always a girl or rather a chunky
young woman with a small skirt and great thighs which she
repeatedly slaps with a large thwack from a small whip. 'Breeches
parts', they used to be called.

But women into men are less evident than men into women.
Widow Twankey has precedence, for the audience, over the Principal Boy. Men like changing into women more than women like
changing into men. The line of drag artists is a long and distinguished one, latterly from Danny La Rue to Barry Humphries; we
seem unable to have enough of it. Soldiers abroad congenitally
dressed as women for the Troops' Entertainment evenings and that
was not only because there were no women available, or because
the men who did it were always homosexual.

There remain two very strong, long-standing and still flourishing
main streams of amateur activity. First, that powered by the urge

for self-improvement. The 1992–3 programme for Adult and Continuing Education classes within the Waverley area alone of the County of Surrey runs to fifty-four treble-columned pages. The different centres include not only Farnham but its outriders such as Farnham College, Heath End, Weydon and St James. There are other centres, based on Cranleigh, Godalming and Haslemere. I have not counted the total of all classes but the subjects include Basic Education, Community Education (five different sections), Access (to yet more education), Art (seven different sections), Craft, Fashion, Design and Textiles, Business and Computing – all with several sections – seven sections of Children's Courses, six on Cookery and Wine, twenty-three sections for GCSE, five on English as a foreign language, eight on General Studies, ten foreign languages in twenty-one sections (including Chinese, Dutch, Polish and Portuguese), three sections on Performing Arts, nine on Physical Education, four on Practical Skills and three on Teacher Training. All that in only one part of Surrey, a fairly lightly populated part.

As I write, the latest Tory government is doing its best to wreck this lovely, complex, delicate but sinewy fabric – by its characteristic insistence that any adult educational provision from public funds should have a clearly defined vocational purpose; the rest is, belittlingly, 'recreational'. Downgrading by reductive labelling. Typewriting stays in, computer operation comes in, philosophy goes out and so do the Principles of Democratic Society; unless you are prepared to pay the full price for them yourself. Since those who may most need such things rarely know their lack and so do not see why they should spend their money in that way, the established divisions within society are thereby deepened. In the land of Tawney and Temple and Albert Mansbridge.

These changes are ironic, too, when one recalls that a century and a half ago adult education began with the assumption that one of its central purposes must be to help its students become more effective citizens of a democracy. One would have thought, one should believe, that in the light of the incessant and barely literate persuasions which abound at all levels of society the need for that kind of democratic education is stronger now than ever; in a largely middle-class stronghold such as Farnham no less than in Northern, industrial, working-class areas.

The Public Library Service offers even less to be cheerful about today. Opening hours were cut during the Thatcher era and after, as were general library budgets virtually throughout the country. This is bad and the Library Service nationally rightly does its best not to let us forget its weakening effects. But it is a less important constraint on purposes than the populism which is now running through the Library Service itself in many counties including Surrey; the North is said to do better. Book-buying is largely determined by best-seller demand ('x' copies of the latest Jeffrey Archer, none of an important new non-fiction book). Farnham's Biography section is better than might have been expected these days; the services for children are very popular; there is a House-bound Service, provision for the disabled and similar facilities; the staff are extremely helpful – and puzzled by criticisms of the Library Service since they know how very busy they are.

The new library building is smart, light and airy. Tables for reading and comfortable chairs are scattered between the shelves; all very different from the Reading Room in Hunslet Public Library in the thirties, where old men not happy to stay in a cheerless home sat picking their noses and hawking, and unemployed men went through the newspaper ads to see if there was 'an opening', and shifty men looked to see whether the racing news had been cut out; it usually had.

You are given little sense, however, that most of the staff know much about why their kind of institution exists, of its history and aims; instead, they seem to take the prevailing policy from headquarters as given. One day there appeared a label on a large stand of CD's for loan: 'Easy Listening'. A thoughtless appropriation from the commercial audio shops. At least they haven't yet gone as far as a Woolworth's label I saw the other day: 'Essential Easy Listening'; that could hardly be boiled down further, a concentrated musical soup-cube. As always it is difficult to imagine adults passing their time on such clichéd promotional exercises; still, if there is money in it . . . It would be much more to the purpose, if portentous, for the libraries to label a CD shelf 'Hard Listening but Worth While'.

It would be harsh to begrudge their pleasures to the considerable numbers of retired people – again, mainly middle-class – who patronise the library. They know just what they want and they get it nowadays – but to a degree which leads to the neglect of purchases of more important books, better books, books which feed the mind and spirit (deliberately old-fashioned language, that).

Should you ask for such a book to be obtained through inter-library loans you are likely to be told, seriously, that it will take months and that, 'If you go on like this, you will make the Council Charge go up.' For example, not one copy of Peter Scott's book on British culture was to be found within the Surrey Service. After four or five months it arrived from that largely working-class South Yorkshire township, Doncaster.

If you point out this manifest fact, that many Library Services have today mistaken their democratic purpose for populist bestseller-chasing, you will find yourself abused as roundly as if you had accused a respectable family grocer of short-changing, or a Methodist minister of Popery. Since those who have deserted their earlier principles like to accuse their critics of exactly that, you will be charged with being 'undemocratic' yourself. You will be told, as I was by the Chief Librarian of a major local authority (not in Surrey), that 'To insist that some books are better than others is pure cultural élitism.' Another senior manager argues for 'getting the maximum reader-value out of available shelf-space'. Letters from schools of librarianship will tell you that the creation of the Public Library Service a century and a half ago was 'merely a bourgeois invention to keep the workers quiet'; and, also by a student or staff member of a School of Librarianship, that 'the Great Victorian novel [surely there's a routine 'so-called' missing there, before the 'Great'] was merely the expression of capitalist individuality'; or 'a device to celebrate and sustain bourgeois hegemony'; 'not in any way a well-intentioned initiative to help workers acquire literacy but a trick to bleed off dissent through the opiate of consoling print'. As Granville-Barker might have said: it's the thin, single-thread simplicity of the argument I resent. In such debates all argumentative sentences containing a 'merely' should be at once skipped; they are protesting too much and too naïvely; they belong in the same linguistic-evasions box as: 'It's as simple as that!' Faced with such outpourings I remember again the postman who was following the philosophy series on television.

Younger people nowadays are much less likely to look back later, as many older people do, on the public library as the place which nourished their emerging intellectual interests.

Some people say that this dereliction of one important aspect of the public libraries' historic purpose is due as much as anything to the common decision by local authorities to bundle libraries in the compendious bag marked 'Leisure Services', along with parks, sports centres and public entertainments; that the people appointed to direct those new umbrella entities are more often chips off the show-biz block than people with much sense of the libraries' origins and traditions. That may be so. But the choosing of such people and their ability to sit at ease in their own Zion are due most to the increasing relativism of the general culture, the dreadful fear of anything which might seem like earnestness, a divisive and 'judgmental' earnestness.

Of all the activities which would need to be recorded in the Doomsday Book of English Leisure, these two great areas are most impressive and admirable: that urge for 'self-improvement', the feeling that life and the understanding of it can be made richer by reading and study; and the urge to help others voluntarily, to help lame dogs over styles, to do something for 'those less fortunate than ourselves'. This impulse recalls that so-much-quoted line of Orwell about England being a family. He went on to say, correctly, that the wrong people were in control, but that is not directly relevant here. Orwell's point in calling England a family was this: he recognised the sense of belonging to one another which so much expresses itself in all that voluntary work for others; he also recognised that families quarrel, some members hate others, there are malicious old aunts and selfish old uncles and cousins who are no better than they should be and siblings whom, we come eventually to realise, we quite simply and powerfully dislike; and most important, that there are invisible but strong nets separating different grades of the family. That is the English situation. But yet underneath we feel bonds.

In the centre of Farnham today there are ten charity shops, full of things – often very decent things – given to them, and manned by the usual posses of well-turned-out ladies. If a charity shop has to move because someone has arrived willing to rent or buy the accommodation, they are likely to find another billet soon; the high incidence of shops which cease trading sees to that.

The town does its duty by all the main national charities and has some of its own, towards which it is especially warm: the Phyllis Tuckwell Memorial Hospice, for example, and Bell's Piece, a Cheshire Home and so treasured as both national and local.

Saturday mornings chink with the sound of shaken and out-stretched collecting boxes – but not so outstretched as to constitute importuning or the police might feel they had to inter-vene. You can, yet again, play Spot the Neighbour all round town, and particularly when the neighbour is in uniform. In this work women predominate, usually women of a certain age and usually lower-middle to middle-class women. That should not cause resentment or disagreement or surprise. It comes with the country, is as it is because that is the way the culture is and has been for centuries. Middle-class women are likely to have more public social skills than working-class women; they are more likely to be used to at least some managing (if only in managing their 'daily helps'); those daily helps free some time for their employers; their houses may be big enough to accommodate a committee meeting and to breathe a flowery-print or Scandinavian-type assurance on being made open to mixed groups of outsiders. The fact that professional pensions are now often index-linked has added to all that assurance and to all that willingness to give time. 'Money pads the edges of things, God help those who have none.' A soft bed of secure available cash can liberate the charitable spirit; in some. But the charitable spirit which does not have, does not need, that assurance, is the finer kind. Above all, such people are likely to have inherited that certain sense of duty, circumscribed and class-bound perhaps but still a call.

We have seen that the condescension and bossiness which one found quite often until about 1960 have now lessened among some people. Those who serve on the Town Council and who run Farnham's charitable societies such as the Citizens' Advice Bureau have learned something over the last three decades. They do not talk down so much; not all of them, at any rate. And some are very competent, conscientious and immensely generous with their time. But one could still sometimes echo Matthew Arnold and wish the remaining few showed 'a shade more soul'.

Soon I shall, I am sure with some difficulty, be trying to tease out how far it is true to say that a place like Farnham still has – or did it ever have? – a sense of community; is it in fact 'a community'? It would be neither sensible nor just to ignore at that point, not to put in the scale, all this voluntary work, so much of it meant to help those less fortunate than the voluntary workers, most of them middle-class women whose sense of community may still be socially three-tiered. A partial, a canted, sense of community perhaps, often still slightly *de haut en bas*, a little red-flannelly, but within the limits of its own vision well-meant, a reaching-out from that sense that we are all in a way related to one another and that debts are owed. These roots are extremely tenacious.

So these two, self-improvement for more than vocational ends and good works towards others, are the major Doomsday Book impulses. Around them flow all the others, domestic or external, solitary or communal, athletic or sedentary. Or, most engaging and intriguing of all, fantastic – the urge to dress up, to throw your voice over large spaces, to change sex, to be someone else – probably bawdy and certainly rhetorical. For good or ill, such things are outside a critically self-aware approach to English – or British – culture. But all in all they present a far from unengaging or unattractive picture, and contain some of the most enduring, appealing and powerful strands in the whole fabric.

CHAPTER 10

IDEAS, OPINIONS, PREJUDICES, ATTITUDES

The wish to spread those opinions that we hold conducive to our own welfare is so deeply rooted in the English character that few of us can escape its influence.

Samuel Butler, *Erewhon*

The English think of an opinion as something which a decent person, if he has the misfortune to have one, does all he can to hide.

Margaret Halsey, *With Malice Toward Some*

Margaret Halsey, perhaps because of being American, is linguistically off-key there. An Englishman – or woman – hides original or carefully examined ideas, thoughts, perceptions; but both men and women are crammed full of opinions, usually unexamined and often prejudicial; and those define attitudes.

About attitudes in towns such as Farnham the most important thing to say – I have said it already and probably will again – the characteristic which strikes an observer early and seems to remain constant, is that change is very slow; for good and ill, in admirable as in dubious ways.

Of these lasting characteristics the most important, noticeable but difficult to talk about, is the practice of neighbourliness. Difficult to talk about because, like the claim to tolerance, it is one of the stubborn clichés among British opinions, one of those deeply embedded substitutes for thought, an over-thumbed card in the island's Happy Families pack.

To some extent I worked my way out of the weightless side of this claim many years ago, gave it – for myself at least – a local habitation, a bit of flesh and blood: by describing neighbourliness in Leeds working-class life as seen by a boy. It is much harder to write about virtue than to delineate vice, especially in a relativist period. Vice is gin, hot, strong and boosting; virtue looks much the same but seems as innocuous, unnoticeable, as water. Virtue embarrasses; if you are writing about an individual, there must be a clay foot somewhere; if about the habits of a group then surely you are being indefensibly 'sentimental' . . . and that is a worse crime than corruption. Some people will more easily accept a politically militant working-class, or a working-class ground down by the bosses to a life of emptiness, than a working-class which had retained at least one – and probably more – remarkable moral conviction and practice of its own.

Now, after twenty years in a southern, largely middle-class town, I have to apologise if my celebration (it was that, though rather more qualified than Orwell's justly remembered lyrical tribute, inspired by a thirties, Northern, working-class interior) seemed to suggest that this quality of neighbourliness was practised only among working-class people.

Neighbourliness is as much a deeply lived-in habit and practice among lower-middle-class and middle-class people as among working-class. It is far more complex an attitude than could be caught in the explanation that it is a way of implying: 'You help me and I'll help you', though that element is certainly there, especially among poor people. It is based more on that sense we have met before, that we are a kind of extended family . . . even though the conventional sayings within which we clothe that attitude when we try to talk about it are just that: conventional, trite, not up to the height of what we are actually doing, carrying out. We are here, as so often, doing better than we know how to say – except in the recurrence of certain words; such as 'helpfulness', a mantra which rings true all the time, which is weighty, borne out, cashed every day.

Yet, and this is the other side of the picture, neighbourliness is not 'community', though related to it; it is a sealed-off form. Neighbourliness stops at the nearby doorsteps; the sense of community is wider, embracing the village or the town; it can exist today though with more and more difficulty. For all the qualifications, the sense of neighbourliness in all classes is still strong and admirable. It simply assumes, sometimes with almost embarrassing alacrity, that when a neighbour needs help of any kind on any occasion that help should be given as a matter of course, meals prepared, the car got out to go on an errand, visits to hospital made, the empty house looked after. More than any other single habit it cuts across differences, beginning with political differences. A society which has plenty of cant, of drawbridge-raising phrases – about not letting people other than family over your doorstep, keeping yourself to yourself, not for ever being in and out of other people's houses, not being fond of living in each other's pockets – such a society here goes against that particularly narrow family insularity and opens itself; if only to the prescribed circle of definable 'neighbours'.

Within the house, the home itself, the predominant mood in places like Farnham and throughout the social range – obviously there are exceptions, families in difficulties, 'at daggers drawn' with each other, suffering from violence or drink, the stresses of teenage or old age, or loneliness and lack of money – nevertheless, within most homes there is usually a mild good nature; not gaiety but a determined cheerfulness, the 'you've got to look on the bright side', 'no use being down in the dumps', 'we did have a good laugh' tradition. Not intellectually neutered because the practice of intellect has hardly any place there; not habitually morose or resentful but ready to 'take everyone as you find them', 'give them the benefit of the doubt', 'give credit where it's due'; a tea-and-teacake or cocoa-and-biscuits amiability; a world which most happily revolves round an unquestioned acceptance of the rightness of family-centred domesticity (a domesticity which has easily absorbed, and made its own, television; as it earlier absorbed radio). Seen through a lighted window on a cheerless evening, this world has its charm, a sort of prelapsarian attraction; the sterner edges of English puritanism tamed or at least modified, in this place, for this time, but yet continuously.

The style is, though in its own way, uxorious; not physically or verbally very expressive in that, but as a matter of custom centred on Mum and Dad or 'the wife' and 'my hubby'. More than any other that last, comfortable 'cumfy'–marriage word, 'hubby', captures much of the snug, inturned warmth, and the limitations, of the style. 'Domesticated' it certainly is, domestic-centred, domestic-revolving; not very if at all reflective; outside the preoccupations of home, not very inventive and even less imaginative; easy, pliant, placable and, when experienced over much time, boring to outsiders, to psychological outsiders. A touch of bloody-mindedness or of the sharp-tempered directness of the French would be a tonic. No wonder university life can be so bewildering, or so cap over the windmill, to those – especially the young women – from the respectable working-class to lower-middle-class who are now in greater numbers leaving home for the campuses.

It is a creaturely life, without wide or deep horizons. The furthest it is likely to branch out from the traditional homely religiosities is into an, again cheerful, mild evangelical mode, the mode and mood of 'Under the spreading chestnut tree' sung with suitable gestures at a jolly camp. It could be called smug as well as snug; but that would be too easy, be like a blanket smothering further teasings-out.

By basic disposition conservative and Conservative and, like many towns of its kind, Farnham is and is likely to remain for as far as we can see massively Tory-voting in national elections. The Liberal Democrats may have made gains recently but they are a long way from unseating the Conservatives. Farnham is a Tory town as securely as South Yorkshire mining communities are Labour towns. The bulk of Farnham's Tory voters are not deferential Tories; they are more secure than that. They vote Tory because they believe – 'assume' would be more accurate – that the Conservatives are the natural party of government. Many of the middle-class citizens take their privileged lives as the norm, unassailable, and feel no guilt or challenge. To be a Socialist is almost unthinkable. They assume that active Labour Party members are loud-mouthed demagogues driven by rancour and envy. They find it difficult, therefore, to believe that anyone from the professional class could, except out of perversity, espouse socialism; and are disconcerted when they find it is so; they can't even tell such people that they'll 'grow out of it'.

Here we remember yet again and get a closer purchase on the group of 'new' professionals who are in increasing numbers choosing Farnham as a home – those in some of the media of

mass-communication, especially, and others in professions which
are to some degree intellectual or artistic. Farnham suits them
not only for its nearness to London but just as much because it
is only 45 minutes from Heathrow. They are not really middle-
class in the sense in which that tag has been used in this book;
they are the at least partly classless members of the newer professions, recruited to an increasing degree on ability and so from all
parts of society, not the public-school-and-City types. But if not
class-conscious in the traditional sense, many are status-conscious
in the contemporary sense. Yet some are likely to be Liberal
Democrats or even Socialists.

More typical middle-class Farnham citizens have a solid assurance in the general rightness, normality, desirable universality of
their own and their kind's ways. They have what Addison called
the 'honest prejudices which naturally cleave to the heart of a
true Englishman' and which made Ogden Nash say: 'To be an
Englishman is to belong to the most exclusive club there is.'
Some even seem not to have noticed that we no longer have an
Empire. Some simply assume that the Empire was overwhelm-
ingly a force for good, a civilising mission; they show little if any
sense of the correlations between the exploitation of colonial
territories, industrial growth and – compared with the standard
of life in those former colonies – a general prosperity. If patriotism is a well-thought-out love of your country, its land, the
nature of the people and their best historic achievements, then
many of these are not patriots, but chauvinists. They half-think
Britain could have won the war without American or Soviet
intervention; they do not believe in America's military efficiency
anyway; they do not want to recognise or know about the
magnitude of the German effort before that country was led to
disaster, as much as anything by the errors of its own leaders.
Like most of us in the developed world, they have rarely thought
about, let alone tried to take the measure of, the Holocaust,
which is both the greatest fully–considered and deliberate sin in
history and the most indigestible instance of 'the banality of
evil'. In the last few years they have hardly registered the plight
of Salman Rushdie. They would be uncomprehending if asked to
consider the challenge from Asia in the decades to come (as
would most people in other parts of the advanced world).

Yet that impression, though it is a strong impression, must surely be misleading? Some people, perhaps many more than one easily recognises, must have by now begun to realise that the terms of life for Britain – and elsewhere in the developed world – have irrevocably changed in the last half-century, that we will have to fight much harder than usual even to maintain our standard of living, that mass-unemployment will not go away unless we learn new and difficult wisdoms; and that in facing these changes Britain looks like having far from a leading and managing role, is psychologically as well as physically insular, on the side-lines; but not insulated.

Though it is said so often that it has become a minor intellectual cliché, it may well be that this insularity has been bred and strengthened by the moat, by the fact that we have not been invaded and occupied for several centuries. Wander only round Alsace-Lorraine, recalling its battle-strewn, to-and-fro history, and you realise how profoundly the experience of occupation, of becoming a refugee in your own land, of seeing everything you and your neighbours have worked for totally destroyed or carted away, sinks into the innermost part of your being so that from then on the world is not the same place, is forever seismically threatened, fundamentally insecure, fragile beneath your feet, not to be trusted, unsettled, temporary. This is not a Farnham experience or outlook. By comparison, Farnham people and their like are emotionally sheltered and sometimes imaginatively purse-proud.

Many still mistrust foreigners and care little for black or Asian people. This seems not to be true of children up to puberty; you can see any day white, Asian and black children (but there are few black families in Farnham), the girls arm-in-arm, walking from school; to some extent that attitude survives into early womanhood and manhood. Later on many adults 'wish coloured people were not around'; they are also still anti-semitic not far below the surface.

Again many, perhaps most, middle-class people mistrust 'State' education and 'State' medicine. These prejudices make an unhappy catalogue. As you finish totting them up, you realise that if you could put people such as these back into Edwardian England, or reverse the process with some Edwardians, and put them today in the right contexts of pub or club, they would all feel substantially and emotionally at home. There are some changes in attitudes and they are interesting; but we are back again with the slowness of change. Some things are slightly adapted; some markers may change, some indicators. But deep down most people's attitudes change very little in themselves; a fixed conventionality of notions holds.

Royalism prevails at all levels. When the newspapers first began full-scale reporting of the marital difficulties of the Prince of Wales and his wife I heard one woman, inevitably at a supermarket check-out, say to another: 'Isn't it a *pity* about Charles and Di!' as though the royal pair were near-neighbours or all members of the same local club. That sentiment, differently phrased, would be common to the majority. The popular news-papers would not be so popular if they did not so accurately tap the shallow sentimentality towards royalty, the braggadocio and the chauvinistic militarism of many working-class people as of many middle-class people. Given a reasonable chance, I would work for a republic, with a non-executive but impressive, wise old president. I know of one or two; they can work well. But the British would be likely to choose a retired party politician or business man or trade unionist or civil servant or amiable aristo-crat, rather than looking for an elderly Cincinnatus. So, apart from casual forays such as this, I will wait awhile until the general mood changes more, before seriously running up the republican flag.

That is not a Farnham view. It would take many times the recent vulgarities by the Royal Family to shift the wide and deep-seated maudlinism, the false comfortable myths, embodied in the com-mon view; it is, after all, an aspect of chauvinism. So whatever shallownesses the rest of the Royal Family may commit, there is always one, we tell ourselves, who represents the best in royalty, and for whom we feel very sorry. In turn, there must always be at least one naughty person in each period; who might slowly change into a well-behaved and admired person – as has happened with the Princess Royal. As for the Queen, only some truly heinous act, such as being caught by the paparazzi drowning corgis in a stable bucket, with a fag hanging from her mouth, might begin to dis-solve the pink fog around her (and her mother).

Attitudes to the established Church come within much the same charmed circle. Many may hardly attend from one year end to another, but they know the Church has a special link with the monarchy, the Tory Party, and perhaps the Almighty. So: weddings, christenings, Christmas, funerals.

Among older people, unfocussed adoration for the Royal Family and a vestigial respect for the established Church are closely linked to an ingrained and diffused nostalgia; indeed, rise from, are an integral part of, that nostalgia, which spreads like golden syrup over many aspects of everyday life – if it truly is nostalgia and not simply an unmeant but slightly comforting potion, verbal Horlick's. Hence televised historical imperialist nostalgia in twelve-part weekly segments. Or, a more homely example: you stand at the check-out and the cashier says she is including the first of the new 10p coins in your change. The man behind says the coins are getting worse all the time, look at the 5p, too small to handle. You know that, he adds, if you are old enough to remember the old ones. Do you remember, he continues, with a smile full of warm memory, the threepenny Johnny? You do, and also remember that the threepenny Johnny was, like the current 5p, inconveniently small. And that the one pound coin is one of the best coins yet, if rather heavy. But of course you don't say so.

Though I have for long resisted the assertion, I have had to admit here that we are an unintellectual nation, that we ignore and often dismiss the life of the mind. But it is an uneasy dismissal. If by chance people find out that I can be addressed as 'Doctor' they become slightly more respectful, and always assume I am a medical doctor. If they hear me referred to as 'Professor' the effect is greater and more edgy; as if a rare and tricky bird had landed in town. 'You must be very *clever*,' they say; or: 'You must have read a lot of books!' It is quite comforting that they do not show the German or French instant deference, but a minor pity that they look at you in so ill-at-ease a way.

Most people are happy to rest within a network of comfortable and unexamined assumptions, are what Cardinal Newman called 'once-born', have from being adults always expected to live securely within a framework of generally received opinions, stable, its myths unshifting; notions but not ideas; the great weight of expectation is firmly invested in seeing this world, this local, contingent, restricted, world, as normal, within a universal frame of reference and behaviour which it is assumed should be sufficient for anybody; and which will not greatly change. After all, why should it, they might say.

In much of the above I have tended to put middle-aged, middle-class people in the centre of attention. There are two reasons, other than the obvious fact that I am myself old; first, that Farnham is, more than anything else socially, a middle-class town and in its composition tipped towards the elderly; and that though many of the attitudes I have just been describing are common to all groups – especially chauvinism and its various forms of expression – their centrepoint here is within the middle-class.

Naturally, from another angle one could detect several somewhat differing worlds, differing by class and by age. Predictably, some young people appear to be in revolt from their parents; some from all classes smoke pot or try something stronger; others, usually from other than the working-class, take a two-year trip round the world with a boyfriend or girlfriend, whatever their parents may think or say; and some, usually from the council estates or the College of Art, go in for the most outré of hair and clothing styles.

The most important agent of change for these younger people is higher education away from home, the introduction it can give to new, less enclosed, styles of living and, a common consequence of those changes, a new kind of work in a different town. But that access is still socially distorted; working-class people are less likely to leave the town; a job in Fleet would be regarded as about the limit. And many lower-middle-class to middle-class teenagers share their parents' lack of interest in higher education, especially not-directly-vocational higher education.

The lack of change between the generations is remarkable: except in attitudes towards sex or at least to frankness about it. The young women I described earlier, when quoting a man in the barber's about the readiness of many who go in pairs to the pubs at weekend to 'do it' behind a convenient wall – a favoured expression, that 'do it', since alternatives are evasive or simply too vulgar – young women like those are not a new phenomenon; they have long been a feature of adolescent and not only working-class life. But frank speaking in public about sex is new and mostly found somewhere above the working-class.

I was sitting a few months ago in the open compartment of a London train. In the next section were two girls in their early or mid-twenties. They were not working-class, or debby middle-class; they were somewhere in between, perhaps liberated lower-middle-class or liberated middle-class, free with themselves and their conversation in public. Which was audible; they saw no reason to lower their voices. One of them said: 'When it came to it, he couldn't get it on. He tried two or three times and said it made him sore. I was killing myself laughing. Then I told him to put spit on it or get moving without it. That's what he did in the end.' Later, I heard two girls laughing loudly as they walked away from a parking meter: 'When she came into work this morning she had love-bites all over her neck.' All generalisations about social change are always tricky, but I do not believe that thirty years ago many young women, even if liberated for their time, would have carried on such conversations in public without any attempt to lower their voices.

Once again, because anecdotes which seem particularly telling often have a striking sexual content, there is a risk of distorting the general picture. At this point, the danger is of undervaluing the amount of voluntary, idealistic work done by young people. Most churches and chapels – St Andrew's, the United Reformed, the Methodists, the Baptists, the Roman Catholics, the Quakers, the Pentecostal Church and the Christian Scientists – have their youth sections; some are not very large but, taken together, they add up to a fair number. Some young people, whether or not prompted by church or chapel, work for local causes; others go off to work for VSO and similar bodies, some support environmental, anti-racist causes, and Human Rights movements. Their interests insofar as they are political are less in national, geographically vertical, political parties, than in multi-national, or fully international, horizontal causes.

Do most – many – young people (except those who leave for full-time higher education elsewhere and then often do not return permanently) get out of Farnham for good as soon as they are able; as they do from many small English provincial towns? Fewer than is normal elsewhere seem to do that. Even if they find work in London, accommodation there is so expensive that it is cheaper to stay in Farnham, probably living at home but socially going their own way. So the first-class commuters are joined, now in the second-class, not only by personal assistants and junior administrative officers but also young secretaries and the like. They might have for a few years a phantom-or-surrogate getting-away-from-Farnham, through music and dress, and the image of American culture which rightly suggests a freer, more liberated world. But that is, after all and in the end, almost always a temporary, in the head, getting-away; most settle back and down. And ten to fifteen years on, married, they could carry on the conversation I heard today, at the check-out of course: 'Is your extension finished yet?' 'Just about.' 'Oh good. You won't know yourself when it's done.' 'That's right. And we'll have to stay in Farnham now. Wouldn't get the cost back if we sold . . . Still; could be worse places.'

The slowness to change arises from a sort of phlegm, and that itself partly explains the fairly consistent good-naturedness and helpfulness. Where there is little determined conviction, and little threat that the social fabric will be torn apart, good nature sets in, the steadiness of the half-shut eye. Sturt wrote admiringly about the settled, phlegmatic decency he found in so many Surrey peasants and Farnham craftsmen at the turn of the century. He saw it, probably rightly, as one of the most enduring and important threads in English life. All in all, it is better than much else which might have evolved. This country has its share of thugs and the incorrigibly self-centred, in both sexes, all classes and all ages; we are in some ways a grossly under-educated and sour nation. But this strain of reasonably fair-minded, laconic considerateness is at least as constant and powerful, perhaps more so, than those unsavoury characteristics.

It is all too easy to see change where none is, to see straws in the wind as firm signposts, to see physical change as the inevitable and speedy gateway to psychological and social movement. Hence all those claims that working-class people are 'becoming middle-class' because they may now be buying their own homes (probably from the Council), may have a car (second-hand), and may take foreign holidays (in easily specified places). But we have seen that often the new material provisions are used in ways which conform with established working-class habits and tastes.

There are certainly important changes underway in the styles of working-class life; but, as I argued earlier, it is confusing and misleading to call the process a movement towards absorption in middle-class mores. We need other language, other identifiers. We could begin by positing that, though some elements of the old three-tiered sense of class are being eroded, the energy which sustained those traditional distinctions is being transferred to a three-tier stratification: by profession, by available money, by styles of consumption of all kinds, material and psychological. But that is another and a very long enquiry.

The more embattled among middle-class people feel such changes, as threats, more clearly and sharply than do most of us. They are acutely aware of 'difference' and seem likely to remain so for a long time. As always, some readers will deny this, angrily. I only ask them to keep their eyes and ears open at key points where the different social groups inevitably meet, for example at those 'junctions' I have constantly returned to – railway booking offices and supermarket check-outs – and to try dispassionately to 'read', interpret, what they see. And this sense of difference does seem to be most evident among middle-class, middle-aged women. Their held-on-to-sense of status affects above all their voices. Like Mrs Tabitha Twitchit they seem always on the edge of being affronted. With those they assume to be socially below them they are watchful, skirt-withdrawing, fearful of theft and anarchy, avatars of 'what I have I hold'.

Here is Sturt in 1912, on habits in this area:

> Jealousy, suspicion, some fear – the elements of bitter class-war, in fact – frequently mark the attitude of middle-class people towards the labouring class. It seems to be forgotten that the men are English. One hears them spoken of as an alien and objectionable race, worth nothing but to be made to work.

It goes on, a long passage and well worth reading as a whole, to describe the uneasy relations between the local people and those who had come to live in the new villas which were then going up in Bourne and Churt and Elstead and other villages round about. Though Sturt was writing eighty years ago that intensely strong and sometimes useful reluctance to change attitudes which I have already described makes the passage as relevant today as then. Well, almost: at the least some palliating devices have been learned by some. They would not actually say now, as they did in Sturt's day about unemployment: 'It will do the men good. It will teach them their place. They were getting too independent.' Not in public, not aloud.

To come back to an earlier question: how far is this settled disinclination to change, this assurance that nothing is ever quite likely to blow up, due to the fact that we are on an island, and have not been invaded for almost a thousand years? That is the usual explanation or guess. Characteristic English phrases, as: 'It'll all come out right in the end / in the long run / in the wash'; or: 'We must grin and bear it / put up with it. Nothing lasts for ever'; or: 'We'll get over it as we've got over worse'; or even: 'Least said, soonest mended' – such phrases are no longer usable when your life lies in ruins all around you. Some parts of Britain had appalling air-raids in the last war; it would be hard to underestimate their effect. But still they are not the same kind of experience as is being occupied, trampled on day after day, month after month, with no settled recourse to law and no adequate system for ensuring even food and shelter.

So, looking at the assured rubbing-along-together attitude of so many in Britain, one is bound to wonder how well they would have survived the strains of occupation. Some would have joined the invader; we have our proto-fascists and our entirely un-ideological brutes. They would have beaten up, tortured and murdered. Such people would have been easily found. Others would have gone underground and lived heroic lives in opposition. Yet wouldn't most have gone on going on, as if blind, not-there? Much as most did in Germany under Hitler, when so many were able to ignore the existence of the death camps? Still, wouldn't our elaborate and highly developed system of checks and balances, air-holes for telling the truth, gatekeepers for the constant transmission of critical opinion, of dissent from the government's line, wouldn't all that, filtering out and down, have saved us? Certainly it would all be useful if a British totalitarianism began to be a threat. But if there were a successful invasion from outside, what then? There would be much resistance; and the phlegm would have to be, would be, modified; but not in all, perhaps not in most.

Meanwhile, what changes have definitely come about in English society? I do not mean changes in the sort of habits which are like froth on a sea-swell: not the Costa Brava instead of Blackpool, not curried scampi instead of fish and chips, not videos at home instead of going to the flicks, not cam-corders instead of the box-Brownie, not chicken-in-a-basket and Bingo instead of talking over a pint, not a fully fitted if cheap and sometimes gimcrack kitchen or bathroom or bedroom. All these mean very little.

The biggest single change in what matters, in attitudes, is sexual. It hasn't or hasn't yet made people marry much across class-lines; class-limits are still stronger than sexual attraction, or at least than sexual attraction leading to marriage. After all, the different classes do not have equality of education, of salaries, of pensions, of health and of life expectancy. But sexual behaviour has altered across the whole of society. Living in partnership rather than in marriage started in the more intellectually liberated areas but has spread up, down and across. To have a child out of wedlock, even when you do not live with a partner, is no longer a general disgrace; nor is it questionable to be no longer a virgin on marriage, if marry you do. To have sexual intercourse with several people with whom you do not expect a continuing relationship but whom you find attractive is, again in many areas, as accepted now as a kiss and what was called 'a bit of a cuddle' in our day; divorce is thought of as a pity but accepted as usually the right thing when the relationship has become very rocky, not often seen as, sometimes at least, a sort of failure and breakdown in a wider sense.

Physically, materially, technically, the contraceptive pill marks the watershed – no, is the icon – of this process of change; it accelerated but did not cause it. For intellectuals and would-be intellectuals the guru writers of the sixties were more important; the pill made it more possible, safer, less troublesome, to live out the new morality. But even earlier, in 1960, the trial apropos *Lady Chatterley's Lover* showed that, underneath, major changes in attitudes had been in play for a long time. That trial did not liberate literature but it put on stage figures who dramatised the old England and others who, not necessarily ideologically driven, thought that that England was out of touch. In sexual matters, in matters to do with sexual relationships and so, by extension, with marriage or the rejection of marriage, with the family and with the commitment to children, that change – one could fairly call it an underground revolution – had been going on for a long time. Its start could probably be dated from the Second World War and the domestic upheavals and shuttlings about the country that that caused. England being England, it came about less because people had read certain books than because that extraordinarily slow-moving organism had nevertheless, secretly even to itself, undergone a secular change – whilst still, as always and in spite of its Established Church, having little (probably less than ever) sense of the transcendent.

CHAPTER 11

COMMUNITY AND COHERENCE

The startling and solemn change which has in a few hours overcast the brightness of our long-planned 'Coronation Week' bids us, one and all, pause and think and pray.

The Rector of Farnham, on the announcement that Edward VII had been rushed into hospital with appendicitis, June 1902

There is something which has never been seen yet, and which, to all appearances, never will be, and that is a little town which isn't divided into cliques . . . where quarrels about precedence don't arise every time a service, a ceremony, a procession, or a funeral are held. . . .

La Bruyère

Between the orotund civic pieties of its Edwardian Rector and the acidity of La Bruyère, where does Farnham stand today? Betwixt and between; even more betwixt and between than ninety years ago.

Some towns of thirty to forty thousand appear to hold together naturally: geography, history, a more or less dominant urban life and probably two or three dominant industries, or a dominant rural life (though there are by now few places of that size with a mainly rural character), all may help bring that about. From the arrival of the railway, Farnham was not likely to hold together in that way; part-urban, part-rural, part-local, part-commutering, with a smallish central core and that ring of villages – some rural, some suburban – a few smallish industries and the usual market-town services: these elements do not of themselves make a whole.

Coherence is not community. A larger town which seems, and in some ways is, coherent may also be firmly divided. Divided above all by class indicators, and so by residential districts, by where the professional middle-class and the industrial executives live, where the foremen and where the rest – these last on both council estates and scattered around. Expensive South Farnham and a few other bits apart, such geographic distinctions are slightly blurred here; a result, I would guess, not only of size but also of precisely the urban/agricultural mixture and the lack of any major industry. The Conservation Area still houses well-to-do middle-class people, most of them professionals, lower-middle-class (shopkeepers, publicans, caretakers, and some – such as teachers and lecturers – who just like living there), and working-class people.

Those who live in such a mixed-up area are not likely to be 'integrated', in the fashionable word. Most can and do inhabit different psychological worlds even though they are not phys-ically separated. Occupations, manners, recreations, speech, a large number of fundamental attitudes, all create a set of differ-ent atmospheres, an ambience no more visible than the air itself but no less all-embracing.

But towns like this, and Farnham no less than any other of its kind, like to think they have, believe they have, a strong sense of community. At least their official spokesmen believe that, and lose few opportunities to assert it in the local newspaper, from the pulpit, in the Council Chamber. You have to reach a certain public and social level before you feel able to make generalisa-tions about where and with whom you live: 'Farnham people believe this, like that, do the other, will not put up with . . .'; 'Farnham will put its hand in its pocket if approached properly, will stand up to be counted if need be, knows what's import-ant to its kind of people . . .'; all the usual invocations by the peacock-end of a small community and rarely heard in working-class homes. But there I go, using that word 'community' at the very moment its validity begins to be doubtful, even in this instance and with this implied meaning.

I do so with great reluctance, for in the last twenty years that word has been so misused, abused, made the toy of ideologies, that anyone who tries to value both the language and the effort at straight thinking has simply to avoid it. In defence of its use, one could say that it might be reaching after a unity felt to be lost, a sense that no man is an island, that – once again – we belong to one another.

People have no doubt referred for a very long time to 'The Farnham Community'. But now no body of people may be referred to, no matter how tenuous their links with each other, nor how wide and powerful and varied the cultural and other differences between them, without being called 'a community'.

Whenever people of any particular area are thrust into the news, especially in tragic circumstances, they are never referred to as inhabitants of that area or of a certain neighbourhood or district. They are always within 'a community', and what is more 'a close community', and even more 'a close-knit community'. This is jargon-hiccup-speak. The word is now entirely threshed clear of substance, is a substitute for thought, a hidden assertion doing duty for direct examination and so a way of avoiding difficulties of definition and unwelcome perceptions. But there are some good Tawneyesque alternatives, full of historical fibre, such as 'fellowship' and 'benignity'.

But here and now, I cannot avoid picking up the word so as to discuss Farnham's possession – or not – of a sense of community. The justification is its use in such towns long before it was misappropriated.

Looking through collections of sepia photographs of Farnham's public occasions (a royal anniversary or that of a battle, a tree-planting, the opening of a bridge or a riverside walk) from the last century to about 1939, and particularly in Edward VII's reign – roughly from the relief of Mafeking to the opening of Gostrey Meadow in 1908 – one can easily believe that there was throughout that period 'a sense of community'. There stand the Town Council members and the other senior citizens (a proper use that, then, not the modern PR use), the Bishop perhaps, Mr Borelli, Mr Trimmer, the Canon – all exuding circumstance from their shiny high hats, down past their high and stiff wing-collars, their black frock-coats, to their highly polished boots. And there too are the common people, standing round in an apparently deferential group watching their betters doing yet one more act of kindness or patriotism for their town.

Assuming for the time being that that apparent sense of unity, of community, was real, has it survived? Or part of it? And if so in what senses? Or, as one is often tempted to think, has it entirely gone? Insofar as it was propped up by unmistakable powers-that-were it is now clearly and considerably weakened. Insofar as it was fed from large groups in solid single occupations – major wood-working, corn, hops – it has also lost what unity those gave.

There are still identifiable groups, of course. And to some extent they are divided by social class, as always. We have seen that most, but not all, sports and leisure pursuits are still class-defined, and that among the main conduits to marriage (together with nearness at work) are such groups. Some sports, usually rather dangerous ones, have long been less defined by class; mountain-climbing is the most striking and long-standing example. To that you could add today hang-gliding and sub-aqua swimming. Ballooning and gliding are too costly to break the class/cash barrier very much. Formation dancing is ineluctably lower-middle-class.

Cricket, especially in the villages, can be another example of class-mixing; as in all those stories where the village blacksmith, called on by his more middle-class captain to save the day against fierce competitors from the next village, knocks up a quick hundred or does great feats of bowling. Farnham is very keen on its cricket and has a picturesque pitch on a corner of the Park. The *Herald* pays great attention, especially when a local young man reaches Test standard. But the social mixture is likely to be less than in a village. Still, most cricket teams are good examples of bonding and networking – for the exchange of information on housing and job opportunities, of goods and services and the like.

Not surprisingly, indoor leisure is less open to irruptions from other than the traditional groups. Whist for the workers, bridge for the bosses – I've just made that up – could still be a motto. Nor would you find many women from the council estates in the fine-needlework or flower-arranging courses.

There must be, there obviously are, other centres of getting-together. The rather grand and well-sited (white chairs and tables on the terrace, extremely generous parking-space) Conservative

Club up Ivy Lane off Downing Street – once a corset-factory and
then a ladies' shooting club – is no doubt such a centre; whatever
its social life, it is likely to have a solid political base also.
Probably not so the early-Lutyens Liberal Club in South Street.
Often closed, it is yet another home to intermittent one-day
spectacular sales of golfing and ski-wear, shell-suits and trainer
shoes. It is affiliated to the CIU, which may be an abbreviated
form of WMCIU, the Working Men's Club and Institute Union,
the Revd Henry Solly's mid-nineteenth-century, well-meant and
at the time teetotal creation. If the Farnham WMCIU-affiliated
Central Club (founded in the 1890s as a worthy Institute for
workers), also in South Street, opposite Sainsbury's, is like the
so-called Liberal Club which my uncle by marriage Jack Birtle
managed in Hunslet Carr, Leeds, it will be a busy, over-heated,
cheaper than the pubs, social centre.

Would the group of professionals which meets or met in the
Bush Hotel have any influence in forming a community? Only
peripherally, if at all. And what role in the 'community' does the
TA unit out on East Street play? They have sometimes advertised
the mixture of good times and patriotic activity they offer, but I
have never heard of other interventions in the town's life.

I surmised earlier that there does not seem to be a Farnham
dinner-party élite; though there may be one so private that no
one seems to have heard of it. There is certainly an annual black-
tie Venison-Dinner-ad-hoc-élite; up at the Castle and regularly
sold out early. All the remaining nobs are likely to be there: the
Lord-Lieutenant, the Bishop, the local mayors, some reasonably
local notables whom they can capture such as the current Lord
Montgomery. It would be easy to be patronisingly accepting,
accommodating, to such a to-do, but that is always a form of
belittling. Some of those who seek tickets – and may hope their
faces will be glimpsed in the photos which appear in the local
paper – could think they were taking part in a medieval ceremony
which links them with the long historic life of Farnham. Not so.
The ceremony as we know it was invented by some nostalgic
character or promoter in the last century, was held in the Bush
Hotel until 1940, then up at the Castle.

Other than that there is, in the way of expensive local events
and focal points, really very little. Not one of the Home Counties'

spectaculars, no Ascot, no Henley, no Glyndebourne, no Sunningdale, no Wimbledon.

There are, of course, all sorts of occasional, amiable groupings, as you may glean at any supermarket check-out. One woman, apparently from one of the nearby Farnham villages and talking to a neighbour about a village occasion, provided a perfect sample of its manners and style as she walked off with her trolley: 'Oh, Charles always provides his own home-made wine.' A small universe in a phrase. For a village whist-drive? More likely for the Harvest Festival or something like it since the phrasing suggests more than a routine weekly event.

And the commuters who see so little of the place, are they part of the community, or at least of one or more of the communities within the community? Golf for many, presumably; and Sunday morning 'drinks' (the word 'cocktail' was left behind soon after the last war, like 'roadhouses' and their culture), drinks with their own kind.

It seems just possible to argue that the main divisions in the groupings are becoming less class-defined and more a matter of different ages. But it would not be easy to prove. One starting-point could be the 'drug-culture' (that's almost as fashionable a phrase as 'drug-community' would be, so I will say 'the drug-taking group' or groups). They come from different classes, with public-school pupils on holiday, those from 'private' day schools (the word 'independent' here is another of those self-flattering, in this instance parent-flattering, misnomers; like 'Independent Television'), and the rest of the group from the maintained schools, the comprehensives and the sixth-form college. This kind of mixture is rare and does not seriously damage the class-sport divisions noted above.

There are still places and occasions at which all parts of the population are present, especially fairs and fêtes; the summer Carnival, the Town Bonfire and the visit of a commercial fair to the Park. But people are then together but separated; they do not mix except in, at some events, an occasional punch-up among young people. The only public occasion at which I have recently seen a reasonably unified group, and it was of a good size, was when the half-marathon started and finished at the Hart car-park, near Safeway's, one Sunday. A closer look showed that they were a group within a group – 'Harriers' and other such groups devoted to running, especially marathons. They came from twenty or thirty miles around with their supporters, so it was likely that only about half to two-thirds of the crowd were inner-locals. But they were clearly coherent, in their enthusiasm for marathons and in their social placing; they were uniformly respectable working-class to lower-middle-class. They had, inevitably, been sponsored. Hence the hectic, logo-heavy Tee-shirts and the frenetic, sub-American-style local commercial radio station's loudspeaker van on site.

Farnham, it is becoming clear, is not a 'wrap-around' place but, rather, is a fissured society most of the time; not so much a closed as a porous society; it will not absorb and retain anything which does not fit its preconceived sense of life's proper picture; it lets any such intruders seep quietly out of sight, as with the College of Art. This is a proceeding which has many advantages. Even before I knew how very porous Farnham is – or like a net which lets through anything not wanted, but is also very strong – it would not have occurred to me to think that the fact that we had come to live in the town would be of any interest to the townspeople. Metropolitan friends, imagining that people in a town of this size and one so concentrated at its centre would live in each other's pockets, simply assumed I would be at least a bit of a figure in the local community as they envisaged it. We have joined the Farnham Society, the Maltings Association, the local Residents' Association, the very active branch of Amnesty International, the Friends of the Earth and the striving-to-be-active local Labour Party, but have attended no meetings of any of them; well, my wife has attended the Residents' Association meetings once or twice. No one, thank goodness, has noticed or notices those or any other of our moves or lack of moves.

After we had lived here a few years, *Private Eye*, reporting on a surprisingly generous decision by the Arts Council towards Farnham's Redgrave Theatre, opened a paragraph with one of its favourite twirls – after this fashion: 'It is no coincidence that Farnham's most celebrated citizen is Richard Hoggart, who is a member of the Arts Council.' The slack attribution was an unwelcome surprise to me and no doubt to many a citizen well-known and celebrated for achievements on behalf of the town. It was also a wrong-headed, as well as a metropolitan-parochial, guess, because I had not been present at the Arts Council meeting where that decision was made. If I had been I would have spoken against it since Farnham's theatre was not then in good shape.

The particular point is that I heard of the *Private Eye* reference only at second-hand, from a London friend; in Farnham, not a whisper. That is as it should be. The local paper, which is assiduous in seeking out and reporting on what it likes to call 'local personalities', has had one piece about me in eighteen years – apropos the Redgrave's production of *Lady Chatterley's Lover*. Probably the PR officer for the theatre jogged their elbows. Again, as it should be and a considerable comfort to us.

But a sort of notoriety caught up with me one sunny afternoon. Walking along The Borough alone, I was accosted by a man of about thirty-five. 'I know who you are,' he slurred, swaying backwards and forwards, 'and I've got one question for you. Who's the better writer, you or Raymond Williams?' I have no idea who he was – perhaps a visitor to town; I do not remember what I answered; but I felt, as well as tickled, mildly and slightly unhappily exposed. Better to be an unknown, to float through town looking and listening, a would-be observant ghost.

That hardly anyone in Farnham knows us is due to three elements: we live unobtrusively, most people in such small towns do not have a wide range of extra-mural intellectual interests, and – the most important and, nowadays, growing feature – people with professional, academic and intellectual interests, though they may practise good neighbourliness, make at least as many national and international links – widely horizontal rather than locally vertical connections. Putting the point another way; we do have local neighbours, of course, meet them socially and like them; we also have national and international acquaintances who share our professional interests. Gardeners can find many similar enthusiasts in any small town and upwards; students of, say, Cultural Studies have most of their friends and neighbours scattered across the world. An obvious point but, when you first think of it, enlightening; the vertical and the horizontal societies; very twentieth-century.

The horizontal society may sound, and in some ways is, more intellectually liberated than the vertical; but is not as liberated as it likes to think. It has its own parochialisms and fashions. Many years ago the American critic R. P. Blackmur, talking over tea at Princeton, set out to identify, after about half-an-hour, the newspapers I read, the journals I took and the opinions I held for the time of year. He was almost entirely, and chasteningly, accurate; the English Literary Happy Family. And even there I am playing the game, using the code, expecting my readers to recognise the phrase from Auden.

So it is hard to claim much of a sense of community for Farnham today; in this it seems at first glance to compare unfavourably, if you value the sense of community, with what is suggested by photographs of fifty to a hundred years ago. But how reliable are those old photos? As a schoolboy, I paraded with my class outside a new public building in Leeds, under orders to cheer as the royal carriage went past. We were also given a decorated mug each and were happy to have them. No doubt the *Yorkshire Post* and the evening paper had large photographs of the town's enthusiastic schoolchildren. It didn't mean a thing, except for the break from school and the mug. I wonder whether they wheeled out the residents of the old folk's homes and the workhouses? They would certainly rope in the Scouts and Guides, the Boys' Brigade, the British Legion and all such. All that soon makes up a crowd; and perhaps some of the many unemployed went along to look and fill yet another idle hour.

Farnham's groups of common people on those Victorian and Edwardian public occasions hardly seem likely to have shown more spontaneous enthusiasm than we did in Leeds round about 1930. Their presence would be inspired by a compound of not-having-much-else-to-do, especially at weekends, by some stimulating by other people of their residual or well-grounded deference, by the prospect of a bit of free roast ox. But if it were a royal celebration towards the turn of the century then the sentimental feeling for the old Queen would have been shared at all levels.

Meanwhile, nowadays, some individuals and some institutions work very hard to maintain and develop, as they would say (others might say to try to revive), the sense of community. Presumably the Canon and perhaps the Nonconformist ministers do their bit. So do the town councillors. They all try to invent or re-invent a coherent Farnham community; the Farnham in Bloom competition, the Farnham Music Festival, historic Town Walks. But one wonders who listens to any of them; and whether they should, whether that is the right way to go about things.

Then there are some of those voluntary groupings which have a general rather than a particular focus (the Townswomen's Guild and Inner Wheel rather than the St John's Ambulance Brigade); they tend to assume a town unity, or to extend their own undoubted sense of common cause into what they wish for the town as an entity.

Most evident of all in making this kind of effort are one or two men's groupings such as the Lions. They seem to attract professional men in early middle-age who live and work in the town; their activities tend to be strenuously in aid of various good causes within the town and to have a boyish, 'up the chaps', air. Most characteristic are The Hedgehogs, 'Farnham's own charitable fund-raising organisation', founded in 1959, and so relatively young. In June 1992 they arranged a Celebration Street Party 'In honour of Her Majesty's Accession to the Throne 40 years ago'. The language is pleasingly old-fashioned, polite, jolly: 'With great pleasure . . . their premier Summer Event for this year . . . a re-enactment of that joyful day . . . will amuse and divert visitors . . . a special day to remember . . . all the fun of the fair . . . we seriously expect all comers to have lots of fun . . . Looking forward to seeing you'. That 'seriously' is an intriguing modern oddity.

Above all, the local paper, the *Farnham Herald* (and, to a lesser extent, its give-away partner under the same ownership, the *Surrey and Hants News*) makes a continuous and strenuous effort to will a sense of community into being; from the *Herald*'s annual Farnham Fun Run to several other amiable initiatives. The *Herald* can of course, be niggly and is predictably conservative with both a small and a large 'C'. But it is also warm-hearted and committed to the English domestic and neighbourly decencies. It can run to one and a half large pages of letters on local issues; it gives generous space to News from the Villages; though resolutely right-wing and devoted to news of the dedicated local MP it lets other kinds of politicians have their say; it debates Sunday opening, the maintenance of roads and footpaths, the strain on the older villages as the commuters' new executive homes encircle them; and whether Christianity still has a meaning. It is, of course, consistently and conventionally outraged about vandalism. But its reporting on such unpleasantnesses is more intelligent than most of its readers' letters – which are, to use one of their favourite words, 'mindlessly' vengeful, and bob like a hop-scotch player from 'thugs', 'yobboes', calls for 'condign chastisement' to, of course, 'mindless'.

Best of all are the Classified Ads for goods and services. Taken in one uninterrupted reading they provide the richest quick introduction to the web of life in and around places like Farnham. They are cheap, they are much used and they work. When advised, during the knee trouble, to buy an exercise bike I wandered round the two or three shops which sell them and baulked at the prices. Then a neighbour said: 'Oh, that's a matter for the *Herald's* classified ads.' One insertion produced fourteen offers, and that led to an interesting sequence of phone conversations, an even more interesting set of visits to houses in and out of town and a splendid machine to which I am devoted, when I remember it.

The *Herald's* pages of goods and services offered, more than any other evidence except the list of Doomsday Book recreations, brings to life much of a local culture if not of a community; often of its areas of breakdown or failure; weddings cancelled, unwanted presents on offer, announcements of loneliness and the need for friends, kissograms and strippograms, stress management, escort services, rewards if lost dogs or cats are found. In with those are the more homely and everyday offerings: entertainment at children's parties, catering for adults' parties, painting and carpentry at 'keen' rates (suggests moonlighting or redundancy), bottled gas (some of the further out villages and small holdings still do not have mains gas. Gilbert White's Selbourne only had it installed in late 1992). Some things on offer seem so cheap as not to be worth even the small cost of putting in the advert.

The *Herald* also gives prominent attention to the publications of the local historians. I do not know how those compare with their counterparts in similar towns but, as I said in Chapter 2, Farnham's are certainly numerous and skilled. They bring to life that sense of community Farnham seems to have once had – well, perhaps; they increase your fondness for the town and make you look even more for signs of community today. But they are not read by the majority of citizens, any more than many citizens regularly look in at the Town Museum; but this is common across much of Europe; any other pattern would be surprising.

The two forms of local activity that are in particularly good health and might be said to express two different forms of the community spirit are, as we have seen, neighbourliness and the intricate network of voluntary good works. But neighbourliness is precisely named, being narrowly neighbourhood-based, physically circumscribed; and voluntary good works – wide, continuous, assiduous – are felt to be a public duty rather than a reaching towards greater social unity.

It seems, then, that Farnham's 'sense of community' is not seamless, but is made up of several overlapping groupings of activities and of impulses. This is not the 'community' so hopefully invoked by the chief burghers; but is certainly no worse, and perhaps better. Perhaps the nearness to London, TV, the trains, motorways, have loosened the commitment to a local core; though not all those features much affect most of the population, even today.

So there are efforts to insist that such a spirit exists and is part of an unbroken historic tradition. The Town Museum is well thought-out and rewarding for those who visit it. But overall the town's face is blurred, contour-less, un-gelled; and of course no longer greatly religious, believing; it seems as though it is waiting for history to happen, or to start again. Given that so much in its earlier sense of itself was willed from above, this may not be a bad condition to rest in; or, if we insist on hoping for better, for more shared conviction, not a bad condition to start from.

*

This aged England . . . pressed upon by transitions of trade and
. . . competing populations, – I see her not dispirited, not weak.

R. W. Emerson, *English Traits*

But of all nations in the world the English are perhaps the least a
nation of pure philosophers.

W. Bagehot, *The English Constitution*

Coming to the end, I have first a sense of a long narrow coloured strip such as you often see on junior schoolroom walls, a procession of different types of people moving along to places just outside the frame; against a background of houses, shops, professional premises, an occasional historic building, a snicket or two.

So: the old men outside Argos, the first-class season-ticket holders, a few Sturt types in from the villages, some Burberry-clad middle-aged women, shop assistants starting or finishing shifts, a line of reliable craftsmen, a parade of would-be independent businessmen and women, some of whom lost their redundancy payments when their subsequent enterprises failed, the great body of 'ordinary' people by whom the town's day-by-day life is kept ticking over; and now in the nineties the professionals sacked from their City firms and the unemployed teenagers.

Then the quite large number of local names still found among the shops; plus the national chains such as Boots and W. H. Smith's; the supermarkets; the old-established and the new privately-owned enterprises. Above all, as signs of the pros and cons of the new consumers' society, the Woolworth's of today; and Argos. And behind them all, the never-ending succession of jumble sales, Saturday markets, bazaars, fairs, fêtes, car-boot sales, table-top sales, bring-and-buys. And, in the first half of the nineties, the increasing number of involuntary 'House for Sale' notices.

Then there are the town authorities, most of them half-hidden much of the time, sometimes evident as at public occasions – town-twinnings, memorial services, the half-marathon – but not much regarded in two senses, as 'thought about' and as 'looked up to'; their virtues and limitations are well exemplified in, on one hand the fine sheltered housing for old people, and on the other the public library's assumptions.

Those authorities and the diligent *Farnham Herald* do their best to invoke – evoke might be better – a sense of community. Perhaps they believe in it, see themselves as celebrating something that firmly exists. I have doubted that it does.

No need to do more here and now than glance at the existing strength of class-separations. Clearly they and some of their manifestations, especially in attitudes towards health-care and education, are both pitiable and silly. But they contribute to the more interestingly cock-eyed elements of the local colour. I would be happy to see the little, turned-up-nosed private schools for very young children go, but would miss the Land-Rovers, the dogs, the countryfied expensively casual outfits donned in the villages each morning so that the pupils in their felt hats, would-be academic-looking jackets and grey gym-slips may reach their classes; and so that they may grow, in those well-raked, social-germ-free, class-allotments into the next generation of suitably modified Joan Hunter-Dunns and their eventual squires. The boys' surrealistically coloured peaked caps would also be missed; a strange style, that; perhaps adapted from cricket. Still, you can't have everything; and retaining the implied and achieved divisiveness of all this is the higher price to pay.

As we have seen, all social groups (obviously, there will be untypical people in each, especially where marriages are under strain) practise neighbourliness to an intense degree. Apart from the mixture in the centre, they tend to live in class-divided areas, though not grossly divided as in some large cities. If they were more socially mixed in their housing would the practice of neighbourliness ignore social differences (as to some extent happened in wartime)? We do not know, but I would be willing to bet that to a significant degree neighbourliness would win; that is, for many, perhaps for most; but not for all; or for always. Perhaps the other strong side of neighbourliness would assert itself even more and in all classes: that fearful incantation against any impulse to break habitual accepted bounds – 'What *would* the neighbours say!'

Similarly, domesticity is the norm in all classes; in the face of the all-embracing strength of that practice the more obvious and off-putting among the distinguishing class-icons (though it is fascinating to note them and try to decipher their meanings) are less important. We intone them too often – the chintz settees as against the pot or plastic ducks flying up the wall, the low, book-laden occasional table and half-hidden TV as against the dominant TV and its accompanying video-recorder with borrowed video-cassettes nearby, the sherry decanter on the solid wood sideboard as against the colourful tray and its endless succession of mugs of tea. The homes of young people, both often working in the early years, show a turning away from many of the symbols of their parents; but, as we saw, changes in attitudes, except in those towards sex-and-marriage, do not yet run deep in a surprising number of young couples.

Here one is reminded of that danger – which was described in the Introduction – of a loss of individuality in discursive descriptions which aim at 'representativeness'. The general point, on the widespread attachment to a mild, good-natured domesticity, is sound. But there is no room in such writing, except as an afterthought or willed coda, for the exceptions, the more colourful and terrible and varied exceptions: the houses which exude meanness (which is different from poverty, looks and smells differently) from the moment you see into the drab, 40-watt-bulb-lighted hall; and the appalling disputes between neighbours which, for instance, excessive noise by one of them can induce. Or the agonised and agonising gentility which some people cannot shake off if their visitors are hard to place. Or, worst of all, the marsh-gas odour of hatred, of people still living together who should long ago have separated. Sickness, desertion, irreparable loss by death, all the vulnerabilities of all lives; obviously Farnham has its share of all of those, but they are hard to include, weigh and measure within the terms of this kind of writing. It is easier to underline again, and again as an inevitable generalisation, that Farnham's apparent public calm hides at least the usual amount of crime of all modern kinds, from plate-window smashing to car theft and all the way up the scales of violence.

It would be interesting to compare Farnham to that in some ways similar French town, Romorantin-Lanthenay, especially for correspondences and differences. The pattern of inhabitants would probably be different – few commuters, fewer commercial chance-takers; the pattern of out-of-doors leisure activities and probably their intensity, would be different. Many attitudes would be similar, especially the more chauvinistic; perhaps the 'bosses' would be recognisable; the sense of class would exist but feel different; and so with 'neighbourliness'. 'Tolerance' might, for good historical reasons, have a shorter fuse; but the sense of 'community', especially because of the local soil fought over more than once in recent times, might remain stronger than in Farnham. But these are first stabs.

To come back to changes. Other kinds of change than the internal ones to do with sex and marriage; especially large-scale physical changes, in housing, types of work, goods and opportunities available or no longer available, all go on briskly. Though few people are consciously in touch with their own past, many of them, especially the born-locals, are still living-out attitudes which Sturt and Sturt's characters would have recognised. Are the commuters who only settled in Farnham because their firm moved to the district or because the estate agents told them, correctly, that it is an agreeable place to live, not quite country and certainly not unpleasantly urban – are such people likely to have the traditional domestic habits? They are likely, those whose marriages last, to have their own inherited, native practices of domesticity and to be neighbourly; they are likely to have been affected by 'the sexual revolution', may be partners rather than spouses. But they too are not likely to have, we saw earlier, much sense of the past, but live foreshortened lives and do not know what they are missing. This is not a novel discovery and most people, invited to recognise it, will find it neither surprising nor regrettable. Yet we should have some sense of the land we stand on and of the generations who have preceded us here.

The innate conservatism (and Conservative voting patterns), the disinclination to think freshly, whether among old residents or newcomers, the almost automatic readiness to pick up the old carpet-bag or executive case – of received ideas for their kind of professional people at any particular time – to carry, on their walk up the professional slope, seems at first glance to sit oddly with that great demand for adult education classes. But the audiences are different. It has to be an article of faith that the second audience, that which is interested in asking out-of-line questions, should be better served and can be broadened.

At times when I am thinking like this, passages I would rather not remember tend to thrust themselves to the front of memory. Such as this from Conrad in *Nostromo*:

> The popular mind [an unusable phrase today and that is a pity; it could fill a gap and be an escape from cant phrases popular with both Left and Right] is incapable of scepticism; and that incapacity delivers their helpless strength to the wiles of swindlers and the pitiless enthusiasms of leaders inspired by visions of a high destiny.

Conrad was not English and this passage, especially in its latter part, could be happily pushed aside as envisaging a future more suitable to inherently unstable continental European countries than to ours.

Coleridge's *Table Talk*, then:

> It has never yet been seen, or clearly announced, that democracy, as such, is no proper element in the constitution of a state. The idea of a state is undoubtedly a government . . . or autocracy. Democracy is the healthful life-blood which circulates through the veins and arteries, which supports the system, but which ought never to appear externally, and as the mere blood itself.

The image is quite difficult to grasp, but well worth tangling with. It would make an excellent start to a discussion in one of those unfashionable adult classes on the nature of a democracy. It is saying something likely to be unpalatable today, particularly to some politicians of all persuasions, to some journalists, to PR people and their kind. Briefly, it is saying: populism is not democracy; but democracy slides inexorably towards populism if it is made the substitute for good government; that government cannot be conducted by head-counting but must proceed on the best judgment available, supported by widespread trust. What Coleridge does not mention at that particular point, though it is implied and though we know he believed in these things, is the need for the citizens of a democracy – us, not the governments – to be educated well enough to provide checks and balances on our governors; and the need for a sizeable body of those citizens to be able to act as the 'clerisy' – the 'gatekeepers', in a less demanding and narrower modern phrase – and for that number to be increased all the time. 'For all of us', some people would demand. Yes, of course, ideally; until then . . . A look at prevailing political attitudes in Farnham as elsewhere suggests that that 'until then' is a very long way off. But that is true in many areas and many countries; democracy is still struggling to be born and many forces – all describing themselves as 'democratic' – are pushing in the opposite direction.

Someone said: 'Oh, so you're writing a book about the Home Counties.' That surprised me. There can be no objective definition of the Home Counties, but certainly their heart is on the other side of the Thames, especially in Bucks and Berks. After that, all is a matter of impressionistic evaluation. Farnham doesn't really qualify because it is still a little too rural, too mixed, psychologically a bit ragged and straggly. But liveable. Ours was an arranged marriage with the town, in that all these years ago we had to find somewhere very quickly. 'Roughnesses, pimples, warts', blindnesses and virtues, it has lasted and lasts; on both sides, I hope.

It will be fitting to end rather by looking at the place as itself, not as standing for this or that kind of English township, not as telling us something about the course of British history, not as evidence of the growth of the mass-consumer society, or of the decline of belief and the rise of relativism . . . but as this unique place, here and now, physically and socially.

The Saxons did well when they chose those river-meadows for their settlement. The place was and is eminently liveable, in an undemonstrative way, manageable. The climate is mild, even though by now the air sometimes seems, as I called it earlier, too much breathed over. The light is less well-washed than that of the Pennines and the horizons not so wide as those of Hull and Holderness; but it has its own mid-blue, breeze-blown clarity. The leaves are beginning to fall just now and I recall that the vegetation here is richer than up north, Tennysonian rather than Brontëan; the trees do not lean over starkly like scarecrows under the pressure of the prevailing wind. I still sometimes miss that sharper northern air but would think it silly to set that against Farnham's climate; each has its attractions. Anyway, catarrh strikes me on the second day of each visit to Yorkshire. I miss the blackened stone and steep hills of the Eastern Pennines now and again and am always glad to go back there, catarrh or

not. But I like the Surrey heath and pine lands, the great massed
trees and those big houses behind enormous yews and rioting
hedges, all suggesting upper-Betjemanesque lives.

In their decencies, their limitations and their inhibitions Farnham
people are much like Yorkshire's and the lives of 'the common
people' were for centuries very hard indeed in both places.
Middle-class Yorkshire accents sound odd down here, as though
being uttered by social interlopers. But sit in one of Harrogate's
grand hotels and you will hear, in those unexpectedly blunt
Yorkshire accents, the same kinds of snobberies of tones and
attitudes as in similar places down here.

A prevailing equability and tolerance; one can at last use those
words though, especially as to the second, cautiously. For what
do they mean? On what are they founded? I have already asked
whether the equanimity is based on the lack for several centuries
of overwhelming threats to the practice of civility; for which we
should be grateful. Tolerance is a harder concept. It can be the
product of lassitude, a feeling that nothing matters enough to be
worth making a fuss and a fight about; 'live and let live' can be,
but isn't always, an empty expression of that state of mind. Its
intellectual relative is the proudly claimed 'open mind', about
which Chesterton remarked that its only virtue is that it can, if
you wish, be closed on something solid. True tolerance must
arise from a respect for other people's opinions which emerges
from respect for your own; 'it wouldn't do for us all to think
alike'. Fanaticism and lassitude both rule out each of those forms
of respect. More English lean to lassitude than to fanaticism, but
some know true tolerance.

Then there is 'fair play' which sounds much less weighty a
value than tolerance, more boy's crickety. Yet that too, if looked
at as if for the first time, can produce a small revelation. In towns
such as Farnham and no doubt in many another kind of English
place 'fair play' and its Siamese twin 'trust' are still on the whole
powerful tenets: call people back if they have over-paid you,
name a fair price and stick to it, 'fair's fair', 'do as you would be
done by' (there's a plain root, in Christianity). We are surprised
and shocked by manifest cheating simply because it breaks a still
largely assumed norm, one so generally assumed that small-time
fiddling thrives. The petty crooks' and double-breasted conmen's

motto 'There's one born every minute' is less a comment on the idiocy of the English than an abusive, unaware acknowledgment of the English capacity for trust, and an indication that trust requires 'rent' to be paid by the trusting. I have seen many societies in which at all levels, for whatever reasons of history, of appalling convulsions, of all sorts of civil disturbance and, above all, of a lack of respect for the individual (especially if that individual is at the bottom of the heap), you would simply go under if you practised 'fair play'. That would be an alien idea. You live in a hostile, rapacious, watch-your-back, cheat-and-assume-cheating-in-others, world.

Seen in that perspective, 'fair play' is a remarkable civic virtue. True, it has been founded in part, and in spite of the manifest historic injustices within Britain, on centuries of relative internal peace and on a majority of lives being able to be lived – as compared with the majority in many other countries – above the level of the direst poverty.

Even today, in some countries of Eastern Europe where salaries, especially in the public service, are appallingly low, it is and has been for decades taken for granted that there is everyday corruption at all levels, in the police, the medical professions, immigration and customs officials, craftsmen in short supply. We are once again with Forster's reminder that money pads the edges of things. 'Fair play' has had with us a much more congenial climate in which to grow, has needed those centuries of comparative peace in which to take hold, to discourage the inclination to seize every chance of a fiddle, large or small. Even so, the practice did not have to grow unless there had been a disposition among individuals and groups to let it grow, to honour it; which remains, even though its Christian foundations have greatly slipped.

All this is to the good. Yet sometimes one thinks that here as in much else we are living on credit, some of it unearned; for the time being still outside a disintegrating world, a very well-protected species – when so many people, outside this small island embedded in the wealthy part of the globe, have existences of great and increasing intolerance, hardship and harshness. Perhaps we will prove to be the last or nearly the last to enjoy that saving illusion of security; even in Farnham; even in Britain.

INDEX

Leeds and Hunslet: xv, xxi, 22, 33, 34, 36, 82, 83, 86, 149, 158, 160, 162, 168, 186, 190
Leicester: 25
Liberal democrats: xix, 12, 136–7, 170–1
Life and Times (by R. H.): xvi
Lilley, Peter: 71
Local government boundary revisions of 1974: 133
Lutyens, Edwin: 36, 124, 186
Lynch, Kevin: 18, 20–21

Magee, Bryan: 66
Magistrates: 34, 87, 136
Magnet (kitchens): 43
Maltings: 46, 59, 138, 144, 149–50, 156, 188
Mansbridge, Albert: 60, 161
Marks and Spencer: 107, 109, 132
Marshall and Snelgrove: 56
Matra Works: 19, 20
Maugham, Somerset: 110
Matthews, Jessie: 35
'Milkman principle': 117
Mohican Style: 51
Montgomery, Field-marshal: 46
Moor Park: 33, 123
Morley, Bishop: 123
Mumford, Lewis: 20
Museum (of Farnham): 63, 193

Nairn, Ian: 126
Nash, Ogden: 171
National Health Service: xviii, 81, 85, 89–99
National Trust: 150, 157
Newbolt, H. J: 83
Newman, J. H. Cardinal: 174
Norwich: 21

Open University: 66, 82
Orwell, George: 126, 164, 168

Pantomimes: 160
Parfitt, G: 64

Patmore, Coventry: 51
Pennines: 22, 199
Pevsner, Nikolaus: 29, 126
Pilgrim's Way: 27, 28
Poggenpohl: 43
Police: 50, 86–88
Post Office: 88–9
Private Eye: 188–9
Public Library: xviii, 162–4

Radio Four: 60
Redgrave Theatre: 138, 156, 189–9
Restaurants: 49, 60, 68, 140
Romorantin-Lanthenay: 18–21, 23, 26, 121, 196
Royal Aerospace Establishment: 5, 48
Royal Family: 173–5
Royal Society Fellows: 12
Royal Surrey County Hospital: xx, 92–6
Rushdie, Salman: 171
Ryle, Bishop: 131

Safeway: 99, 103–8
Sainsbury's: 61, 104–8, 146
Schools: 69–70, 83–5
Selbourne: 192
Smith, W. H: 81, 109–10, 111, 194
Solly, Rev. Henry: 186
Sologne: 19, 20
Southern California: 126
South Kingdom of Middle Saxons: 26
Spar: 68, 69, 115
Sports centre: 144, 153–5
Stephenson, R. L: xiii
Sturt, George: 6, 7, 15–18, 26, 28, 42–3, 45, 52, 63, 65, 67, 72–3, 110, 122, 123, 126, 177–9, 194, 197
Sunday dinner: 157–8
Surrey county show: 159
Surrey and Hants News: 139–40, 191
Swift, Jonathan: 54, 123, 137